Ancient History
from
Primary Sources

Also by Harvey and Laurie Bluedorn

Teaching the Trivium, 2001

Also by Harvey Bluedorn

Books

A Greek Alphabetarion, 1993
Handy English Encoder & Decoder, 1994
Vocabulary Bridges from English to Latin & Greek, 1994
*Homeschool Greek: A Thorough Self-teaching Grammar
 of Biblical Greek*, 1996
*The Covenantal Allegory: A Study of the Covenant
 Promises Made to Abraham*, 1997

Pamphlets

The Biblical Evidence for House Assemblies, 1993
Observations on the Order of the Assembly, 1994
An Acceptable Sacrifice of Praise, 1995
Woman's Role in the Gathered Assembly, 1995
On Family Worship, 1997
The Sabbath Syllogism, 1998
The Logical Defense of the Faith, 1998

Herodotus reading his history to the Greeks

Ancient History
from
Primary Sources
A LITERARY TIMELINE

*And hath made of one blood
all nations of men for to dwell
on all the face of the earth,
and hath determined the times
before appointed, and the bounds
of their habitation. Acts 17:26*

by Harvey & Laurie Bluedorn

April 2003
TRIVIUM PURSUIT

Ancient History from Primary Sources
by Harvey & Laurie Bluedorn

Library of Congress Control Number: 2003090983

Trivium Pursuit
PMB 168, 429 Lake Park Blvd.
Muscatine, Iowa 52761
309-537-3641
www.triviumpursuit.com

"Thou shalt not muzzle the ox that treadeth out the corn. And, The labourer *is* worthy of his reward." (I Timothy 5:18; cf. I Cor. 9:9; Deut. 25:4; Luke 10:7; Matt. 10:10; Deut. 24:15)
"Therefore, behold, I *am* against the prophets, saith the LORD, that steal my words every one from his neighbour." (Jeremiah 23:30)
". . . Thou shalt not steal. . . . Thou shalt love thy neighbour as thyself." (Romans 13: 9; cf. Matt. 19:18; Mark 10:19; Luke 18:20; I Cor. 6:8,10; Eph. 4:28; Exod. 20:15; Lev. 19:11,13; Deut. 5:19 and Lev. 19:18; Matt. 5:43, 7:12, 19:19, 22:39; Mark 12:31; Luke 10:27; Gal. 5:14; Jam. 2:8)
"Render therefore to all their dues: . . . honour to whom honour." (Romans 13:7)
"That no *man* go beyond and defraud his brother in *any* matter: because that the Lord *is* the avenger of all such, as we also have forewarned you and testified." (I Thessalonians 4:6; cf. Lev. 19:13; Deut. 32:35; Prov. 22:22,23)

Biblical quotations are either from the King James Version, common 1769 edition of Dr. Benjamin Blayney, or else they are our own very literal translation, abbreviated V.L.T. Occasional corrections of the KJV are enclosed in brackets. Alternate translations follow a forward slash [/abc]; more literal translations follow a backward slash [\xyz].

Contents

Introduction
    How to Use This Book 13
    Using Primary Sources to Study History 19
Timeline of Ancient Literature 27
Author & Primary Source Index 73
    The Bible 75
        The Hebrew Scriptures 75
        The Greek Scriptures 83
    Literature of Egypt 91
    Literature of the Hebrew People 93
        The Hebrew Scriptures 93
        Apocrypha 93
        Pseudepigrapha 94
        Talmud 95
        Midrash 95
        Targum 96
        Dead Sea Scrolls 96
    Literature of Mesopotamia (Sumer, Accad,
        Babylonia, Assyria, and Persia) 97
    Literature of Greece and Rome (including early
        literature of Christians) 101
        Accius 101
        Aeschines 101
        Aeschylus. 101
        Aesop. 102
        Ambrose 102
        Ammianus. 103
        Anaxagoras 103
        Anaximander 103
        Antiphon. 103
        Appian of Alexandria 104
        Archimedes of Syracuse 105
        Aristarchus of Samos 107
        Aristides 107
        Aristophanes 107

Aristotle. 108
Arrian 110
Athanasius. 111
Augustine 113
Augustus 114
Avianus 114
Caesar 114
Cato the Elder 116
Catullus. 116
Celsus 116
Chrysostom 117
Cicero 117
Clement of Alexandria. 119
Clement of Rome 120
Commodianus 120
Cyprian 120
Demosthenes 121
Dio Cassius 122
Dio Chrysostom 122
Diodorus Siculus 122
Diogenes Laertius 124
Dionysius of Halicarnassus 125
Ennius 126
Epictetus 126
Epicurus 126
Eratosthenes 127
Euclid 127
Euripides 129
Eusebius 129
Eutropius 130
Frontinus 131
Galen 131
Gellius 132
Herodian 132
Herodotus 134

Hesiod 135
Hippocrates 136
Homer 138
Horace 138
Ignatius of Antioch 138
Irenaeus of Lyons 139
Isocrates 139
Jerome 140
Josephus 141
Julian the Apostate 143
Justin 143
Justin Martyr 143
Juvenal 144
Lactantius 144
Livy 145
Lucan 146
Lucian 146
Lucilius 147
Lucretius 147
Lysias 147
Marcus Aurelius 148
Martial 148
Menander 148
Nepos 148
Nicolaus of Damascus 149
Nicomachus of Gerasa 149
Origen 149
Ovid 150
Pacuvius 150
Pausanias 150
Pericles 151
Philo 151
Pindar 152
Plato 152
Plautus 153
Pliny the Elder 154
Pliny the Younger 154
Plutarch 155
Polybius 157
Priscus 158
Prudentius 158

Pyrrho of Elis 159
Pythagoras 159
Quintilian 159
Quintus Curtius 160
Sallust 160
Salvian 161
Sappho 161
Seneca 161
Socrates 162
Socrates Scholasticus 164
Solon 165
Sophocles 165
Sozomen 166
Strabo 166
Suetonius 169
Tacitus 169
Terence 170
Tertullian 170
Thales 172
Theocritus 172
Theodoret 172
Theodosius II 172
Thucydides 173
Tyrtaeus 174
Varro 174
Vegetius 174
Velleius 175
Virgil 175
Vitruvius 176
Xenophon 176
Zeno of Citium 178
Appendices
  1. Four Approaches to the Study of Ancient
     Literature 183
  2. Nothing Is Neutral 187
  3. Was Paul a Classical Greek Scholar? 195
  4. The Bible Chronology Puzzle 203
  5. Sources Consulted 215
  6. History Curricula and Resources Which Can Be
     Used with This Book 221

Introduction

How to Use This Book

This book is not a history curriculum, nor a textbook, nor an all-inclusive timeline. Others have written such things (see Appendix 6: "History Curricula and Resources"), and this book supplements them.

This is a reference book which guides the student on a selective timeline tour through ancient history, outlining the major events and personalities, and noting the primary literary sources from which these things are known. Time-wise, this book covers the period from the creation of the world to the fall of Rome in A.D. 476. Space-wise, this book covers the civilizations of the Near East and West. Each event or person in history is accompanied by suggested readings from various ancient sources.

❧ WHY WE WROTE THIS BOOK ☙

We like to go back to the sources whenever we can. (We discuss the value of primary sources in the next section, "Using Primary Sources to Study History.") We couldn't find a book which helped us find the primary sources, so we decided to write one. This book makes it much easier for anyone to study history from the real sources of history – the ancient writings themselves. Here, in one place, you will find listed in chronological order all of the major primary literary sources for the events of ancient history.

❧ HOW THIS BOOK IS LAID OUT ☙

In "Using Primary Sources to Study History," you will find a general discussion of history, a discussion of primary sources, and suggestions on how to analyze historical documents.

In the second section of this book, "Timeline of Ancient Literature," you will find each page divided

into rows and columns.

The rows (labeled down the left side of the page) represent the progression of time. They begin in fifty-year increments, narrow to twenty-five-year increments, and finally to ten-year increments.

Each column (labeled across the top of the page) represents a culture, civilization, or empire:

Column 1: Hebrew and Christian

Column 2: Egyptian

Column 3: Mesopotamian (Sumer, Accad, Babylonia, Assyria, Persia)

Column 4: Greek

Column 5: Roman

There is not enough room to include every historical event or every person on the timeline. Within this grid, you will find selected events and persons noted, along with the literary citations of selected excerpts from the primary sources for each event or person. Each source is identified by author, work, and citation. By using the "Timeline of Ancient Literature," the student can study history chronologically and by civilization.

The third section of this book, "Author & Primary Source Index," is divided into five sections:

1. The Bible
2. Literature of Egypt
3. Literature of the Hebrew People
4. Literature of Mesopotamia (Sumer, Accad, Babylonia, Assyria, Persia)
5. Literature of Greece and Rome (including Early Literature of Christians)

The authors identified on the "Timeline of Ancient Literature" are listed in alphabetical order under one of these five categories. Each author is accompanied by a brief biographical sketch, a list of his works, citations of important passages, and descriptions of those passages. By using the "Author & Primary Source Index," the student can study in greater depth the authors of ancient history.

Following this, there are six Appendices:
1. Four Approaches to the Study of Ancient Literature
2. Nothing Is Neutral.
3. Was Paul a Classical Greek Scholar?
4. The Bible Chronology Puzzle
5. Sources Consulted
6. History Curricula and Resources

Finally, in the accompanying compact disk, *Primary Literary Sources for Ancient History,* you will find an English translation of all of the ancient literature mentioned in this book which is available in the public domain. At the end of this introduction, we will list several other sources for ancient literature.

❧ GENERAL GUIDELINES ❧

This book can be used profitably by youth (twelve and up) as well as by adults. However, each family has its own standards, and a parent should not assume that all literary selections meet their standards of appropriateness for their children. In classical literature, particularly Greek and Roman literature, one may occasionally encounter suggestive and descriptive passages of foul and degenerate thought and behavior which are simply inappropriate for anyone, and particularly inappropriate for children.

In the "Timeline of Ancient Literature," we have taken care to cite better examples of literature, but even in some of the best literature, an author will sometimes insert an occasional (and unnecessary) comment which many parents will not find acceptable. (We may compare this to modern media, which often inserts a moment of unnecessary profanity, lewdness, or depravity in the middle of what might otherwise be an acceptable presentation.) So we recommend that a parent or teacher read the literature first, then make an independent determination regarding its acceptability.

Below, we have divided Greek and Roman authors into three main classifications according to our own considered opinion of general standards of "acceptability," with several categories within each classification. None of these classifications is absolute, and we note only a few of the many exceptions.

1. Authors Who Are Useful (But Should Be Pre-Read)

Generally speaking, the more useful works are found in the categories of history, geography, biography, oratory, rhetoric, logic, grammar, science, medicine, mathematics, architecture, military, agriculture, and fables. We recommend that they be pre-read by parents. Remember, all of these works are written from a pagan worldview, so none of them can be considered truly "neutral."

Historians, Geographers, & Biographers	
Ammianus	Nepos
Appian of Alexandria	Nicolaus of Damascus
Aristotle	Pausanias
Arrian	Philo
Augustus	Plutarch
Dio Cassius	Polybius
Diodorus Siculus	Priscus
Diogenes Laertius	Quintus Curtius
Dionysius of Halicarnassus	Sallust
Eusebius	Socrates Scholasticus
Eutropius	Sozomen
Herodian	Strabo
Herodotus	Suetonius
Josephus	Tacitus
Julian the Apostate	Theodoret
Julius Caesar	Theodosius II
Justin	Thucydides
Livy	Velleius
Lucan	Xenophon

Orators	
Aeschines	Isocrates
Antiphon	Lysias
Cicero	Pericles (included in Thucydides)
Demosthenes	Pliny the Younger
Dio Chrysostom	

Rhetoricians, Logicians, & Grammarians	
Aristotle	Gellius
Cicero	Quintilian
Dionysius of Halicarnassus	Varro

Scientists, Physicians, Mathematicians, Architects, Military, & Agriculture	
Aristarchus	Galen
Aristotle	Hippocrates
Archimedes	Nicomachus of Gerasa
Cato the Elder	Pliny the Elder
Celsus	Varro
Eratosthenes	Vegetius
Euclid	Vitruvius
Frontinus	

Fables	
Aesop	
Avianus	

2. Authors for Mature Christians

After they are firmly grounded in Christian philosophy and theology, more mature Christians may read the philosophers and the Christian apologists. Remember, there is nothing truly neutral about the philosophers, and even the Christian apologists have many unbiblical ideas in their thinking.

Philosophers	
Anaxagorus	Plato
Anaximander	Pyrrho – founder of Skeptic
Aristotle	school
Cicero – Stoic	Pythagoras
Epictetus – Stoic	Seneca – Stoic
Epicurus – founder of Epicurean	Socrates (found in Plato and
school	Xenophon)
Lucretius – Epicurean	Thales – first philosopher
Marcus Aurelius – Stoic	Xenophon – follower of Socrates
Philo – Jewish	Zeno – founder of Stoic school

Christian Apologists	
(Some of these writings may be appropriate for younger students, but many of these writings are philosophical in nature.)	
Ambrose	Jerome
Aristides	John Chrysostom
Athanasius	Justin Martyr
Augustine	Lactantius
Clement of Alexandria	Origen
Clement of Rome	Prudentius
Commodianus	Salvian
Cyprian	Tertullian
Ignatius	Theodoret
Irenaeus	

3. Authors with Much Questionable and Graphic Content

With few exceptions, the poets, satirists, tragedians, and comedians wrote questionable and graphic content which is simply inappropriate. Mature adults who have a special purpose may find a need to handle this material, but put on the chore boots first, and take a thorough shower after you're finished.

Poets and Satirists	
(Some exceptions: The political poetry of Solon and Tyrtaeus is useful. Virgil's *Georgics* may be useful. Lucian's *Life of Peregrinus* is useful.)	
Catullus	Menander
Hesiod	Ovid
Homer	Pindar
Horace	Sappho
Juvenal	Solon
Lucian of Samosata	Theocritus
Lucilius	Tyrtaeus
Martial	Virgil

Tragedians and Comedians	
(Exception: The historical play *The Persians* by Aeschylus may be useful.)	
Accius	Pacuvius
Aeschylus	Plautus
Aristophanes	Seneca
Ennius	Sophocles
Euripides	Terence

A FEW GENERAL COMMENTS ON AUTHORS AND LITERATURE

Many persons begin in classical literature with the fables of Aesop (Greek) and Avianus (Latin). These are suitable for all ages, young and old.

Some literature suitable for ages ten and up:
    Caesar – *Gallic War* and *Civil War*
    Josephus – *War of the Jews*
    Xenophon – *Anabasis*

Some literature suitable for ages twelve and up:
    Ammianus – *The History*
    Appian of Alexandria – *The Roman History*
    Arrian – *Anabasis of Alexander*
    Cato the Elder – *On Agriculture*
    Eusebius – *The History of the Church*
    Gellius – *Attic Nights*
    Herodotus – *The History of the Persian Wars*
    Julian the Apostate – *Letters*
    Livy – *The Early History of Rome*
    Pliny the Elder – *Natural History*
    Plutarch – *Lives*
    Quintus Curtius – *History of Alexander*
    Socrates Scholasticus – *History of the Church*

The works of Xenophon are a mixed bag. Some are appropriate for even a ten-year-old (*Anabasis*), while others are quite inappropriate (*Symposium*).

On the Deaths of the Persecutors, by the Christian apologist Lactantius, is more historical than philosophical, and may be read profitably by students age twelve and up.

Most of Herodotus may be fine to read for students age twelve and up, but the very beginning and other short sections of Book 1 may be skipped because of content.

Aristotle's historical work (*The Athenian Constitution*) and his works on natural history (*History of Animals*, *On the Parts of Animals*, etc.) may be valuable for students age twelve and up, while his works on logic (*Categories*, *Prior Analytics*, etc.) and physics (*Physics*, *On the Heavens*, etc.) are better suited for rhetoric-level students. We suggest that Aristotle's philosophical works (*Metaphysics*, *Politics*, *Nicomachean Ethics*) be reserved for mature Christians with a good foundation in theology and with sharpened analytical and critical skills.

Cicero is listed among orators, rhetoricians, and philosophers, but his letters provide us with much valuable historical information, so he could also be listed under historians. Most of Cicero's works are appropriate for students age twelve and up, except perhaps his Stoic philosophical works (*On the State*, *On the Supreme Good and Evil*, etc.), which could be left for the mature

Christian.

The mythological works and love poetry (works of Homer, Sappho, Ovid, Martial, Juvenal etc.) have a great reputation with the world, and that is one very strong reason for the Christian to handle them with utmost caution. There is no question that Hesiod and Homer are fundamental to understanding Greek culture, but that is no justification for sacrificing the tender conscience of a child to their fantasies, brutalities, and perversions.

Historical poetry and plays (*The Persians* by Aeschylus, the political poetry of Solon) can be read by ages twelve and up.

The "Timeline of Ancient Literature" lists selected excerpts, and the "Author & Primary Source Index" lists more selected excerpts.

For more of our own philosophy on reading classical literature, see our Appendices, "Four Approaches to the Study of Ancient Literature," and "Nothing Is Neutral."

❧ GROUND RULES & TERMINOLOGY ❧

1. Spelling

There is no universally accepted standard for the spelling of ancient names. So if the spelling in your curricula doesn't match the spelling in this book, this does not necessarily mean there is a misspelling.

2. Chronology

There is no universally accepted chronology of ancient dates. So if the dates in your curricula don't match the dates in this book, this does not necessarily mean there is a mistake. See Appendix 4, "The Bible Chronology Puzzle," for an explanation of some of the difficulties of chronology.

3. Terminology

We offer the following explanations for some of the terminology we use in this book:

a. By *extant works*, we mean we have listed *all* of the author's works which survive today.

b. By *extant works include*, we mean this is a selected list of the major works of the author. (A complete list of all surviving works of every author would overburden this book.)

c. By *significant excerpts*, we mean this is a selected list of passages which you should consider reading from among the extant works of this author. (There may be many more significant or important excerpts worth reading, but the *significant excerpts* we supply may either help you to begin, or they may help you to pare your own selections down. If we do not list any significant excerpts for a particular author, you may consider that as a caution about the author's works.)

d. By *significant excerpts from others writing about _____ or including his writings in their works*, we mean this is a selected list of the comments from others about the particular author.

e. By *B.C.*, we abbreviate *Before Christ*, which means "before (the customary date for the birth of) Christ." (The customary date for the birth of Christ is year A.D. 1 by our modern calendar.)

f. By *A.D.*, we mean *Anno Domini*, "in the year of the Lord," that is, after the customary date for the birth of Christ. We choose not to use C.E. (Common Era) and B.C.E. (Before Common Era).

g. By *A.M.*, we mean *Anno Mundi*, "in the year of the world," that is, from the date of creation.

h. By *c.* (used in conjunction with B.C., A.D., or A.M.) we abbreviate *circa*, "around (that date)," so that c. A.D. 150 means "approximately the year 150 after the customary date for the birth of Christ."

i. By *FL.*, we mean *flourished*, that is, the person lived somewhere around the date given.

4. Citations

When we cite a passage of the Bible, we give the book, then the chapter, then the verse (Matt. 5:3 = Matthew, Chapter 5, Verse 3). There are some translations and editions of the Bible which do not give the chapter and verse divisions, which makes it difficult to cite a particular passage. Similarly, there are some translations and editions of ancient literature which do not divide the text up into sections for reference purposes, and if you use one of these editions, then you will have difficulty finding the passages which we cite.

Many of the ancient authors, especially during the period when the great library of Alexandria flourished, actually divided their works into smaller numbered "books." During the Renaissance, humanists added numbering systems to many ancient works, such as Plato and Aristotle. In the nineteenth century, the Germans produced "scholarly" editions of every piece of ancient literature which they could lay their hands upon, often establishing a new numbering system.

The citation numbers identify progressive divisions of the text. Hence:

1 would represent the largest division, usually a book or chapter

1.1 would represent the next largest division, usually a chapter or section

1.1.1 would represent the next largest division, usually a section or passage

1.1.1.1 would represent the next largest division, usually a passage or verse

❦ HOW TO FIND THE ANCIENT ❦ LITERATURE MENTIONED IN THIS BOOK

Where can we find the texts for classical Greek and Latin literature?

1. Compact Disks

There are several compact disks which contain ancient literature in English translation:

a. *Primary Literary Sources for Ancient History* (the accompanying compact disk) which is also available from Brainfly, Inc., 10540 NW 26th Street, Suite 103, Miami, Florida, 33172. (www.brainfly.net) This company also produces compact disks of other literature as well.

b. The B & R Samizdat Express Classical Literature on CD. (www.samizdat.com) This company also produces compact disks of other literature as well.

c. *Christian Classics Ethereal Library* – 300 classic Christian books and the complete early church fathers on CD. (Wheaton College, 630-752-5119)

d. *Perseus 2.0* – Thirty-one Greek authors on CD. (800-987-7323; www.perseus.tufts.edu)

2. Online Sources

Websites for English translations of the classics:

http://classics.mit.edu The Internet Classics Archive by Daniel C. Stevenson – Select from a list of 441 works of classical literature by 59 different authors. Mainly Greco-Roman works (some Chinese and Persian), all in English translation.

http://www-gap.dcs.st-and.ac.uk/~history The MacTutor History of Mathematics Archive – an integrated collection of over 1000 biographies and historical articles of a mathematical nature.

http://www.fordham.edu/halsall The Internet History Sourcebooks Project by Paul Halsall – collections of public domain and copy-permitted historical texts presented cleanly for educational use. Includes ancient, medieval, and modern history.

www.perseus.tufts.edu The Perseus Digital Library – Greek and Latin classics.

www.ipl.org The Internet Public Library – numerous online texts.

www.digital.library.upenn.edu/books The On-Line Books Page – search their 12,000+ listings.

www.eserver.org Eserver.org – publishes online quality works (31,742 of them) in arts and humanities.

www.ukans.edu/history/VL History Central Catalog.

www.ccel.org Classic Christian books, including all the Church Fathers, in electronic format.

www.gutenberg.net Fine literature digitally republished.

http://un2sg4.unige.ch/athena/html/athome.html Athena – nearly 10,000 links to books on all subjects.

www.earlychristianwritings.com All of early Christianity – New Testament and Fathers.

www.stoa.org Electronic publications in the humanities.

3. Large public, college, or university libraries

a. In libraries with the Library of Congress numbers, Greek and Latin literature can be found from PA 3301 to the end of the PA's.

b. The *Loeb Classical Library* is a series of volumes which include the text of classical authors in the original language along with an English translation.

4. Purchase from catalogs

Besides the ordinary book catalogs which may provide many of the literary sources, some catalogs have a special focus on classical and historical materials.

a. American Home-School Publishing, 5310 Affinity Court, Centreville, Virginia, 20120 (800-684-2121, www.ahsp.com).

b. Bolchazy-Carducci Publishers, 1000 Brown St., Unit 101, Wauconda, Illinois, 60084 (800-392-6453, www.bolchazy.com)

c. Greenleaf Press, 3761 Highway 109N, Unit D, Lebanon, Tennessee, 37087 (615-449-1617, www.greenleafpress.com).

d. Veritas Press, 1250 Belle Meade Drive, Lancaster, Pennsylvania, 17601 (800-922-5082, www.veritaspress.com)

❧ SUGGESTIONS ON HOW THIS BOOK CAN BE USED ❧

This book is not a history curriculum, nor a textbook, but it will serve as a curriculum supplement, a reference book, or a resource for curriculum development. As a reference or resource book, it provides the student or teacher access to the very best of all existing material. As a curriculum supplement, it takes the student back to the sources from which the history textbook was written, adding light and color, depth and perspective. It may be used in connection with any course in ancient history. We have compiled an Appendix of "History Curricula and Resources" which can be used along with this book.

Here are a few suggestions as to how this book might be used: The student may read a section or a chapter in his history textbook, then read from the corresponding sources listed on the "Timeline of Ancient Literature." A younger student (ten through twelve) may read those passages, then give oral narration, do copywork, or write from dictation. Older students (thirteen and up) may give oral or written narration or summary, or write essays on assigned topics dealing with the sources. A teacher may choose to give special attention to the study of certain authors by assigning the reading of their biographies or assigning the reading of more of their writings.

❧ THE COVER ❧

The cover is from an oil painting by our daughter, Johannah, who researched the furniture, writing materials, scrolls, and clothing in order to represent accurately Tertullian dictating to his servant.

Using Primary Sources to Study History

Imagine having no knowledge of the past beyond our own personal recollections. That would place us at the beginning of all we knew, which would naturally give us a self-centered perspective. Such is the perspective of little children. A limited perspective makes someone a little child. A person who has a very limited knowledge of the world around him will behave in childish ways toward his environment. Likewise, a person who has a very limited knowledge of the history which came before him will behave in childish and self-centered ways toward his future. A knowledge which stretches beyond our own life and experience will lay the foundation for broader understanding and deeper wisdom. Any study of history will, by the nature of the case, broaden and deepen the character of an individual.

❧ WHAT IS HISTORY? ❧

History is the teller of stories. It is a narration of events in the order in which they occurred, and an attempt to explain their causes, their connections, and their consequences. Apart from the record of history revealed in Scripture, history is a rather inexact science. The activities of the past can only be reconstructed from what remains from the past – in whatever state it may be preserved. So history must depend upon other sciences to develop methods to improve its accuracy.

❧ THE BIASED NATURE OF THE ❧ HISTORICAL RECORD

We must sharply distinguish historical *fact* from historical *record*. The historical *fact* is what indeed actually happened. The historical *record* of the fact is what someone believes happened from his own narrow perspective. (The historical *record* of someone viewing an illusionist's performance may be very different from the historical *fact* of what the illusionist actually did.) First, an objective historical event (fact) takes place. Then the event is subjectively recorded in one or more ways, from one or more perspectives. Ignorance, prejudice, passion, and the tricks of the mind and memory become a part of the record – along with any physical defects in the way the record is preserved. Even if the record is relatively unbiased, it is nevertheless always incomplete – the event could never be perfectly recreated from the record. The historian collects the physical remains of an event and the recorded descriptions of the event, and he interprets these sources in order to form an opinion of what really happened. This adds still another level of opinion and bias to history. Because of this interpretive element, absolute certainty about historical fact is impossible – apart from direct revelation from God.

❧ REVEALED HISTORY ❧

The one great history book is the Bible. It is an anchor in the midst of man's conflicting records of history. The Bible teaches historical facts – such as the origin of all things, the division of the languages, and the causes of God's judgments upon men and nations. These historical facts may be used to discern principles which we can then turn around and apply to man's record of historical events in order to discern some of the truth about an historical event.

One approach to the study of history is to study how the philosophies of men have influenced their actions. What men believe eventually works its way out into what they do. If we can discern the philosophy which prevails in any given age, then we may observe what the fruits of that philosophy are within that age. The next step is to study God's philosophy and actions, which explain man's philosophy and actions. Only the principles of the Bible can explain universal history, because the Bible is the Word of the universal God.

❧ THREE BIBLICAL PRINCIPLES ❧ FOR THE STUDY OF HISTORY

1. Knowledge Level: "History repeats itself."

What has been is what will be; and what has been done is what will be done: and there is nothing entirely new under the sun. (Ecclesiastes 1:9 V.L.T.)

To quote the historian Thucydides, "The lack of the fabulous may make my work dull. But I shall be satisfied if it be thought useful by those who wish to know the exact character of events now past which, human nature being what it is, will recur in similar or analogous forms."

God so rules over circumstances that similar actions regularly have similar consequences. This is the basis for all scientific study.

Though this Biblical philosophy is what founded scientific study, much of modern science has strayed far from this principle by remaking scientific study into the image of man. It adopts the philosophy of naturalism: *all* things *must* be explained *only* as natural phenomena. This philosophy excludes the notion that God created and sustains the universe, and that He reserves the prerogative to intervene in His own property when He pleases and as He pleases. Naturalist philosophy eventually degenerates into a materialist determinism which makes the study of history pointless.

2. Understanding Level: "The past is the key to the future."

What is now has been long ago; and what is yet to be has already been; and God seeks [/requires an account of] what has been pursued in the past. (Ecclesiastes 3: 15 V.L.T.)

If we know what has happened leading up to the moment, then we will know where things are likely leading. As we stand in the stream of events, what we see coming down the stream will eventually pass by us. Given a certain set of circumstances, there is no escaping the consequences of our actions.

Man wants to escape the consequences of his actions. That is at the heart of humanism – giving creation a makeover according to man's imagination – "man is the measure of all things." Natural man thinks he can figure out a way to disobey God's law with impunity.

3. Wisdom Level: "He who does not study history is doomed to repeat it."

If we do not study history and learn its lessons, then we are less likely to interrupt the pattern discerned by those who do study history. If we know how similar things have concluded, and we know what has happened leading up to the present moment, then we may know how to intervene to change events and to interrupt the pattern.

. . . the men of Issachar, who had understanding of the times, to know what Israel ought to do . . . . (I Chronicles 12:32 V.L.T.)

But if we do not know these things, then we are less likely to recognize the significance of the moment and to act in order to alter the pattern. Therefore, we will repeat the pattern.

. . . Hypocrites! Ye indeed know enough to discern the face of the heaven, yet ye cannot discern the signs of the times? (Matthew 16:3 V.L.T.)

If God should grant repentance, then we can change the given circumstances and the resulting consequences.

The moment I speak concerning a nation, or concerning a kingdom, to uproot, and to break down, and to cause it to perish; yet if that nation, against which I have spoken, turns from its evil way, then I will repent regarding the evil which I intended to do to it. And the moment I speak concerning a nation, or concerning a kingdom, to build and to plant it; yet if it does evil in My sight, not obeying My voice, then I will repent regarding the good, which I had said was to benefit it. (Jeremiah 18:7 V.L.T.)

And Jonah began to enter into the city a journey of one day, then he cried out, and said, Yet forty days, then Nineveh shall be overthrown. . . . Who knows? God may turn and He may repent, and turn away from the fierce glow of His anger, such that we will not perish. When God saw what they did – how they turned from their evil way – then God repented concerning the evil, which He had declared He was to do to them, so He did not do it. (Jonah 3:4,9,10 V.L.T.)

❧ AN OUTLINE FOR EVALUATING ❧ HISTORICAL DOCUMENTS

What Is the Value of a Primary Literary Source?

Perhaps the most important part in determining the trustworthiness of an historical account is knowing how close that source was to the actual historical event. A *primary source* is about as close as one can come to the actual event, because it is a direct link between us and someone who was actually present when the event which we are studying occurred. Eyewitness accounts, original documents, surviving objects, photographs, audio or video recordings – these are all examples of primary sources. A *primary literary source* is an account of an historical event which was composed in and around the period of time when the event actually occurred, and which was composed by someone who had direct acquaintance with the persons, events, and conditions which he described. A *primary literary source* has not been "handled" by others, each contributing his own interpretations and biases to the record. Certainly, all authors have their biases, and these must be identified. Nevertheless, *a primary literary source* would have fewer layers of biased interpretation to work through. Therefore, a *primary literary source* is ordinarily a more accurate record of the original event. For example, a detailed account of the burning of Rome would be more credible if the author was actually there when it happened.

A history textbook may supply a larger perspective through a skeleton outline of the subject, but the study of history should consist of something more than just reading a textbook. With textbooks, names and dates may seem most important, but when the original accounts are read, the names and dates become part of a larger picture. *Primary literary sources* give flesh to the skeleton by adding fuller and more lively accounts, bringing the reader into closer touch with the persons and events which made the history.

Literature from a Period May Be Considered a Primary Source for That Period

The authors of *Greek and Roman Classics in Translation* state:

> Every work of literature can be treated as an historical document; since every writer, as a human being, lives in space and time, his physical environment and the history of his age must contribute something to his view of life and hence to the meaning and purpose of his art. Works of art are not produced in a vacuum, and often the historical background of a masterpiece will enable us to interpret its significance more fully; conversely, a knowledge of works of art will often help us to understand better the history of the age which produced them. (Charles Theophilus Murphy, Kevin Guinagh, and Whitney Jennings Oates, *Greek and Roman Classics in Translation* [New York: Green and Company, 1947])

What Is a Secondary Source?

A *secondary source* obtains its information from *primary sources* or other *secondary sources*. In the courtroom, a *secondary source* is called "hearsay evidence." It is information given by someone who was not at the original scene, but who heard about it from someone else, who in turn may have heard about it from someone else, eventually tracing its way back to the original event. Ordinarily, the more times a story has been handled, the less reliable the story becomes, because interpretations and biases are usually attached with each handling. History textbooks, encyclopedias, and historical novels are all examples of *secondary sources*.

If we wrote a history of WWII, that history would be a *secondary source* because we were not alive during WWII, and our record is "secondhand."

What Is a Principal Source?

If we have only one early record of an event, and it is a *secondary source*, then we call this a *principal source*. This is less reliable than a *primary source*, but it is all we have. Homer could not be considered a *primary source* for the Trojan War because he was not there. Yet we have no record from someone who was there, so Homer is our most useful source. Regarding ancient history, much of the literature we have is not primary in the strictest sense, but because it is all we have, most historians refer to ancient literature as *primary sources*, even though, technically speaking, much of it is only *principal sources*.

When we study history, we must consider *primary sources* first. People who actually witness an historical event are considered *primary sources* for the time period of the event, and the literature which was written during a particular time period is considered a *primary source* for that time period.

Examples

In about 472 B.C., a man named Aeschylus wrote an historical play called *The Persians*, which presents in dramatic form the invasion of Xerxes (King of Persia) and his overthrow by the Greeks at Salamis. This play is considered a high quality *primary source* for two reasons: first, this play was written only a few years after the battle of Salamis (literature written during a time period is considered a *primary source* for that time period); and secondly, Aeschylus was actually present at the battle of Salamis (eyewitnesses to an historical event are considered *primary sources*).

Herodotus wrote a book called *The History*, which is an historical account of the wars which Persia waged against Greece from the time of Cyrus to about 479 B.C.

Herodotus was born in about 484 B.C., so he was not alive for most of the time about which he wrote. Neither was he an eyewitness to any of the events he described. Technically speaking, he would not be a *primary source* for the events. Yet, because Herodotus wrote his history shortly after the events he described, and because we have almost no other records of the events for that time period, historians prefer to consider Herodotus a *primary source*, though not of as high a quality as our example of Aeschylus above. So Herodotus is a *primary source* by default. Because of the scarcity of evidence for ancient history, much of ancient historical literature falls into the category of *primary source* by default.

Biases, Interpretations and Other Distortions

Even if we begin with a *primary source*, there is no guarantee that this record is characteristically accurate. A *secondary source* which has passed through one or more intermediaries may actually be more accurate than a *primary source*. How can this be? Our *secondary source* may have received its information from a *primary source* which was less biased than our *primary source*, and the intermediaries may have altered very little of the story.

Criteria for Critical Evaluation of Sources

1. DOES THE WITNESS HAVE ANY PECULIAR BIASES OR AGENDAS?

The witness himself does not need to be aware of his bias for it to affect his record. A witness who grew up in Alabama may express an unconscious bias in his account of the battle of Gettysburg. This fact needs to be carefully weighed, but it must not be stereotyped. ("He says the South was right only because he is from the South.") The fact that one is from the losing side does not mean he cannot give accurate information, nor does it mean the winning side is more accurate.

2. DOES THE WITNESS HAVE A REASON TO LIE OR DISTORT THE EVIDENCE?

Someone present on Lexington Green in 1775 might have a reason to lie about who fired the first shot, depending upon which side he was on. Someone with no discernible reason to distort or lie about an event is a more desirable witness.

3. WAS THE WITNESS KNOWLEDGEABLE ENOUGH CONCERNING A SUBJECT TO BE CAPABLE OF DESCRIBING IT ACCURATELY FOR OUR PURPOSES?

An ordinary landsman may not know enough about ships to describe a naval battle correctly.

4. WAS THE WITNESS TELLING US WHAT HE ACTUALLY SAW, OR ONLY WHAT HE INFERRED?

"Russians don't smile very much" or "Russians are a depressed race."

5. WAS THE WITNESS IN A GOOD POSITION TO CHRONICLE THE EVENT ACCURATELY?

He may not have been close enough, or the conditions may have been too difficult for him to have grasped the events fully. ("He said it was a good play, but he was too far away in the balcony to see it well." "He may not have been close enough to have known why the president made that decision.") For the same reasons, even tape recorders, video cameras, and other solid evidence may give us improper or incomplete evidence. An artifact which has been found on the scene may not match well with others found in the same area, so it would be a misrepresentative sample.

More Than One Point of View

Was there more than one witness to an event? If so, do the witnesses agree? If they do not agree, then the matter must be investigated more deeply. Two persons may view the same event from different angles, and their descriptions from their perspectives may be accurate, yet they may not seem to agree. If, from the perspective of the audience, we watched an illusionist perform, we would see one thing. If we were backstage, or if we were one of the illusionist's assistants, then we would see it all another way. The audience might have seen quite accurately, but incompletely, which, in their minds, produced an illusion contrary to fact. When we have apparently conflicting accounts, it would be necessary to disqualify at least a portion of the testimony – unless a way is found to reconcile them. In the case of the illusionist, the conflicting accounts could be easily reconciled simply by taking into account the different perspectives.

Historical Fallacies

When analyzing historical events, we are more likely to commit certain errors in reasoning:

1. POST HOC ERGO PROPTER HOC (AFTER THIS, THEREFORE, BECAUSE OF THIS)

This argues that if one thing happened after another, then the first thing must have caused the second. "The Boston Tea Party caused the War for Independence because it happened right before the war."

2. FALSE SCENARIO

Arguing that if something in history had not happened, then all the events following it would never have happened either. "If General MacArthur had never been born, then we would all be speaking Japanese now."

3. FAULTY ANALOGY

Arguing that two things which are similar in some ways are similar in virtually all ways. "Both the American Revolution and the French Revolution involved an unhappy populace getting rid of a king, therefore both revolutions must have pursued the same ideals."

4. HASTY GENERALIZATION

Overgeneralizing without enough of a sample. "Cretans are liars, evil, and lazy. I've met several who were that way."

5. PROOF BY FAILURE TO FIND CONTRARY EVIDENCE

Assuming something has been proven true just because it has not been proven false yet. "Cretans are liars, evil, and lazy. I have yet to meet one who wasn't."

6. PROOF BY APPARENCY

Something must apparently be true because "everybody knows" it. "Everybody knows that Cretans are liars, evil, and lazy."

7. PROOF BY MASSIVE AMOUNTS OF EVIDENCE

Proving an argument's validity by the sheer number of arguments or evidence in favor of it – even though all the arguments or evidence may be based on false assumptions. "We have checked literally hundreds of documents, and they all say the Romans had lead poisoning."

8. APPEAL TO AUTHORITY

Arguing based on views of people in authority. "This historian says that the cause for the fall of Rome was lead poisoning. He must be right. After all, he's famous."

9. EITHER-OR REASONING

Presenting an issue as if there were only a few possible explanations, when there could be more. "The fall of Rome was either caused by lead poisoning, or else aliens from outer space infiltrated them. Rome had no lead mines, so it must have been the aliens."

10. AD HOMINEM ATTACK

Discrediting a man's argument by discrediting the man, not his argument. "Don't trust what that man says. He's a Cretan. Everybody knows they are liars, evil, and lazy."

This is obviously only a partial list, but we all understand the principle that historians are subject to the same infirmities of fallacy as are we all.

The remainder of this "Using Primary Sources to Study History" is an excerpt from Martin Anstey, *The Romance of Bible Chronology,* (London: Marshall Brothers, 1913) volume one, pages 54-60. Anstey describes and discusses the different kinds of evidence, contrasts the character of Biblical evidence with that of all other ancient evidence, then lists seven "Canons of Credibility."

THE TRUSTWORTHINESS OF TESTIMONY

The Science of History stands upon a different basis from that of the Science of Nature. In all matters relating to the facts and events of past history there is one and only one kind of proof possible, and that is, not deductive proof, as in Mathematics, and not inductive proof of the kind which is admissible in the Natural Sciences, but legal, evidential, or historical proof, of the kind required in a Court of Law.

If a man denies a mathematical truth, that truth can be demonstrated in such a way as to compel belief. If for example, a man denies that two and two make four, or that the three angles of a triangle are equal to two right angles, it is not the propositions that become of doubtful validity, but the competence or the sanity of the man who denies them.

Or again, if he denies that oxygen and hydrogen under certain given conditions combine to form water, he can be taken into a chemical laboratory, in which the fact is verified, and ocular demonstration of its truth is given so as to again compel belief.

But when we come to the sifting of evidence, and the proof of the truth of events belonging to the past, the case is essentially different. If a man denies that there ever was such a person as Alfred the Great, or William the Conqueror, or Napoleon, or Jesus Christ, Moses, Abraham, or Adam, the only kind of proof which it is possible to adduce in support of the fact of the past existence of these persons is that of evidence, or testimony. The lawyer "proves" his case by calling his witnesses; the historian by adducing Monumental, documentary, or other evidence.

The trustworthiness of testimony is the fundamental postulate of all history. If this be called in question it is impossible to proceed a single step in the Science of History. But some testimony is not trustworthy, and it is the business of the historian, or the Chronologer, to sift the evidence, to probe the character of the witness, and to test the trustworthiness of the testimony given. For the prosecution of this task certain rules have been laid down which define the limits within which testimony may be regarded as worthy of acceptance and belief.

A credible witness is one who is at once both honest, capable and contemporary.

The fact that all the writers of the Old Testament were aided by Divine Inspiration gives a double sanction, and a supernatural authority to their writings. As mere human witnesses, and altogether apart from Divine Inspiration, their evidence would be valid for the periods on which they wrote.

The testimony they bear is one and undivided, it is continuous and uninterrupted from the Patriarchal period to the Theocratic; from that to the Monarchic, the period of the Captivity, the Return, the Scribes, the Talmudists, and the Masoretes, the writings of the Old Testament have been handed down in one continuous, unbroken line of succession, until the time of their publication in the printed Hebrew Bibles of the present day. They are therefore worthy of acceptance as the work of honest, capable and contemporary witnesses, whose testimony has been faithfully preserved, and duly accredited to each succeeding generation, right down to, and including, our own.

Canons of Credibility

The Hebrew Records of the Old Testament possess, from the very earliest times, a definite historical character, in marked contrast with those of other nations. The antiquities of the Greeks are full of poetic fictions. They wrote nothing in prose till after the conquest of Asia by Cyrus. "Their own times," says Sir Isaac Newton, in his *Chronology of Ancient Kingdoms Amended*, "were divided into three parts. Those before the Flood of Ogyges they called 'Unknown,' because they had no history of them. Those between the Flood of Ogyges and the first Olympiad they called 'Fabulous' because it was full of fables. Those subsequent to the first Olympiad, B.C. 776, they called historical, but they had no Chronology of the times preceding the Persian Empire," except in so far as they subsequently constructed one by means of inference and conjecture. The antiquities of all other nations are likewise lost in the mists of early legend, myth and fable. The religious systems of Greece and Rome, Egypt and India, Persia and other nations of the East, did not even postulate a historical basis. The farther back we trace their past history, the more obscure and uncertain it becomes.

With the Hebrew Records the case is quite different. The history of the race begins with an epoch which is quite definite, and the record of the first 2369 years, the period covered by the Book of Genesis, is stated with such minute accuracy and precision, that for those who accept the Hebrew Text there is no possible alternative to that of Ussher, as shown in the margin of the Authorised Version of our English Bibles. The chronological record is accurately continued, and may be definitely traced through the succeeding Centuries. It is only when we reach the latest records of Ezra and Nehemiah that chronological difficulties become acute, and only after the close of the Canon that the count of the years is altogether lost.

The annals of the Hebrew nation are authentic narratives by contemporary writers. The Biblical Record is the Record of the redeeming activity of God. This Record is embedded in a human history, but it is a miraculous history throughout.

It is not only a history of the external events of the life of men. In its primary significance it is a history of God, and of His activity within the realm of human history. Hence, none but men informed by the Spirit of God could write it, and only by faith in the truth of the Revelation can we ever hope to be able to understand it. The essence of Revelation is redemption, and redemption is a deed of God, done, as it were, within the veil, yet manifesting itself to us in the Revelation given in Holy Scripture, as a Divine movement in human history.

We trace the history in one unbroken line, from the Creation of Adam to the Crucifixion. Bible Chronology is an exact science. It is not built upon hypothesis and conjecture. It rests ultimately upon evidence, or testimony, but it does occasionally require the use of the method of scientific historic induction.

. . . [T]he supposed parallelism between the early records of other nations, with their prodigies, and miracles, and Divine appearances, their myths and legends, and fictitious personages, does not really exist. Accurate historical investigation establishes the authenticity of the facts, and the reality of the persons presented to us in the writings of the Old Testament, so far as these can be tested by the application of the laws of history or the Canons of historic Truth.

These Canons are of universal applicability. They are aptly formulated by George Rawlinson in his Bampton Lectures for 1859, on "The Historical Evidences of the Truth of Scripture Records." They may be briefly summarized as follows:

Canon I. When the record which we possess of an event is the writing of a contemporary, supposing that he is a credible witness, and had means of observing the fact to which he testifies, the fact is to be accepted as possessing the first, or highest degree of credibility. Such evidence is on a par with that of witnesses in a Court of Justice.

Canon II. When the event recorded is one which the writer may reasonably be supposed to have obtained directly from those who witnessed it, we should accept it as probably true, unless it be in itself very improbable. Such evidence possesses the second degree of historical credibility.

Canon III. When the event recorded is removed considerably from the age of the recorder of it, and there is no reason to believe that he obtained it from a contemporary writing, but the probable source of his information was oral tradition; still, if the event be one of great importance, and of public notoriety, if it affected the national life, or prosperity – especially if it be of a nature to have been at once commemorated by the establishment of any rite or practice – then it has a claim to belief as probably true, at least in its general outline. This, however, is the third, and a comparatively low degree of historical credibility.

Canon IV. When the traditions of one race are corroborated by the traditions of another . . . the event which has this double testimony, obtains thereby a high amount of probability, and, if not very unlikely in itself, thoroughly deserves acceptance.

Canon V. Direct records, such as those which proceed from the agents in the occurrences, public inscribed Monuments such as have frequently been set up by Governments and Kings, state papers, such as those contained in the Books of Ezra and Esther, autobiographies and memoirs, deserve the very highest degree of credit, and are the best and most authentic sources of history.

Canon VI. Indirect records, embodying the result of personal enquiry and research, are to be placed on a much lower footing, and must be judged by the opportunity, the competency, and the veracity of their composers.

Canon VII. The cumulative evidence of two or more independent witnesses to the same event, increases the probability of the event, not in an arithmetical, but in a geometrical ratio. "At the mouth of two or three witnesses" the word to which such witness is borne is "established" (Deut. 19:15).

Canon Rawlinson enters a caveat [warning] against the exaltation into a Canon of historical truth, of the false assumption now almost universally prevalent, of "the inviolability of the chain of finite causes, and the impossibility of miracles." Events are not self-caused, and self-sustained, possessing powers that lie beyond the control of the Divine Will, and working by their own inherent power of self-determination, or necessity. They take place either mediately, in obedience to the Laws of Nature, which are simply so many expressions of the will of God, or else immediately, as a result of the direct immediate act of God, in which case they are described as miraculous, or supernatural. The sacred records themselves are the proof of the miraculous events contained in them. The principles of historical criticism do not force us to reject them, but compel us to accept them as true.

Timeline
of Ancient Literature

How to Use the Timeline of Ancient Literature

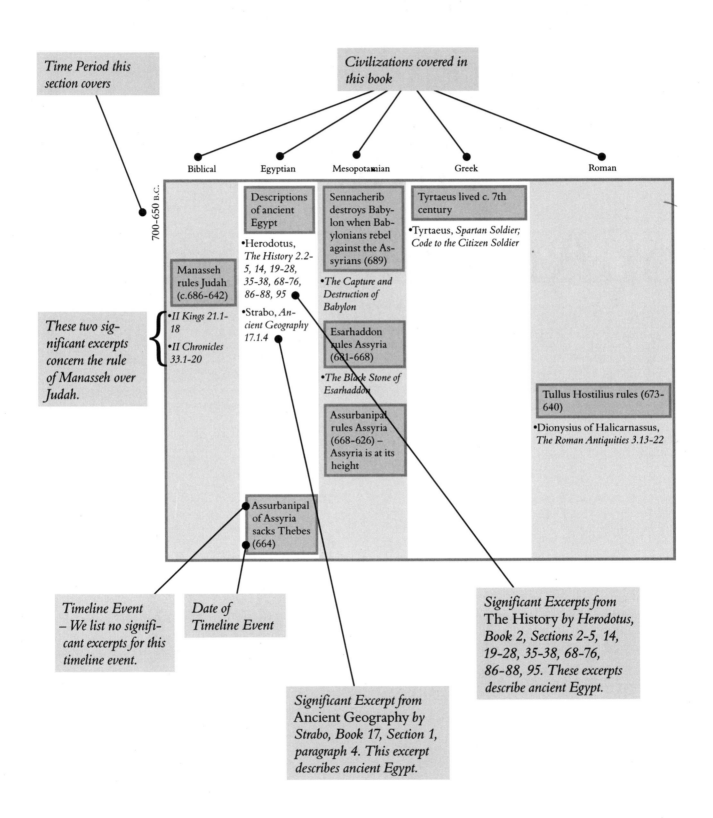

Time Period this section covers

Civilizations covered in this book

Biblical   Egyptian   Mesopotamian   Greek   Roman

700-650 B.C.

These two significant excerpts concern the rule of Manasseh over Judah.

Manasseh rules Judah (c.686-642)

•II Kings 21.1-18

•II Chronicles 33.1-20

Descriptions of ancient Egypt

•Herodotus, *The History 2.2-5, 14, 19-28, 35-38, 68-76, 86-88, 95*

•Strabo, *Ancient Geography 17.1.4*

Sennacherib destroys Babylon when Babylonians rebel against the Assyrians (689)

•*The Capture and Destruction of Babylon*

Esarhaddon rules Assyria (681-668)

•*The Black Stone of Esarhaddon*

Assurbanipal rules Assyria (668-626) – Assyria is at its height

Tyrtaeus lived c. 7th century

•Tyrtaeus, *Spartan Soldier; Code to the Citizen Soldier*

Tullus Hostilius rules (673-640)

•Dionysius of Halicarnassus, *The Roman Antiquities 3.13-22*

Assurbanipal of Assyria sacks Thebes (664)

Timeline Event – We list no significant excerpts for this timeline event.

Date of Timeline Event

Significant Excerpt from Ancient Geography by Strabo, Book 17, Section 1, paragraph 4. This excerpt describes ancient Egypt.

Significant Excerpts from The History by Herodotus, Book 2, Sections 2-5, 14, 19-28, 35-38, 68-76, 86-88, 95. These excerpts describe ancient Egypt.

Timeline from Creation through A.D. 476

Before Christ

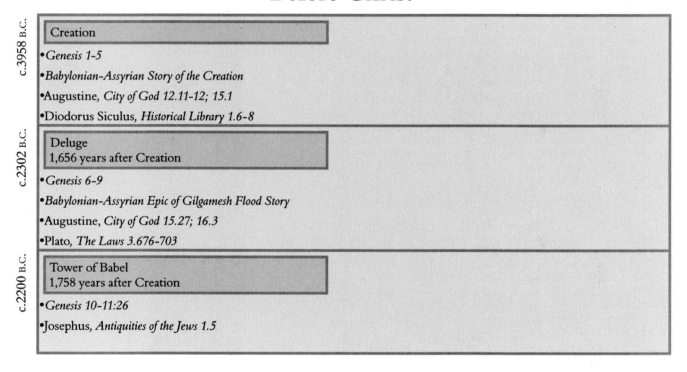

c.3958 B.C.

Creation
- *Genesis 1-5*
- *Babylonian-Assyrian Story of the Creation*
- Augustine, *City of God 12.11-12; 15.1*
- Diodorus Siculus, *Historical Library 1.6-8*

c.2302 B.C.

Deluge
1,656 years after Creation
- *Genesis 6-9*
- *Babylonian-Assyrian Epic of Gilgamesh Flood Story*
- Augustine, *City of God 15.27; 16.3*
- Plato, *The Laws 3.676-703*

c.2200 B.C.

Tower of Babel
1,758 years after Creation
- *Genesis 10-11:26*
- Josephus, *Antiquities of the Jews 1.5*

2200 B.C. to 1500 B.C. [Dates during this period are uncertain.]

Hebrew & Christian	Egyptian	Mesopotamian	Greek	Roman
	Menes – possibly the first pharaoh of Egypt		The rise of the Minoan civilization on the island of Crete (c.2100-1400)	
	•*Egyptian Precepts*		•Diodorus Siculus, *Historical Library 4.79; 5.78, 84*	
	Cheops (Khufu) rules – builds the largest pyramid.	Sargon of Accad builds an empire in Babylonia and Assyria.		
	•Herodotus, *The History 2.124-128*	•*Chronicle of the Reign of Sargon*		
Abram born in Ur of the Chaldeans (2,008 years after Creation, or c.1950)	•Diodorus Siculus, *Historical Library 1.63-64*			
	Pepi II rules – longest reign in human history.			
Abram is called by God and travels to Canaan (2,083 years after Creation, or c.1875).	•*Letter of Pepi II* •*Edwin Smith Surgical Papyrus* •*Epitaph of Beka* •*The Laboring Classes* •*Story of Sinuhe* •*The Shipwrecked Sailor*			
	Amenemhat III rules (c.1678-1632).			
Jacob is established in Egypt (2,298 years after Creation, or c.1660).		Hammurabi – ruler of the Old Babylonian Empire (c.1565)		
•*Genesis 11:27-50:26* •*Job*		•*Achievements of Hammurabi* •*Code of Hammurabi*		

	Hebrew & Christian	Egyptian	Mesopotamian	Greek	Roman
1500-1450 B.C.				Mycenaean Civilization flourishes on Greek mainland (1500-1120). •Herodotus, *The History 1.171; 3.122*	
1450-1400 B.C.	Moses leads the Israelites out of Egypt (2,513 years after Creation, or c.1445) •*Exodus* •*Leviticus* •*Numbers* •*Deuteronomy* Israel enters Canaan (2,553 years after Creation, or c.1405). •*Joshua*	Dudimose rules – possibly the pharaoh of the Exodus (c.1448-1445). The Hyksos rule Egypt (c.1445-1200).		Minoan Civilization disappears (c.1400).	
1400-1350 B.C.	The period of the judges (c.1399-1050) •*Judges* •*Ruth*				
1350-1300 B.C.					
1300-1250 B.C.			Ninus founds the Assyrian Empire c.1267.		
1250-1200 B.C.					

	Hebrew & Christian	Egyptian	Mesopotamian	Greek	Roman
1200-1150 B.C.		Ahmose rules (c.1194-1170).		The Achaeans move into Greece and establish themselves (c.1200-1000).	
		Amenhotep I rules (c.1170-1150).		Mycenaeans destroy the city of Troy (c.1200).	
		Thutmose I rules (c.1150-1139).			
1150-1100 B.C.		Thutmose II rules (c.1139-1138).			
		Thutmose III rules (c.1138-1085).			
		•*Products of Arabia*			
		Hatshepsut rules (c.1131-1116).			
			Tiglath-Pilesar I rules Assyria (c.1120-1100) – moves capital of Assyrian Empire to Ninevah.	Dorians invade Greece and destroy Mycenae. Dorians found Sparta. Refugees of Mycenae found Athens (c.1120).	
			•*Inscription of Tiglath-Pilesar I*	Kings rule Greece.	
1100-1050 B.C.		Amenhotep II rules (c.1085-1059).			
		•*Pharaoh Amenhotep II as a Sportsman*			
		Thutmose IV rules (c.1059-1050).			

	Hebrew & Christian	Egyptian	Mesopotamian	Greek	Roman
1050-1000 B.C.	Saul rules Israel (c.1050-1010). •*I Samuel* David begins to reign in Hebron (c.1010-970). •*II Samuel* •*I Chronicles* •*Psalms*	Amenhotep III rules (c.1050-1012). Akhenaten (Amenhotep IV) rules (c.1022-1006). •*Tablets of Tel El-Amarna* Smenkhkare rules (c.1006-1003). Tutankhamun rules (c.1003-994).			
1000- 950 B.C.	Solomon rules Israel (c.970-930). •*I Kings 1-11* •*II Chronicles 1-9* •*Proverbs* •*Ecclesiastes* •*Song of Solomon* Solomon begins to build the temple (c.966). •*I Kings 6.1*	Ay rules (c.994-989). Haremheb rules (c.989-960). Haremheb is possibly the pharaoh who gave his daughter to Solomon. Ramesses I rules (c.961-959). Seti I rules (c.959-940).			

950-900 B.C.

Hebrew & Christian	Egyptian	Mesopotamian	Greek	Roman
Kingdom is divided c.930.	Ramesses the Great rules (c.940-873).			
Rehoboam rules Judah (c.930-913) and Jeroboam rules Israel (c.930-909).	•*Ramesses II, Son and Second Self of the God Ptah-To-tunen*			
•*I Kings 12-14*	Battle of Kadesh – Ramesses fights the Hittite king Muwatallis II.			
•*II Chronicles 10-12*	•*Ramesses at Kadesh*			
Ramesses the Great (called Shishak in the Bible) sacks Jerusalem (925).	•*Treaty between Ramesses II and the Hittite King Hattusilis III*			
•*I Kings 14:25-26*	•*Apology of Hattusilis III*			
•*II Chronicles 12: 2-9*	•*The Israel Stela of Merneptah*			
Abijah rules Judah (c.913-910).				
Asa rules Judah (c.910-869).				
Nadab rules Israel (c.909-908).				
Baasha rules Israel (c.908-885).				
•*I Kings 15-16:7*				
•*II Chronicles 13-16*				

	Hebrew & Christian	Egyptian	Mesopotamian	Greek	Roman

900-850 B.C.

Hebrew & Christian

Elah rules Israel (c.885-884).

Zimri rules Israel (c.884).

Tibni rules Israel (c.884-880).

Omri rules Israel (c.880-873).

Ahab rules Israel (c.873-853).

Jehoshaphat rules Judah (c.869-848).

Elijah begins to prophesy (865).

Ahaziah rules Israel (c.853-852).

Joram rules Israel (c.852-841).

•*I Kings 16:8-22*

•*II Kings 1-3*

•*II Chronicles 17-20*

Egyptian

Ramesses III rules (c.866-835).

Mesopotamian

Assurnasirpal II rules Assyria (c.884-860).

•*Moabite Stone*

Shalmaneser III rules Assyria (c.860-825).

Greek

Rise of Sparta and Lycurgus's Laws

•Plutarch, *Lives, Lycurgus 1-6, 8-10, 16-20, 27-31*

•Xenophon, *Constitution of the Lacedaemonians 2-5, 7-8, 10*

•Herodotus, *The History 6.56-58*

	Hebrew & Christian	Egyptian	Mesopotamian	Greek	Roman
850-800 B.C.	Elisha begins to prophesy (850).				
	Jehoram rules Judah (848-841).				
	Ahaziah rules Judah (841).				
	Athaliah rules Judah (841-835).				
	Jehu rules Israel (841-813).				
	Joash rules Judah (835-796).				
	Jehoahaz rules Israel (813-798).	Ramesses IX rules (c.835-816).			
	II Kings 4-13:9	•*Spoliation of Tombs*			
	II Chronicles 21-24				

	Hebrew & Christian	Egyptian	Mesopotamian	Greek	Roman

800-750 B.C.

Hebrew & Christian	Greek	Roman
Jehoash rules Israel (c.798-781).		
Amaziah rules Judah (c.796-767).		
Jeroboam II rules Israel (c.781-753).		
Uzziah rules Judah (c.767-739).	First Olympic Games (776) - True Greek history begins with this date.	
Zechariah rules Israel (c.753-752).		
Shallum rules Israel (c.752).		Founding of Rome (753)
Menahem rules Israel (c.752-741).		Kings rule Rome (753-509).

•*II Kings 13:10-15:22*

•*II Chronicles 25-26*

•*Jonah*

•*Amos*

•*Hosea*

Roman column:

•Strabo, *Ancient Geography 5.3*

•Pliny the Elder, *Natural History 3.5*

•Virgil, *Georgics 2.136-225*

•Dionysius of Halicarnassus, *The Roman Antiquities 1.3, 72-75*

•Eutropius, *A Concise History of Rome 1.1-20*

•Livy, *The Early History of Rome 1.1-7*

Romulus rules (753 -715).

•Dionysius of Halicarnassus, *The Roman Antiquities 1.88; 2.7-14, 16, 18-21, 26-27*

•Cicero, *On the State 2.5-17*

	Hebrew & Christian	Egyptian	Mesopotamian	Greek	Roman

750-700 B.C.

Hebrew & Christian

Pekahiah rules Israel (c.741-739).

Jotham rules Judah (c.739-731).

Pekah rules Israel (c.739-731).

Ahaz rules Judah (c.731-715).

Hoshea rules Israel (c.731-722).

Sargon of Assyria carries away the people of Israel (722).

Hezekiah rules Judah (c.715-686).

Assyrian campaign against Judah (701)

•*II Kings 15: 23-20*

•*II Chronicles 27-32*

•*Isaiah*

•*Micah*

Mesopotamian

Tiglath-Pileser III rules Assyria (747-728).

Shalmaneser V rules Assyria (728-722).

Sargon II rules Assyria (721-705).

•*Sargon's Capture of Samaria*

Sennacherib rules Assyria (705-681).

•*Annals of Sennacherib*

•*Letter of an Assyrian Physician Reporting Upon a Patient*

Greek

Homer lived c. eighth century.

•Homer – *The Iliad; The Odyssey*

Monarchy ends. Development of the City-States c.750-550

•Aristotle – *The Athenian Constitution 2-3*

Hesiod lived c. eighth century.

•Hesiod – *Works and Days 342-345, 571-581, 618 ff.*

Roman

Numa Pompilius rules (715-673).

•Livy – *The Early History of Rome 1.19-20*

•Plutarch – *Lives, Numa 17*

700-650 B.C.	Hebrew & Christian	Egyptian	Mesopotamian	Greek	Roman
		Descriptions of ancient Egypt	Sennacherib destroys Babylon when Babylonians rebel against the Assyrians (689).	Tyrtaeus lived c. seventh century.	
		•Herodotus, *The History 2.2-5, 14, 19-28, 35-38, 68-76, 86-88, 95*	•*Sennacherib: The Capture and Destruction of Babylon*	•Tyrtaeus, *Spartan Soldier; Code of the Citizen Soldier*	
	Manasseh rules Judah (c.686-642).	•Strabo, *Ancient Geography 17.1.4*	Esarhaddon rules Assyria (681-668).		
	•*II Kings 21:1-18*		•*The Black Stone of Esarhaddon*		Tullus Hostilius rules (673-640).
	•*II Chronicles 33: 1-20*		Assurbanipal rules Assyria (668-626). Assyria is at its height.		•Dionysius of Halicarnassus, *The Roman Antiquities 3.13-22*
		Assurbanipal of Assyria sacks Thebes (664).			

	Hebrew & Christian	Egyptian	Mesopotamian	Greek	Roman

650-600 B.C.

Hebrew & Christian

Amon rules Judah (c.642-640).

Josiah rules Judah (c.640-609).

Jehoahaz rules Judah (c.609).

Jehoiakim rules Judah (c.609-598).

Daniel is taken captive to Babylon by Nebuchadnezzar (605).

•*II Kings 21:19-24:7*

•*II Chronicles 33:21-36:8*

•*Zephaniah*

•*Joel*

•*Habakkuk*

•*Jeremiah*

•*Lamentations*

•*Daniel*

•*Nahum*

Mesopotamian

Nabopolassar rules Chaldea (626-605).

Chaldeans (with the Medes and Scythians) destroy Nineveh (612) and defeat the Assyrians; Babylon becomes their capital.

Nebuchad-nezzar rules (605-562).

•*An Inscription of Nebuchadnezzar*

Greek

Thales born – mathematician and scientist (c.624-546).

•Diogenes Laertius, *Lives of the Philosophers, Thales*

•Aristotle,

Metaphysics 983b 20-28

On the Soul 405a 20-22; 411a 7-8

On the Heavens 294a 28-66

Politics 1.11

•Herodotus, *The History 1.74-75*

•Josephus, *Against Apion 1.2*

•Plato, *Protagoras 342e-343a*

Draco's Bloody Laws (621)

•Aristotle, *The Athenian Constitution 4*

Anaximander born – philosopher (611-547).

•Diogenes Laertius, *Lives of the Philosophers, Anaximander*

	Hebrew & Christian	Egyptian	Mesopotamian	Greek	Roman
600-575 B.C.	Jeconiah rules Judah (c.598-597). Nebuchadnezzar captures Jeconiah and takes him to Babylon and makes Zedekiah ruler (597). Zedekiah rules Judah (c.597-586). Nebuchadnezzar takes Jerusalem and burns temple (586). •*II Kings 24:8-25:30* •*II Chronicles 36.9-21* •*Ezekiel* •*Obadiah* •Josephus, *Antiquities of the Jews 10.8.1-7*		Descriptions of ancient Babylon •*A Babylonian Lawsuit* •Strabo, *Ancient Geography 16.1.5* •Herodotus, *The History 1.195* •Diodorus Siculus, *Historical Library 2.7-12, 29-31*	Reforms of Solon at Athens (594) •Plutarch, *Lives, Solon 14, 24, 29-31* •Aristotle, *The Athenian Constitution 5-12* •Herodotus, *The History 1.29-33* •Demosthenes, *On the Embassy 255* •Diodorus Siculus, *Historical Library 9.1, 3-4, 17, 20, 26-27* •Diogenes Laertius, *Lives of the Philosophers, Solon* Aesop lives c. sixth century •Aesop, *Fables* Early Greek history •Herodotus, *The History 5.49-51, 58, 66-77, 97, 99-101* •Thucydides, *The History of the Peloponnesian War 1.2-11* Pythagoras born (582-500) – Greek philosopher and mathematician. •Diogenes Laertius, *Lives of the Philosophers, Pythagoras* •Strabo, *Ancient Geography 10.3.10* •Diodorus Siculus, *Historical Library 10.3-11*	Servius Tullius rules (578-535). •Livy, *The Early History of Rome 1.43-44*

	Hebrew & Christian	Egyptian	Mesopotamian	Greek	Roman
575-550 B.C.		Amasis II rules (570-526).	Nabonidus/ Belshazzar rules Chaldean Empire at Babylon (562-539). Persia rises to power. •Herodotus, *The History 1.95-106* Cyrus the Great rules the Persians (559-529). •Herodotus, *The History, 1.107-130, 190-191* •Xenophon, *Cyropaedia, 1.2-4; 8.7*	Pisistratus rules Athens (560-527). •Aristotle, *The Athenian Constitution 13-19* •Diodorus Siculus, *Historical Library 9.17, 20, 37*	

	Hebrew & Christian	Egyptian	Mesopotamian	Greek	Roman

550-525 B.C.

Hebrew & Christian

Cyrus allows Jews to return to their land and rebuild temple (537).

•*II Chronicles 36: 22-23*

•Josephus, *Antiquities of the Jews 11.1.1-3*

•*Ezra 1-4*

Egyptian

Psammetichus III rules (526-525).

Persia conquers Egypt (525).

Mesopotamian

Cyrus the Persian captures Babylon, and Chaldean Empire comes to an end (538).

•*How Cyrus Took Babylon (538)*

Cambyses rules the Persian Empire (529-522).

Roman

Tarquinius Superbus rules (534-509).

Hebrew & Christian	Egyptian	Mesopotamian	Greek	Roman

525-500 B.C.

Mesopotamian

Darius rules Persia (522-485).

•Herodotus, *The History 3.80-97*

•*The Behistan Inscription of King Darius*

•*Letter of Darius*

Description of Persians

•Herodotus, *The History 1.131-140*

Hebrew & Christian

Temple completed (516).

•*Zechariah*

•*Haggai*

•*Ezra 5-6*

Roman

Fall of monarchy at Rome; institution of two annual consuls; Roman Republic established (509)

•Cicero, *On the State 2.30, 32*

•Livy, *The Early History of Rome 2.1-2, 5, 9-10*

•Polybius, *The Histories 3.22*

The Dictators rule (509-450)

•Dionysius of Halicarnassus, *The Roman Antiquities 5.5-8, 75; 6.95.1-2; 9.41*

•Livy, *The Early History of Rome 2.18*

Growth of plebeian rights (509-367)

•Livy, *The Early History of Rome 2.23-24, 32-33; 3.26-29; 4.1-2, 4-6, 8, 35, 42*

•Cicero, *On the State 2.34*

•Dionysius of Halicarnassus, *The Roman Antiquities 11.45, 53-63*

Greek

Reforms of Cleisthenes at Athens (508)

•Aristotle, *The Athenian Constitution 20-22*

Popular democracy develops in Greece; Pre-Persian War.

•Gellius, *Attic Nights 7.17*

	Hebrew & Christian	Egyptian	Mesopotamian	Greek	Roman
500-475 B.C.				Anaxagorus born (500-427) – philosopher.	
				•Diogenes Laertius, *Lives of the Philosophers, Anaxagorus*	
				Persian Wars between Persia and Greece (490-449)	
				•Herodotus, *The History 5.102-106; 6.102-117, 120; 7.1-7, 22-24, 33-56, 60-83, 100-105, 118-120, 138-147, 175-177, 196-234; 8.40-43, 74-86, 96-99, 143; 9.52-70, 82*	
				•Aeschylus, *The Persians*	
		Xerxes I (Aha-suerus) rules Persia (485-465).	•Plutarch, *Lives, Themistocles 6-15, 19; Aristides 6-8, 22-24*	
				•Aristotle, *The Athenian Constitution 23-24*	
			•Herodotus, *The History 8.118*	Herodotus born (484-425) – Greek historian.	
	Esther marries Xerxes I of Persia (483)				
	•*Esther*				

475-450 B.C.	Hebrew & Christian	Egyptian	Mesopotamian	Greek	Roman
				Cimon is leading politician of Athens (474-462).	
				•Plutarch, *Lives, Cimon 10-11*	
				Socrates born (469-399) – Greek philosopher.	
				•Diogenes Laertius, *Lives of the Philosophers, Socrates*	
				•Plato, *Symposium 219e*	
			Artaxerxes I rules Persia (474-425).	•Augustine, *City of God 8.1-3*	
				•Salvian, *Of God's Government 7.23*	
				Hippocrates born (460-377) – Greek "Father of Medicine."	
	Second return of the Jews to Judea under Ezra (458)			•Hippocrates, *On Ancient Medicine 1-7, 13, 16, 19-20*	
				– *The Oath of Medical Ethics*	
				– *On Airs, Waters, and Places 1-16*	
	•*Ezra 7-10*			– *On the Sacred Disease*	
				– *The Instruments of Reduction 1*	
				– *The Epidemics I, 1-3*	
					The first Decemvirate; The Law of the Twelve Tables (451)
					•Livy, *The Early History of Rome 3.33-34*
					•Cicero, *The Making of an Orator 1.43-44*
					•Gellius, *Attic Nights 11.18*

	Hebrew & Christian	Egyptian	Mesopotamian	Greek	Roman

450–425 B.C.

Third return of Jews to Judea under Nehemiah (445)

•*Nehemiah*

Herodotus visits Egypt (440).

Pericles leads the Athenians in a democracy (443-429).

•Thucydides, *The History of the Peloponnesian War 1.139-146; 2.13, 34-46, 59-65*

•Plutarch, *Lives, Pericles 3-5, 7-9, 12-13, 29-33*

•Aristotle, *The Athenian Constitution 25-27*

•Plato, *Gorgias 515-517*

Peloponnesian War between Athens and Sparta (431-404)

•Thucydides, *The History of the Peloponnesian War 1.12-23, 31-44, 66-71, 89- 99, 103-113; 2.2-9, 47-54; 3.20-24, 36-50, 82-84; 4.3-14; 5.17-19, 77-79, 84-116; 6.1-5, 24-32; 7.70-87; 8.1-2, 48*

•Xenophon, *Hellenica 1.6.24-38; 2.1*

•Diodorus Siculus, *Historical Library 12.38-40*

Plato born (427-348) – philosopher

•Plato, *The Republic 7.514-21, 525-530*

– *The Laws 7.817e-820d*

•Augustine, *City of God 8.4-8, 10-16*

•Gellius, *Attic Nights 3.13; 14.3*

425–400 B.C.

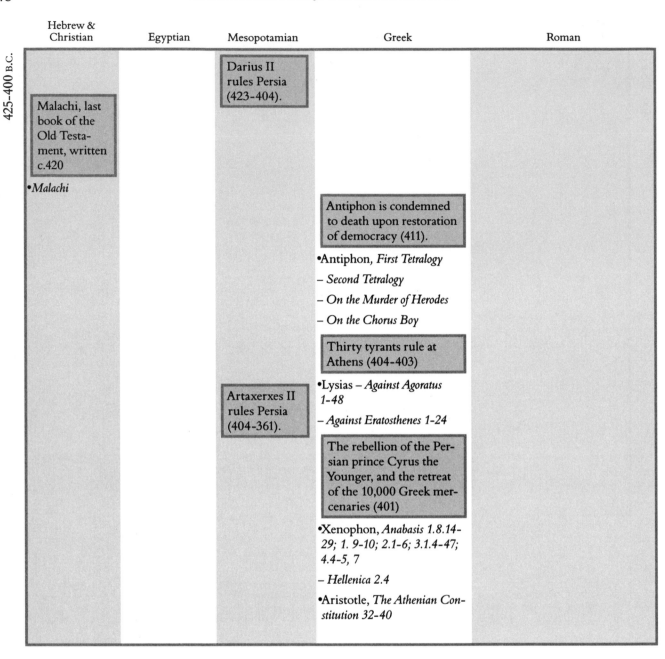

Hebrew & Christian	Egyptian	Mesopotamian	Greek	Roman
Malachi, last book of the Old Testament, written c.420		Darius II rules Persia (423-404).		
•*Malachi*				
			Antiphon is condemned to death upon restoration of democracy (411).	
			•Antiphon, *First Tetralogy*	
			– *Second Tetralogy*	
			– *On the Murder of Herodes*	
			– *On the Chorus Boy*	
			Thirty tyrants rule at Athens (404-403)	
		Artaxerxes II rules Persia (404-361).	•Lysias – *Against Agoratus 1-48*	
			– *Against Eratosthenes 1-24*	
			The rebellion of the Persian prince Cyrus the Younger, and the retreat of the 10,000 Greek mercenaries (401)	
			•Xenophon, *Anabasis 1.8.14-29; 1. 9-10; 2.1-6; 3.1.4-47; 4.4-5, 7*	
			– *Hellenica 2.4*	
			•Aristotle, *The Athenian Constitution 32-40*	

	Hebrew & Christian	Egyptian	Mesopotamian	Greek	Roman
400-375 B.C.				**Execution of Socrates (399)** •Plato, *The Phaedo, 113d-118a* – *Crito 50-54* – *Apology of Socrates 17a-42a* **Aristotle born (384-322) – philosopher** •Aristotle, *Politics, 1.1-2; 3.4-7; 4.10-12; 7.4-5, 11; 8.1-3* – *On the Parts of Animals 2.4-5, 7, 9-10, 17; 3.1* – *On the Progression of Animals 8,11* – *Poetics 15, 17-18, 20-25* •Gellius, *Attic Nights 13.5; 20.4* **Demosthenes born (384-322) – orator** •Plutarch, *Lives, Demosthenes 5-11* **Isocrates writes *Panegyricus* (380).** •Isocrates, *Panegyricus 110-122*	**Gauls sack Rome (390).** •Plutarch, *Lives, Camillus 18, 22, 27-30* •Livy, *The Early History of Rome 5.39-43, 47-49*

375-350 B.C.

Hebrew & Christian	Egyptian	Mesopotamian	Greek	Roman
		Artaxerxes III rules Persia (361-338).	Pyrrho born (365-275) – philosopher. •Diogenes Laertius, *Lives of the Philosophers, Pyrrho* Philip of Macedon rules (359-336). •Diodorus Siculus, *Historical Library 16.1-3, 14* •Justin, *Epitome of the Philippic Histories 7.5; 9.3-5, 8; 50.100* •Isocrates, *On the Areopagiticus 1-28, 76-84* •Xenophon, *Hellenica 5.3-4; 6.4; 7.5* •Aristotle, *The Athenian Constitution 42-69* •Demosthenes, *The First Philippic 2-12, 40-41, 47-51* •Plutarch, *Lives, Demosthenes 16-18*	The Licinian Laws (367); plebeians win their rights. •Polybius, *The Histories 6.2-19, 21-24, 38-39, 43-57* •Livy, *The Early History of Rome 6.34-42; 8.8, 14* •Gellius, *Attic Nights 16.13* •Velleius, *History of Rome 1.14*

Hebrew & Christian	Egyptian	Mesopotamian	Greek	Roman

350-338 B.C.

Egyptian

Artaxerxes III conquers Egypt (343).

Mesopotamian

Arses rules Persia (338-336).

Greek

Isocrates writes *To Philip* (346).

•Isocrates, *To Philip 14-16, 30-41, 68-71, 154*

Aeschines delivers *On the Embassy* (343) and *Against Ctesiphon* (330).

•Aeschines, *Against Ctesiphon; On the Embassy*

Demosthenes delivers *The Third Philippic* (341) and *On the Crown* (330).

•Demosthenes, *The Third Philippic 1-5, 36-40, 67-76*

– *On the Crown 1-8, 42-51, 66-72, 95-101, 168-179, 188-194, 199-210, 232-235, 321-324*

Epicurus born (341-270) – philosopher.

•Epicurus, *Letter to Menoeceus*

•Diogenes Laertius, *Lives of the Philosophers, Epicurus*

•Ambrose, *Letters 63*

•Athanasius, *On the Incarnation of the Word 2*

	Hebrew & Christian	Egyptian	Mesopotamian	Greek	Roman
338-325 B.C.	How Alexander the Great treats the Jews •Josephus, *Antiquities of the Jews 11.8.1-7*	Alexander the Great conquers Egypt (332). The founding of Alexandria (331)	Darius III rules (336-330). Alexander the Great conquers Persian Empire (331).	Alexander the Great rules (336-323). •Diodorus Siculus, *Historical Library 17.1-7, 20-22, 49-51, 70-72, 84-107* •Strabo, *Ancient Geography 1.4.9* •Plutarch, *Lives, Alexander 4-8, 14-15, 20-21, 38, 45* •Gellius, *Attic Nights 5.2; 9.3.21* •Arrian, *Anabasis of Alexander 1.6, 11-16; 2.4, 6-14; 3.1, 3-4, 7-16; 4.8-14, 22-30; 5.1-29; 6.1-29; 7.1, 9, 24-30* •Quintus Curtius, *History of Alexander 3.11; 4.4.1-5, 10-21; 4.7; 4.9; 4.10.1-7; 5.1.17-35; 5.7; 7.4.20-25; 8.9; 9.9; 10.5* •Livy, *The Early History of Rome 9.17-19* Zeno born (336-264) – philosopher. •Diogenes Laertius, *Lives of the Philosophers, Zeno* Euclid born (330-275) – mathemetician. •Euclid, *Elements Book 7 prefix*	
325-300 B.C.	Ptolemy Soter rules Palestine (323-283).	Ptolemy Soter rules Egypt (323-283). City of Alexandria becomes "The University of the East."	Seleucus and Lysimachus rule Asia.	Alexander the Great dies at Babylon (323) and his Empire is divided among 4 generals. Cassander rules Greece and Macedon. The Hellenistic Age – Greek language is widely diffused. •Strabo, *Ancient Geography 8.1.2* Aristarchus born – Greek astronomer (310-230). •Aristarchus, *On the Sizes and Distances of the Sun and Moon*	

	Hebrew & Christian	Egyptian	Mesopotamian	Greek	Roman
300-275 B.C.	Ptolemy II rules Palestine (283-247).	Ptolemy II rules Egypt (283-247).		Archimedes (287-212) – Greek mathematician and inventor •Archimedes, *The Method, Introduction* – *On Floating Bodies, 2.318-336* – *The Sand-Reckoner, 3* •Plutarch, *Lives, Marcellus 14-19* •Polybius, *The Histories 8.5.3-5* •Livy, *The Early History of Rome 24.34* •Diodorus Siculus, *Historical Library 1.34.2; 5.37.3* Eratosthenes (276-195) – Greek scientist •Strabo, *Ancient Geography 1.4.1-9*	
275-250 B.C.	Ptolemy II causes the Hebrew scriptures to be translated into Greek (255) – called the Septuagint. •Augustine, *City of God 15.10-11* •Josephus, *Antiquities of the Jews 12.2.1-15*				The First Punic War (264-241) •Polybius, *The Histories 1.56-63; 2.1* •Appian, *The Roman History 8.3-4* •Horace, *Odes 3.5*
250-225 B.C.					

	Hebrew & Christian	Egyptian	Mesopotamian	Greek	Roman
225-200 B.C.			Antiochus III, the Great, rules the Syrian Empire (223-187).		Hannibal becomes general in Spain (221-182). •Polybius, *The Histories 9.22-26; 11.19* •Nepos, *On Famous Men: Life of Hannibal 1-13* •Livy, *The Early History of Rome 21.1, 3-4; 39.51* The Second Punic War (218-201) •Polybius, *The Histories 3.6-10, 14-15, 20-22, 27-30, 33-56, 91; 5.84-86* •Livy, *The Early History of Rome 21.10, 18, 30-38; 22.4-6, 44-49; 23.17; 26.7, 9-11; 27.45; 28.27; 30.32-35, 44-45* •Dio Cassius, *Roman History 8.21-22* •Appian, *The Roman History 6.6-13; 7.1-4*
200-175 B.C.	Antiochus III, the Great, of the Syrian Empire takes Palestine from the Ptolemies (198).				

	Hebrew & Christian	Egyptian	Mesopotamian	Greek	Roman
175-150 B.C.	Antiochus IV, Epiphanes, rules Palestine (175-164).		Antiochus IV, Epiphanes, rules the Syrian Empire (175-164).		Agriculture in second century B.C. Rome •Cato the Elder, *On Agriculture 1, 49, 98, 111, 120*
	Persecution of the Jews by Antiochus IV and desecration of the Temple at Jerusalem (168) •Josephus, *Antiquities of the Jews 12.5.3-4*				
	Jews revolt against Syria under Judas Maccabaeus (166).				
	Government of the Maccabees (166-37)				
150-125 B.C.					The Third Punic War (149-146)
				Greece conquered by Rome (146) •Pausanias, *Description of Greece 7.16*	Carthage destroyed by Rome (146) •Polybius, *The Histories 38.3-7, 9-11* •Plutarch, *Lives, Cato the Elder 25-26* •Appian, *The Roman History 8.132-135*
	Jews free from Syrian rule (135)				The Gracchus Brothers (133-121) •Appian, *The Roman History 13.7-12*

	Hebrew & Christian	Egyptian	Mesopotamian	Greek	Roman
125-100 B.C.					**Gaius Marius and Sulla (106-78)** •Sallust, *The Jugurthine War 63-65, 84-86* •Plutarch, *Lives, Marius 13, 32-35; Sulla 31-33* •Appian, *The Roman History 13.61, 76-84, 95-106* •Cicero, *Discussions at Tusculum 5.56*
100-75 B.C.					

	Hebrew & Christian	Egyptian	Mesopotamian	Greek	Roman
75-50 B.C.			Rome conquers the Syrian Empire (65).		Pompey and Caesar rule (78-49). •Plutarch, *Lives, Pompey 24-29; Caesar 15, 57-59* •Appian, *The Roman History 13.108, 114-119; 14.2-3, 7, 19, 83-87* •Cicero, *Against Catiline 1; Letter to Atticus 7.1, 20; Letters to Friends 7.5; 8.14* •Lucan, *The Civil War 1.120-157* •Caesar, *Gallic War 2.16-28; 4.20-36; 5.44; 6.13-14, 19, 21-23; 7.69-89* – *Civil War 1.1-11; 3.47, 88* •Sallust, *The Conspiracy of Catiline 1, 31, 51* Slave revolt in Rome (73) •Plutarch, *Lives, Crassus 8-11* The First Triumvirate rules Rome (60) – Crassus, Pompey and Julius Caesar. First century B.C. Roman life and philosophy •Lucretius, *On the Nature of Things 3.894-977* •Cicero, *Moral Duties 1.150-151* – *Letters to Atticus 4.4* –*Letters to Friends 4.5; 7.1; 14.1-2, 14; 16.21* –*On the State 1.35-71* – *Against Verres* – *The Making of an Orator 1.16, 25, 61; 2.12-15, 86; 3.11* •Dio Cassius, *Roman History 37.15-19*

	Hebrew & Christian	Egyptian	Mesopotamian	Greek	Roman

50–40 B.C.

The Roman Empire is founded (49).

Julius Caesar rules as dictator (49-44).

•Plutarch, *Lives, Julius Caesar 62-69*

•Suetonius, *Lives of the Twelve Caesars, Julius Caesar 1-2, 10, 14, 20, 25, 31-36, 55-56, 82*

•Appian, *The Roman History 14.106-117, 120,136-154*

•Nicolaus of Damascus, *Life of Augustus 19-22*

•Cicero, *Letters to Atticus 13.52; In Defense of Sestius 96-100, 102-103, 136-139; Second Philippic 1, 25-30, 84, 112-114, 116-119; Letters to Friends 10.28; Letters to Brutus 1.16*

•Dio Cassius, *Roman History 44.12-22*

The Second Triumvirate rules Rome (44)– Gaius Octavian, Marcus Lepidus, and Mark Antony.

•Appian, *The Roman History 15.15-20; 16.1-4, 89-101*

40–30 B.C.

Judea comes under Roman rule (37).

Herod the Great rules Judea (37-4).

Battle of Actium (31) – Octavian defeats Antony.

•Dio Cassius, *Roman History 51.9-14*

	Hebrew & Christian	Egyptian	Mesopotamian	Greek	Roman
30-20 B.C.		Rome conquers Egypt (30).			Augustus rules Rome as Emperor Augustus Caesar (30 B.C.-14 A.D.). •Suetonius, *Lives of the Twelve Caesars, Augustus 5, 8, 28, 31, 35, 47-49, 76-77, 81* •Dio Cassius, *Roman History 52.14-19, 23, 27-30, 34, 36, 39; 53.11-12, 16-22, 30-32; 55.13-21* •Tacitus, *Annals 1.1-15* •Augustus, *The Acts of Augustus* •Seneca, *Essay on Benefits 3.27* •Virgil, *Georgics 1.176-203, 351-392, 461-483; 2.109-225, 458-460; 3.9-18; 4.67-85, 149-280* •Horace, *Satires 1.1; 1.6.65-88; 2.6.78-115*
20-10 B.C.					
10-1 B.C.	Jesus is born (c.4 B.C.). •Josephus, *Antiquities of the Jews 17.8.1*				Life in first century B.C. Rome •Varro, *On Agriculture 1.17.4* •Nepos, *On Famous Men, Life of Atticus 13*

Anno Domini

	Hebrew & Christian	Egyptian	Mesopotamian	Greek	Roman
A.D. 1-10		Description of Egypt in first century A.D. •Strabo, *Ancient Geography 17.1.6-10, 52-54, 17.2.4-5*		Science and geography in first century A.D. •Strabo, *Ancient Geography 1.1.20-21; 3.5.11; 4.1.4-5; 6.3.1;7.6.2; 9.1.16-17; 11.14.2; 16.2.22-24, 26*	Architecture in first century A.D. •Vitruvius, *On Architecture 1.2.1-7; 1.4.1-7, 9-12; 1.5.1-4; 5.8.1-2; 7.7.1-5; 7.11.1-2; 7.13.1-3; 8.1.1-7; 8.4.1-2; 10.9.1-7*
A.D. 10-20					Tiberius rules (14-37). •Tacitus, *Annals 1.16-30; 2.47, 86-87; 4.1-2, 57-58, 64; 6.51* •Velleius, *History of Rome 2.104.3-4; 2.126.1-4* •Suetonius, *Lives of the Twelve Caesars, Tiberius 36*

	Hebrew & Christian	Egyptian	Mesopotamian	Greek	Roman
A.D. 20-30	Jesus begins His ministry (29). •Josephus, *Antiquities of the Jews 18.1.2-6; 18.3.3; 18.5.2* •Strabo, *Ancient Geography 16.2.34-46*				
A.D. 30-40	Jesus is crucified and resurrected; He appears to more than 500 disciples at one time (32). •Lactantius, *On the Deaths of the Persecutors 2* Pentecost (32) Stephen is stoned to death (35). Paul is converted (35). •*Matthew* •*Mark* •*Luke* •*John* •*Acts 1-11*				Caligula rules (37-41). •Philo, *Embassy to Gaius 349-373; On the Creation of the World 1-30; The Therapeutae 1-4; Every Good Man Is Free 75-87* •Suetonius, *Lives of the 12 Caesars, Caligula 8.1,9,11,13,19,22; 8.23.2; 8.26.2-5; 8.30.1; 8.50; 8.54; 8.55.3; 8.57.1-2; 8.58* Conditions at Rome in first century A.D. •Tacitus, *Annals 6.16-17* •Celsus, *On Medicine 2.1-2; 2.6.1-6; 5.27.1-2; 7.5.3-4*

	Hebrew & Christian	Egyptian	Mesopotamian	Greek	Roman
A.D. 40–50	The Apostle James is martyered (44). •*Acts 12-15* •*James (written 46)* •Josephus, *Antiquities of the Jews 20.9.1* •*Galatians (written 48)*				Claudius rules (41-54). •Suetonius, *Lives of the Twelve Caesars, Claudius 4; 25.4; 30* •Tacitus, *Annals 11.13-14, 23-25; 12.23-24*
A.D. 50–60	•*Acts 16-28* •*I Thessalonians (written 50)* •*II Thessalonians (written 51)* Rome expels Jews from the city (53). •*I Corinthians (written 56)* •*II Corinthians (written 57)* •*Romans (written 57)*				Nero rules (54-68). •Suetonius, *Lives of the Twelve Caesars, Nero 6-10, 20, 30-31, 38, 49, 57* •Tacitus, *Annals 13.15-17, 31-32, 50-51* •Seneca, *Moral Letters 7, 47, 84*

	Hebrew & Christian	Egyptian	Mesopotamian	Greek	Roman
A.D. 60-70	•*Philippians (written 61)* •*Colossians (written 61)* •*Ephesians (written 61)* •*Philemon (written 61)* •*Titus (wr. 63)* •*I Timothy (written 63)* •*I Peter (wr. 65)* •*II Peter (wr. 66)* •*II Timothy (written 67)* •*Hebrews (written 67)* •*Revelation (written 67-68)* •*Jude (wr. 69)* Peter and Paul martyred in Rome (67) •Eusebius, *The History of the Church 2.25* •Clement of Rome, *Epistle to the Corinthians 5.6* Temple is destroyed (70) •Josephus, *War of the Jews 2.17.1; 2.18.2; 5.2.1; 5.3.1; 5.6.3; 5.6.5; 5.10.2; 6.3.3-4; 6.4.1-8; 6.10.1* •Josephus, *Antiquities of the Jews 20.8.5*				Nicomachus born (60-120) – mathematician •Nicomachus, *Introduction to Arithmetic; Manual of Harmonics* Epictetus born (c.60-135) – philosopher •Epictetus, *The Discourses of Epictetus 1.1, 9, 14; The Manual 33* Fire in Rome – blamed on Christians (64) •Tacitus, *Annals 15.38-44* •Suetonius, *Lives of the Twelve Caesars, Nero 16.2* •Dio Cassius, *Roman History 62.16-18* Roman philosophy and life in first century A.D. •Seneca, *Essay on Providence 4* •Pliny the Elder, *Natural History 2.2, 4, 6-7, 32-36, 41-43; 3.1.3-5; 7.21-23; 11.69; 25.9-11; 29.112-113; 33.6, 13; 35.6 f; 36.24* •Dio Chrysostrom – *Oration 7.34 ff.; 14.18; 16.1-11; 17.1-22; 18.1-21; 41.11-14* Galba rules (68-69). •Tacitus, *Histories 1.1-50* Otho rules (69). Vitellius rules (69). •Tacitus, *Histories 1.2* •Suetonius, *Lives of the Twelve Caesars, Vitellius 13* Vespasian rules (69-79). •Suetonius, *Lives of the Twelve Caesars, Vespasian 1, 4-5, 7-9, 16, 18, 25* •Tacitus, *Histories 3.32*

	Hebrew & Christian	Egyptian	Mesopotamian	Greek	Roman
A.D. 70-80					Titus rules (79-81). Eruption of Vesuvius destroys Pompeii (79). •Pliny the Younger, *Letters 6.16, 20* •Strabo, *Ancient Geography 5.4.8*
A.D. 80-90	Domitian persecutes Christians. •Eusebius – *The History of the Church 3.18* •Lactantius – *On the Deaths of the Persecutors 3* •Dio Cassius – *History of Rome 67.14 ff.*				Domitian rules (81-96). •Tacitus – *Agricola 2, 19-21, 39-40; Dialogue on Orators 28-29, 34-35; Germania 4-23, 45-46* •Suetonius – *Lives of the Twelve Caesars, Domitian 4* •Quintilian – *The Education of an Orator 1.1-3, 8, 10; 2.1, 7, 15, 19; 3.3; 10.1.105-112; 10.3, 7* •Frontinus – *On Water 2.74-76, 119-124*
A.D. 90-100	•*I John (written 90)* •*II John (written 90)* •*III John (written 90)* Clement of Rome writes earliest Christian document outside of NT (97). •Clement of Rome, *Epistle to the Corinthians 5.1-7* Apostle John dies (99). •Eusebius, *The History of the Church, 3.31* •Irenaeus, *Against All Heresies, 2.22.5; 3.3.4* •Jerome, *Commentary on Galatians, 26:462*				Nerva rules (96-98). Trajan rules (98-117). •Pliny the Younger – *Letters 1.6, 13; 2.6; 4.13; 6.4; 9.6, 36; 10.16-17, 33-34, 42-43, 62-63, 96-97; Panegyric on Trajan 1-5, 12-13, 16, 21-24, 44-45, 47, 65-68, 80, 83, 94-95*

	Hebrew & Christian	Egyptian	Mesopotamian	Greek	Roman
A.D. 100-110					
A.D. 110-120	Ignatius is martyred (117). •Eusebius, *The History of the Church 3.36* •Ignatius, *7 Letters*				Hadrian rules (117-138).
A.D. 120-130	Aristides writes apologetical text (c.126). •Aristides, *To the Emperor Hadrian Caesar from the Athenian Philosopher Aristides 1-2, 4, 13, 15-16*			Galen born (129-199) – physician. •Galen, *On the Use of the Parts of the Human Body I, 2-3* – *On the Natural Faculties 1.2, 5* Description of Greece in second century •Pausanias, *Description of Greece 1.28.8-11; 1.35; 2.28.1-2; 2.37.4-6; 5.7-9, 11-12*	
A.D. 130-140					Antonius Pius rules (138-161).
A.D. 140-150					

	Hebrew & Christian	Egyptian	Mesopotamian	Greek	Roman
A.D. 150-160	Justin Martyr writes his *First Apology* (155). •Justin Martyr, *First Apology 1.5, 14, 31, 46, 53, 61-67; Second Apology 2.10, 13* Polycarp is martyred (155). •Eusebius, *The History of the Church, 4.15, 23*				
A.D. 160-170	Marcus Aurelius persecutes Christians. •Eusebius, *The History of the Church 5.1, 10* •Lucian, *Life of Peregrinus, 11-16*				Marcus Aurelius rules (161-180). •Marcus Aurelius, *Meditations 1.1 ff.; 2.1, 17; 4.23, 41, 48; 5.27; 6.7, 10, 44, 54; 7.18, 28, 49; 8.16, 59; 9.23; 10.10; 11.3-4; 12.26, 32, 36* •Eutropius, *A Concise History of Rome 8.12-14* •Gellius, *Attic Nights 2.7; 4.13; 5.14, 16; 7.3; 10.7; 12.1; 13.18* •Tertullian, *Apology 5*
A.D. 170-180					Commodus rules (176-192).
A.D. 180-190	Irenaeus lists 20 New Testament books as canonical (180). •Irenaeus, *Against All Heresies 3.11.8*				

	Hebrew & Christian	Egyptian	Mesopotamian	Greek	Roman
A.D. 190-200					Pertinax rules (193) for 3 months).
					•Herodian, *History of the Emperors 2.1-6*
	Persecution of Christians under Septimius Severus				Septimius Severus rules (193-211).
					•Herodian, *History of the Emperors, 4.2*
	•Tertullian, *Apology, 2, 5, 29-32, 39; Prescriptions against Heretics 7; On Idolatry 10-12, 18; Against the Jews 7*				
	•Eusebius, *The History of the Church 6.1*				
	23 New Testament books recognized as canonical (200).				
	•Tertullian, *Against Marcion 4.5*				
A.D. 200-210					
A.D. 210-220	Clement of Alexandria (150-215) claims Scriptures are misused by heretics.				
	•Clement of Alexandria, *Miscellanies 7.16*				

	Hebrew & Christian	Egyptian	Mesopotamian	Greek	Roman
A.D. 220-230	Origen founds school in Caesarea (220). •Eusebius, *The History of the Church, 6.18* •Origen, *Against Celsus Books 1-2*				
A.D. 230-240					
A.D. 240-250	Christianity in the Roman Empire in third century •Commodianus, *Instructions 3, 17, 22, 63, 74* Decius persecutes the church. •Lactantius, *On the Deaths of the Persecutors 4* •Eusebius, *The History of the Church, 6.39* •Cyprian, *Letters 55.9, 14; 58* – *The Lapsed 1-17, 27-28*				Philip rules (244-249). •Eusebius, *The History of the Church, 6.34* Decius rules (249-251).
A.D. 250-260					
A.D. 260-270					

	Hebrew & Christian	Egyptian	Mesopotamian	Greek	Roman
A.D. 270-280					
A.D. 280-290					Diocletian rules (284-305).
A.D. 290-300					
A.D. 300-310	Diocletian persecutes Christians (303-304). •Eusebius, *The History of the Church 8.2, 6* •Lactantius, *On the Deaths of the Persecutors 7-14* •Salvian, *Of God's Government 5.4*				Constantine rules (306-337). •Sozomen, *Ecclesiastical History 1.15, 20-21; 2.32* •Eusebius, *Life of Constantine 1.24 ff.; History of the Church, 10.5-7* •Lactantius, *Divine Institutes 3.13-15, 18-19* •Socrates Scholasticus, *History of the Church 1.2, 17-18, 40*
A.D. 310-320	Edict of Milan (313) •Lactantius, *On the Deaths of the Persecutors 48*				

	Hebrew & Christian	Egyptian	Mesopotamian	Greek	Roman
A.D. 320-330	Eusebius writes *The History of the Church* (324). Council of Nicaea confronts heresies against Christianity (325). •Socrates Scholasticus – *History of the Church 1.9*				Founding of Constantinople (324) •Socrates Scholasticus, *History of the Church 1.16* •Sozomen, *Ecclesiastical History 2.3*
A.D. 330-340					
A.D. 340-350					
A.D. 350-360					
A.D. 360-370	Canon of the New Testament confirmed at 27 books (367).				Julian the Apostate rules and tries to restore paganism (361-363). •Socrates Scholasticus, *History of the Church, 3.1, 11-13, 16* •Sozomen, *Ecclesiastical History, 5.3, 5, 16, 18* •Julian, *Letters 23, 36-41, 49, 56* •Ammianus, *The History 22.4; 25.4.4-26* •Theodoret, *Ecclesiastical History 3.1-28*

	Hebrew & Christian	Egyptian	Mesopotamian	Greek	Roman
A.D. 370-380					Barbarian invasions of Roman empire begin (376). •Ammianus, *The History 31.2-4, 12-14* Theodosius rules (379-395). •Theodoret, *Ecclesiastical History 5.17-18*
A.D. 380-390	Nicene Creed finalized – condemns heresies (381) •Socrates Scholasticus, *History of the Church 4.12*				
A.D. 390-400	Augustine writes numerous theological works (395-430). •Augustine, *Confessions 1.8-9, 13-14, 19; 5.8, 12*				
A.D. 400-410	Jerome translates Bible into Latin, called the Vulgate (404). Christianity in fifth century Rome •Prudentius, *Against Symmachus* •Jerome, *Letters 107, 125, 128* •Augustine, *City of God, 1.1, 2.6, 8.9* •Avianus, *Fables*				Theodosius II rules (408-450). •*Theodosian Code (438)* •Vegetius, *Military Institutions of the Romans 1.3-4, 6-12, 14-20, 26* •Socrates Scholasticus, *History of the Church 7.22, 42* Sack of Rome (410) •Jerome, *Letters 60.16-18; 127; Commentary on Ezekiel, Preface* •Socrates Scholasticus, *History of the Church 7.10*
A.D. 410-420					

	Hebrew & Christian	Egyptian	Mesopotamian	Greek	Roman
A.D. 420-430					
A.D. 430-440					
A.D. 440-450					
A.D. 450-460	Council of Chalcedon confirms orthodox theology and condemns heresy (451).				Attila the Hun dies (453). •Priscus, *History, fragment 8*
A.D. 460-470					
A.D. 470-480					Fall of western Roman Empire (476) •Salvian, *Of God's Government 6.1-18; 7.6, 16*

Author and
Primary Source
Index

How to Use the Author & Primary Source Index

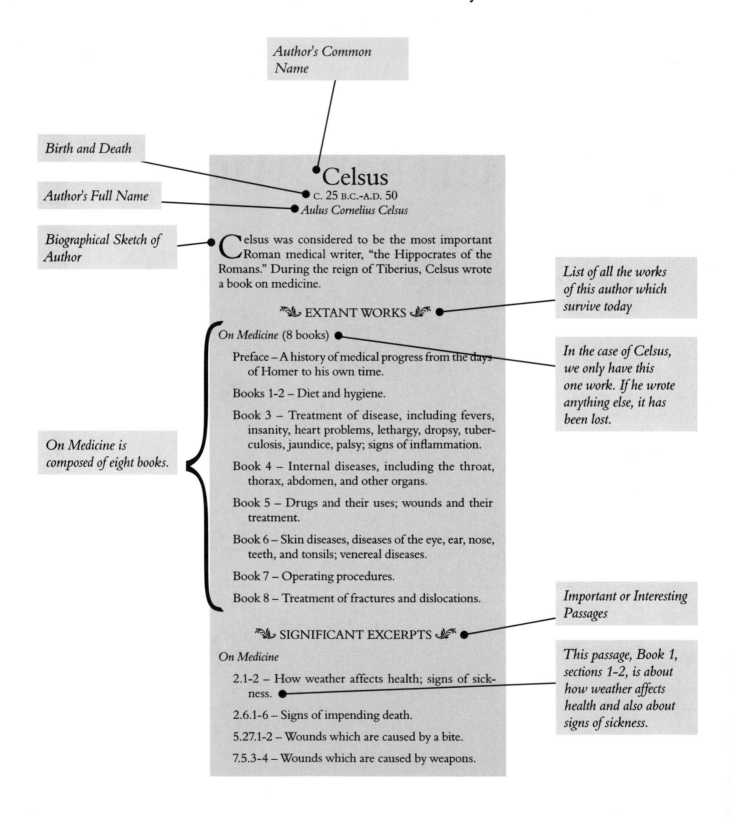

Author's Common Name

Birth and Death

Author's Full Name

Biographical Sketch of Author

Celsus
c. 25 B.C.-A.D. 50
Aulus Cornelius Celsus

Celsus was considered to be the most important Roman medical writer, "the Hippocrates of the Romans." During the reign of Tiberius, Celsus wrote a book on medicine.

❧ EXTANT WORKS ❧

On Medicine (8 books)

Preface – A history of medical progress from the days of Homer to his own time.

Books 1-2 – Diet and hygiene.

Book 3 – Treatment of disease, including fevers, insanity, heart problems, lethargy, dropsy, tuberculosis, jaundice, palsy; signs of inflammation.

Book 4 – Internal diseases, including the throat, thorax, abdomen, and other organs.

Book 5 – Drugs and their uses; wounds and their treatment.

Book 6 – Skin diseases, diseases of the eye, ear, nose, teeth, and tonsils; venereal diseases.

Book 7 – Operating procedures.

Book 8 – Treatment of fractures and dislocations.

❧ SIGNIFICANT EXCERPTS ❧

On Medicine

2.1-2 – How weather affects health; signs of sickness.

2.6.1-6 – Signs of impending death.

5.27.1-2 – Wounds which are caused by a bite.

7.5.3-4 – Wounds which are caused by weapons.

List of all the works of this author which survive today

In the case of Celsus, we only have this one work. If he wrote anything else, it has been lost.

On Medicine is composed of eight books.

Important or Interesting Passages

This passage, Book 1, sections 1-2, is about how weather affects health and also about signs of sickness.

The Bible

The *Bible* is the Anglicized form of the Greek τα` βιβλία, *the little books*, and this name came into common use in the fifth century A.D. The more ancient term, and the term used commonly in the Bible itself, is *The Scripture* [ἡ γραφή, *The Writing*] or *The Scriptures* [αἱ γραφαί, *The Writings*].

It would be more accurate to refer to the two great divisions of the Bible as the *Hebrew Scriptures* and the *Greek Scriptures*. The common labels – *Old Testament* and *New Testament* – came from a Latin misunderstanding and mistranslation of II Corinthians 3:6,14 (cf. Heb. 8: 13; 9:15). These common mis-labels have endured because, as a matter of fact, they do not stray too far from the truth. The *Hebrew Scriptures* do mostly reveal matters which occurred under the old covenant (mistranslated *testament*) formally instituted through Moses, and the *Greek Scriptures* do mostly reveal the content of the new covenant (mistranslated *testament*) formally instituted through Jesus Christ.

If the Bible is the inspired record of God, and we believe it is, then we should treat the Bible as the primary source of the highest possible quality. We list the Bible first because it is to the Bible that we must compare and measure everything else.

The Hebrew Scriptures

It was the duty of the priesthood to instruct the people, so the records were entrusted to them (Deut. 17:18; 24: 8; 33:8-10; II Chron. 15:3; 17:8,9; Mal. 2:7). Many of the books of the Hebrew Scriptures were compiled and edited from the records of the priests, and internal evidence suggests that the historical books of the Hebrew Scriptures were edited several times by different persons. In all likelihood, Ezra the priest and scribe edited the entire Hebrew Scriptures into their final form, altering vocabulary and adding explanatory notes where appropriate.

The Hebrews commonly named the books of the Scriptures by their introductory words (Genesis is named Bereshith: In the beginning; Exodus is named Ve-Aleh Shemoth: These are the words). The common English names given to the books of the Old Testament are derived from the names given to them in the Greek Septuagint translation (Genesis is named Γένεσις: Generation; Exodus is named Ἔξοδος: Departure;). We will list each book under its common English name.

❧ THE ORIGINAL ORDER ❧

The Hebrew Scriptures were originally arranged into 22 books (Josephus, *Against Apion* 1.8; Eusebius, *The History of the Church*, 4.26.14; 6.25.1; many other places). We have listed them below in their original order in the Hebrew canon.

1. Five books of the *Law* (Torah) (a.k.a. Pentateuch): Genesis, Exodus, Leviticus, Numbers, Deuteronomy.
2. Six books and collections of the *Prophets* (Nevi'im):
   a. The two *Former Prophets*: Joshua & Judges (as one book); (I&II) Samuel & (I&II) Kings (as one book called Kingdoms)
   b. The three *Latter Prophets*: Isaiah, Jeremiah, Ezekiel (some say Jeremiah came first)
   c. The one collection of *The Twelve* minor prophets (as one book):
      Assyrian Captivity: Hosea, Joel, Amos, Obadiah, Jonah, Micah, Nahum
      Babylonian Captivity: Habakkuk, Zephaniah

Persian Restoration: Haggai, Zechariah, Malachi

3. Eleven books of the *Holy Writings* (Kethuvim):
   a. *3 Wisdom Books*: Psalms, Proverbs, Job
   b. *5 Festival Books*: Song of Songs (Passover), Ruth (Pentecost), Lamentations (Ab 10th), Ecclesiastes (Tabernacles), Esther (Purim)
   c. *3 Books from the Captivity and Restoration*: Daniel, Ezra & Nehemiah (as one book), (I&II) Chronicles (as one book)

❧ THE WESTERN ORDER ❧

Our English versions follow the Greek or western order of the Old Testament, which divides these 22 books into 39 books and rearranges them:

1. Five Books of The Law of Moses: Genesis – Deuteronomy
2. Twelve Books of History: Joshua – Esther
3. Five Books of Wisdom and Poetry: Job – Song of Solomon
4. Seventeen Books of Prophecy:
   Five Major Prophets: Isaiah – Daniel
   Twelve Minor Prophets: Hosea – Malachi

A SURVEY OF ❧ THE HEBREW SCRIPTURES ❧

Genesis

Compiled by Moses, using ancient records, covering about 2,369 years, from creation down to Jacob's family going down into Egypt. It records the origin of the world (1-2); the fall of man (3); the history of man from Adam to Noah (4-5); the Flood (6-7); the history of man from Noah to Abraham (8-11); the history of Abraham (12-25); of Isaac (25-26); of Jacob (27-36); of Joseph (37-50).

Exodus

Compiled and recorded by Moses, covering about 145 years down to A.M. 2514. It describes the oppression of the people (1); the early life of Moses (2-6); the hardening of Pharaoh's heart under the ten plagues (7-11); the Exodus from Egypt (12-14); the parting of the Red Sea and other miracles (17); the government of Israel and the giving of the Law (18-23); the ceremonial law and the construction of the tabernacle (24-40).

Leviticus

Recorded by Moses, covering the history of one month, from the construction of the tabernacle at the beginning of the second year until the numbering of the people in the second month. It records the laws of sacrifice (1-7); the institution of the priesthood (8-10); the laws of purification (11-22); the laws of festivals, vows, and tithes (23-26).

Numbers

Recorded by Moses, covering the history of 38 years and ten months, from the numbering of the people in the second month until the eleventh month of the 40th year. It records the census of the people (1-4); describes the institution of various ceremonies (5-10); rehearses eight murmurings on the way to Moab (11-21); transactions in the plains of Moab, including the prophecies of Balaam; the second census of the people, and the appointment of Joshua (22-36).

Deuteronomy

Recorded by Moses (chapters 33 and 34 were probably completed by Joshua), covering the history of less than two months, from the first day of the 11th month of the 40th year after the Exodus to the 11th day of the 12th month of the same year, A.M. 2553. It repeats the history of the wandering in the wilderness (1-4); repeats the laws in a form adapted to entrance into the land (5-26); confirms the law with blessings and curses (27-30); records the final acts of Moses (31-34).

Joshua

Recorded by Joshua (and completed by others), covering the history of about 17 years until the death of Joshua in A.M. 2570. It tells the story of Joshua's leadership in the conquest of the land Canaan (1-12); the division of and the settlement in the land Canaan (13-22); the final counsels of Joshua (23-24). The book may be rearranged into chronological order: 1:1-9; 2:1-24; 1:10-18; 3:1-11: 23; 22:1-34; 12:1-21:45; 23:1-24:33

Judges

Probably compiled by the prophet Samuel from previous records, covering the history of about 300 years, down to A.M. 2870. It describes the history of the elders who outlived Joshua (1-3:4); the history of the oppressions of the Israelites and their deliverance by judges (3:5-16); an appendix of earlier history describing how idolatry was introduced into the land, for which cause God repeatedly delivered them to the oppressions of their enemies (17-21).

Ruth

Probably compiled by the prophet Samuel from previous records, serving as a positive appendix to Judges (offsetting the negative Judges 17-21), covering the life of Ruth, a Moabitess, who may have lived in the time of Gideon, around A.M. 2750. It describes Naomi's departure into Moab and return into Canaan with her daughter-in-law Ruth (1); the events which led to Ruth's marriage to Boaz (2:1-4:12); the relations of Boaz down to David (4:13-18).

Samuel I & II

Probably recorded by the prophets Samuel (I Sam.1-24), Nathan (I Sam. 25-31; II Sam. 1-5), and Gad (II Sam. 6-24) (see I Chron. 29:29). I Samuel covers about 80 years, down to A.M. 2949, and II Samuel covers about 40 years, down to A.M. 2989. I Samuel describes the judgeship of Eli (1-4); of Samuel (5-7); the inauguration of Saul as king (8-12); Saul's war with the Philistines (13-14); the rejection of his family for the line of kings (15); the choice of David as king (16); David's victory over Goliath (17); Saul's persecutions of David (18-22); David's rise and Saul's fall (23-27); the final demise of Saul (28-31). II Samuel describes David's confirmation as king (1-4); his many military triumphs (5-10); his many troubles leading to his removal from the throne (11-19); his restoration to the throne (20-21); his psalm of praise (almost the same as Psalm 18) (22); the last words of David and a list of his mighty men (23); David's great offense in numbering the people (24).

Temple of Solomon

Kings I & II

Probably recorded by the prophets Nathan, Ahijah, Iddo (I Kings 11:41; II Chron. 9:29), Shemaiah (II Chron. 12:15), Jehu (I Kings 16:1; II Chron. 20:34), Isaiah (II Chron. 26:22; 32:32; Isa. 1:1), and later compiled by Ezra the priest and scribe. I Kings picks up right where II Samuel left off, covering about 126 years, from the anointing of Solomon A.M. 2988 down to the death of Jehoshaphat A.M. 3114, and II Kings covers about 257 years, down to the destruction of Jerusalem and the temple A.M. 3371 or 586 B.C. I Kings describes the latter days of David and the inauguration of Solomon (1:1-2:11); the reign of Solomon from David's death until the building of the temple (2:12-4:34); the building and consecration of the temple (5-8); the remainder of Solomon's reign (9-11); the accession of Rehoboam and the division of the kingdom (12); the reigns of Rehoboam of Judah and Jeroboam of Israel (13-14); the reigns of Abijam and Asa of Judah, and Nadab, Baasha, Elah, Zimri, Omri, and Ahab of Israel (14-16); the reigns of Jehoshaphat of Judah and Ahab and Ahaziah of Israel, including an account of the prophet Elijah (17-22). II Kings describes the reigns of Jehoshaphat and Jehoram of Judah and Ahaziah and Joram of Israel, including an account of the prophet Elisha (1:1-8:2); the reigns of Jehoram and Ahaziah of Judah and Jehoram of Israel (8:3-29); the reign of Jehu, who killed both Jehoram of Israel and Ahaziah of Judah, and the usurpation of Athaliah as queen of Judah (9:1-11:3); the reign of Jehoash of Judah and Jehoahaz and Jehoash of Israel, including an account of the death of Elisha (11:4-13:25); the reigns of Amaziah, Azariah (Uzziah), and Jotham of Judah and Jehoash (Joash), Jeroboam II, Zechariah, Shallum, Menahem, Pekahiah, and Pekah of Israel (14-15); the reign of Ahaz of Judah, and Hoshea of Israel through the Assyrian captivity of Israel (16-17); the decline and fall of Judah including the reigns of Hezekiah (18-20); Manasseh and Amon (21); Josiah (22:1-23:30); Jehoahaz, Jehoiakim, Jehoiachin, and Zedekiah (23:31-24:20); the destruction of Jerusalem and the temple and the captivity of Judah by Babylonian king Nebuchadnezzar in the eleventh year of Zedekiah, in A.M. 3371 or 586 B.C. (25:1-21); subsequent rebellion (25:23-26); a final mercy to Jehoiachin while in captivity (25:27-30).

Shalmaneser receiving tribute from Jehu

Chronicles I & II

Tradition assigns this book to Ezra, with the help of Zechariah and Haggai, who compiled the document from all court records at hand (I Chron. 29:29; 32:32; II Chron. 9:29; 12:15; 16:11; 20:34; 25:26; 33:19). The Hebrew title means *Accounts of Days*, as if compiled out of diaries. The Greek title means *The Things Which Were Omitted*, as if this is a supplement to previous records, which in fact it is, for though it retraces much of Samuel and Kings in a brief way, it also adds many details. These books record genealogies which stretch from Adam down to the return from Babylonian captivity, about 3,420 years (1:1-9:34); the history of Saul (9:35-10:14); the inauguration and worthies of David's reign (11-12); the bringing of the ark to Jerusalem and placing it in the tabernacle of David (13-16); David's intention of building a temple (17); victories over Israel's enemies (18-20); David's census and the plague which followed (21:1-27); David's regulations for the temple (21:28-26:32); regulations for David's administration and a list of officers (27); preparations for building the temple (28:1-29:22); the death of David, inauguration of Solomon, and the grandeur of his reign (29:23-II Chron. 1:17); the building and consecration of the temple (2:1-8:16); the remainder of Solomon's reign (8:17-9:31); the accession of Rehoboam, division of the kingdom, and plundering of Jerusalem (10-12); the reigns of the kings of Judah (13-35); the final days of the kingdom and of the temple ending in its destruction A.M. 3371 or 586 B.C. (36:1-21). The last two verses (36:22-23) are almost identical to the first two verses of the book of Ezra. The foci of the two books are the temple and priesthood, and the genealogical line of David.

Assyrian king blinding a prisoner

Ezra

Tradition assigns this book to Ezra, the priest and scribe, who would have compiled this book from such things as legal documents (4:7-16), genealogies (2:1-70), and personal records (7:27-9:15). Portions are written in Aramaic instead of Hebrew (4:8-6:18; 7:12-26). The book tells the history of the Hebrew people's return from exile under Zerubbabel by decree of Cyrus A.M. 3420 or 538 B.C. (1-2); the building of the temple begun but hindered (3-4); the temple finished A.M. 3443 or 515 B.C. (5-6); Ezra's departure from Babylon and arrival at Jerusalem (7-8); Ezra's reformation (9-10).

Nehemiah

Tradition assigns this book to Nehemiah, cupbearer to Artaxerxes Longimanus, and governor of the province by Artaxerxes' appointment. The book tells the history of Nehemiah's departure from Shushan in the twentieth year of Artaxerxes Longimanus A.M. 3499 or 459 B.C. (1:1-2:11); the building of the walls despite the opposition of Sanballat (2:12-7:4); the genealogy of those who returned from Babylon (7:5-72); the reading of the law at the feast of tabernacles (8); a solemn feast and renewal of the covenant (9-10); registry of those who dwelt in Jerusalem, of high priests, chief Levites, and principal singers (11:1-12:26); the completion and dedication of the wall (12:27-47); the correction of abuses after Nehemiah's return (13).

Esther

Whoever wrote this book (perhaps Mordecai and Esther) consulted the annals of the kings of Media and Persia (10:2). The name of God is never explicitly mentioned, but His hand of providence is apparent throughout, and His name does appear several times in Hebrew acrostics (compare: Let's Owe Respect Due = LORD). The book tells the history of Esther's promotion to queen of Persia, and Mordecai's exposure of a plot against the king of Persia (1-2); the promotion of Haman and his affliction of the Jews (3-4); the defeat of Haman's plot against Mordecai in particular (5-7) and against the Jews in general (8:1-9:16); the institution of the feast of Purim (9:17-32); the advancement of Mordecai (10). This history may fit between the sixth and seventh chapters of Ezra.

Job

This book may have been written by Job himself, probably before the time of Abraham, though it probably has been edited by later copyists from Moses on down. The long lifespan of Job (42:16) was nevertheless considered only a shadow of the lifespan of fathers of the former age (8:8-9) which suggests a time after the Flood but before Abraham. Complicated astronomical considerations (9:9; 38:31-32) suggest a date 184 years before the birth of Abraham A.M. 1814. or 2134 B.C. Job is referred to elsewhere in the Bible as an historical figure (Ezek. 14:14,18,20; Jam. 5:11) and the book is quoted throughout the Hebrew and Greek Scriptures, the most notable occurence being I Corinthians 3:19, which declares Job 5:13 to be Scripture. The subject of this poem is how God afflicts not only the wicked, but also the righteous. It describes Job's circumstances and two trials under Satan (1-2); his subsequent trials in dialogue with three antagonist friends (Eliphaz, Bildad, and Zophar) in regular rotation beginning with the complaint of Job (3); the three reproofs of his friends, each followed by Job's response (4-14); the second rotation of the same (15-21); the third rotation of the same, except Zophar does not speak (22-31); the contribution of Elihu's observations (33-37); the intervention of the Lord in judgment (38-41); the restoration of Job. The book is filled with remarkable testimonies to the creation and governance of the world by God, and contains an early testimony to faith in the resurrection (29:25-29).

Psalms

This book is composed of 150 lyric poems (poems adapted to music) collected over a millennium, from the time of Moses down to the time of Ezra, though most of them were likely written in the time of David and Solomon. The Hebrews call this collection *The Book of Praises*, but the Greek Septuagint entitles it *The Book of Psalms*. It contains a wide variety of poems, from praise to lament, from teaching to commanding, from alphabetical to dramatic dialogue. The Psalms are divided into five books: I (1-41), II (42-72), III (73-89), IV (90-106), V (107-150); each book ending with a colophon of praise which divides it from the next book (41:13; 72:18-20; 89: 52; 106:48; 150:6). One hundred Psalms are traditionally ascribed "of" "for" or "to" certain persons: of David – 73 Psalms (3-9; 11-32; 34-41 [to Jeduthun 39;62]; 51-65; 68-70; 86; 101; 103; 108-110; 122; 124; 131; 133; 138-145); of or for Asaph – 12 Psalms (50; 73-83 [to Jeduthun 77]); for the sons of Korah – 11 Psalms (42; 44-49; 84-85; 87-88 [of Heman – 88]); for Solomon – 2 Psalms (72; 127); of Moses – 1 Psalm (90); of Ethan – 1 Psalm (89). These and other ascriptions in the titles of the Psalms are of uncertain origin and are not considered inspired, and though many of them may be valuable, the meaning of some is uncertain, and some appear to be in error.

Proverbs

Tradition assigns this book to Solomon, and there is no necessary reason to doubt that he authored most of it (1:1; 10:1), though King Hezekiah's scribes selected (25: 1) from among Solomon's 3,000 proverbs (I Kings 4:32), and one chapter (30:1) is attributed to Agur, and another (31:1) to King Lemuel's mother, though it is possible that

Agur and Lemuel are aliases for Solomon. Proverbs is divided into five books: I – precepts addressed to youth (1-9); II – short proverbial sayings for grown men (10: 1-22:16); III – miscellaneous longer proverbs for rich men and nobles (22:17-24:34); IV – more miscellaneous longer proverbs, repeating some earlier proverbs (25-29); V – ethical precepts and a prayer of Agur (30) and the instruction of Lemuel's mother, including the description of a virtuous wife (31).

Ecclesiastes

Tradition assigns this book to Solomon, and there is no necessary reason to doubt his authorship (1:1,12,16; 2:4-9; 12:9-10). The book describes the emptiness of the pursuits of life considered by themselves "under the sun" and apart from God (1-6); counsel on what to do in view of this emptiness (7:1-12:8); the conclusion: fear and serve God (12:9-14).

Song of Solomon

Tradition assigns this book to Solomon, and there is no necessary reason to doubt his authorship (1:1; 3:7,9,11; 8:11-12), as he wrote 1,005 songs (I Kings 4: 32), and many internal features agree with his life and circumstances. The Hebrew name means *Song of Songs*, which is idiomatic for *The Most Beautiful of Songs*. It has been divided and interpreted many ways, such as a dramatic nuptial song in the customary seven days: 1 – The Courtship (1:1-2:7); 2 – The Betrothal (2:8-3:5); 3 – The Marriage (3:6-5:1); 4 – The Honeymoon (5:2-6: 9); 5 – The Deepening Love (6:10-7:10); 6 – Renewed Love (7:11-8:4); 7 – The Maturing Marriage (8:5-14). A common Hebrew interpretation is that it is an historical allegory of God and Israel. A common Christian interpretation is that it is a mystical allegory of Christ and the church. The Hebrews regarded Proverbs as the temple, Ecclesiastes as the Holy Place, and the Song of Solomon as the Holy of Holies. The Christian fathers taught Solomon's ladder: Proverbs is moral instruction, Ecclesiastes is natural instruction, and the Song of Solomon is mystical instruction.

Isaiah

Tradition assigns this book to Isaiah, and there is no necessary reason to doubt his authorship. Some have asserted the book had three different authors (1-39, 40-55, 56-66), but the internal evidence does not require this, and the testimony of the New Testament forbids it. For example, John 12:38-41 quotes both Isaiah 6 and Isaiah 53, and ascribes them both to Isaiah. Isaiah prophesied 740-680 B.C. The book begins with prophecies under

Uzziah [767-739 B.C.] denouncing Judah; prophecies under Jotham [739-731 B.C.] and Ahaz [731-715 B.C.] predicting deliverance from Assyria (7-12); denunciations of other nations and cities – Babylon, Assyria, Philistia, Moab, Damascus, Ethiopia, Egypt, Edom, Arabia, Jerusalem, Tyre (13-23); prophecies under Hezekiah [715-686 B.C.] describing a future kingdom (24-27); denouncing Israel and Assyria (28-35); recording the history of Sennacherib's invasion and the answer of God to Hezekiah's prayer, his sickness, his recovery, and the Babylonian embassy (all of which is almost the same as II Kings 18:13-20:19) (36-39); the trial of the nations (40-55); the rebirth of Israel's kingdom (56-66). Tradition suggests that under Manasseh [686-642 B.C.], Isaiah was sawn in two while inside a hollowed log (cf. Heb. 11:37).

Jeremiah

Tradition assigns this book to Jeremiah, a priest (son of Hilkiah) (1:1), and there is no necessary reason to doubt his authorship. Jeremiah began his prophetic ministry 627 B.C., the thirteenth year of Josiah [640-609 B.C.] (1:2; 25:3). His writing ministry began 605 B.C., the fourth year of Jehoiakim [609-598 B.C.] (36:1-2), and ended some time after the fall of Jerusalem 586 B.C. (1:3), so in all he prophesied 627-586 B.C. He was contemporary with five or seven other prophets: Ezekiel, Daniel, Nahum, Habakkuk, Zephaniah, and perhaps Joel and Obadiah. His book consists of collections of his prophecies, somewhat topically arranged: prophecies concerning Judah and Jerusalem (2-45) and concerning all other nations (46-51). We may rearrange them chronologically: the call of the prophet (1); prophecies under Josiah (2-12); prophecies under Jehoiakim (13-20; 22-23; 25-26; 35-36; 45:1-49:33); prophecies under Zedekiah (21; 24; 27-34; 37-39; 49:34-39; 50-51); prophecies under the rule of Gedaliah the governor (40-44); historical supplement introducing Lamentations, taken largely from II Kings (52). Even this rearrangement is not chronological within the new collections.

Lamentations

Tradition assigns this book to Jeremiah, and there is no necessary reason to doubt his authorship. Jeremiah wrote Lamentations shortly after the fall of Jerusalem 586 B.C. It is divided into five elegies (mournful poems): grief over the destruction of Jerusalem (1); suffering following the destruction of the city (2); exhortation to patience and hope (3); painful remorse (4); memorial of the past and humble request to be restored (5). The first four chapters are acrostics (alphabetical poems) of the twenty-two letters of the Hebrew alphabet, each verse beginning with one letter, except that in chapter 3 the verses come in triplets.

Ezekiel

Tradition assigns this book to Ezekiel, a priest (son of Buzi), who was taken captive with Jehoiachin [598-597 B.C.] in 597 B.C. (1:1-3), and there is no necessary reason to doubt his authorship. Of all the prophets, Ezekiel provides us with the most detailed dating. His prophecy covers 593-571 B.C. in four periods: 593-588 B.C. (1:1-25:17); 587-585 B.C. (26:1-29:16; 30:20-39:29) 573 B.C. (40:1-48:35); 571 B.C. (29:17-30:19). His book describes Ezekiel's call (1-2); delivers prophecies against Judah and Jerusalem (3-24); delivers oracles against foreign nations (25-32); prophecies concerning Israel (33-39); (after the fall of Jerusalem) gives a vision of the temple and law of the future kingdom (40-48).

Daniel

Tradition assigns this book to Daniel, who served in the courts of foreign kings during the captivity, and all internal and external evidence points in that direction. Though there is no necessary reason to doubt his authorship, there are many who attack the book's authenticity because it so precisely predicts numerous events of history, which they think is impossible. Daniel was removed to Babylon by Nebuchadnezzar 605 B.C. and was in Babylon during the entire captivity, while Jehoiakim [609-598 B.C.] Jehoiachin [598-597 B.C.] and Zedekiah [597-586 B.C.] ruled, until Nebuchadnezzar destroyed Jerusalem and the temple in 586 B.C., and Daniel lived beyond Cyrus' decree to rebuild the temple 537 B.C. His book begins with historical events (1-6) describing: how Daniel rose to favor in Nebuchadnezzar's court (1); how Daniel told and interpreted Nebuchadnezzar's dream of four world empires and was further promoted (2); how the faith of Shadrach, Meshach, and Abed-Nego, in not succumbing to demands to practice idolatry, brought the Lord's deliverance for them from the fiery furnace (3); how the Lord humbled Nebuchadnezzar to confess the sovereignty of the Lord over all (4); how the Lord removed the kingdom from Belshazzar (5); how the Lord delivered Daniel from the lions' den (6). His book ends with four prophetic visions: the vision of four beasts (representing Babylon, Persia, Greece, and Rome) (7); the vision of the ram (Persia) destroyed by the goat (Greece), which would divide into four kingdoms (Greece, Thrace, Syria, Egypt), and the little horn (Antiochus Epiphanes) which would rise from them (8); the prophecy of seventy weeks to bring in a final everlasting atonement through the death of the Messiah, and the final destruction of Jerusalem (9); the panoramic vision of the future of Persia, Greece, Egypt, Syria, Rome, and the sealing up of the book until the time of its fulfillment (10-12).

Hosea

Tradition assigns this book to Hosea, and there is no necessary reason to doubt his authorship. Hosea prophesied under Uzziah [767-739 B.C.] Jotham [739-731 B.C.], Ahaz [731-715 B.C.], Hezekiah [715-686 B.C.], and Jeroboam II of Israel (1:1). His book describes five discourses: the infidelity of Israel, her punishment, restoration, and redemption (1-3); a warning against Israel for her bloodshed and idolatry, and a plea to repent (4:1-6:3); the complaint of God against Israel's obstinacy, and the pronouncement of her sentence – captivity (6:4-8:14); the threat of captivity and dispersion for Israel, the prediction of Israel's return, and more denunciation of idolatry (9:1-13:8); more threats of punishment and promises of restoration, exhortations to repentance and prayer, and predictions of full restoration (13:9-14:9).

Joel

Tradition assigns this book to Joel, and there is no necessary reason to doubt his authorship. Some have conjectured that Joel prophesied before or during the reign of Joash [835-796 B.C.] or else under Jehoiakim [609-598 B.C.] or later. Internal evidence points to the earlier date. It mentions Phoenicians, Philistines, Egypt, and Edom as enemies (3:4,19), which agrees with the time of Joash, while there is no mention of Assyria, Babylon, or Persia, which might be expected with a later date. The book mentions priests and elders, but no king, and in his early years, Joash relied upon priests and elders to rule (II Kings 11:4-12:21). Joel's book describes a plague of locusts and exhorts the priests to repentance lest further calamities befall them (1:1-2:11); exhorts them to keep a solemn feast, with the promise of immediate deliverance (2:12-32); predicts the day of the Lord coming with judgment for the nations and blessings on Jerusalem (3:1-21).

Amos

Tradition assigns this book to Amos, and there is no necessary reason to doubt his authorship. Amos prophesied under Uzziah of Judah [767-739 B.C.] and Jeroboam II of Israel [781-753 B.C.] (1:1). Uzziah was stricken with leprosy 739 B.C., and his son Jotham shared his power. The prophecy consists of the prophet's commission (1:1-2); judgments of the Lord against neighboring Gentile nations, Damascus (Syria), Philistia, Tyre, Edom, Ammon, Moab (1:3-2:3); turning to judgments against Judah and Israel (2:4-16); finally focusing on the imminent judgment of Israel (3:1-15); with a thorough reprimand of the nation (4-6); three visions (locusts, fire, plumbline) of the of the impending disaster (7:1-9); then an historical account of the confrontation between Amos and Amaziah the priest (7:10-17); then more visions of the Israel's end (8); the Lord judging (9:1-10); the future raising up of the tabernacle of David (9:11-15).

Obadiah

Tradition assigns this book to Obadiah, and there is no necessary reason to doubt his authorship. This book is addressed to the nation of Edom. Some have conjectured that Obadiah prophesied under Jehoram of Judah [848-841 B.C.] (II Kings 8:20; II Chron. 21:16-17, cf. Joel 3:3-6 with Obad. 11-12, and notice the use of Obad. 1-9 in Jer. 49:7-22). This would make Obadiah the earliest of the writing prophets. Others conjecture a time between Nebuchadnezzar's taking of Jerusalem and his destruction of the Edomites, some time after 586 B.C. The book announces the destruction of Edom for its pride and confidence (1-9) and its cruelty against "brother Jacob" (10-16); predicts the restoration of the house of Jacob and their victory over their enemies (17-21).

Jonah

Tradition assigns this book to Jonah, the son of Amittai, a native of Gath-Hepher in Zebulun, and there is no necessary reason to doubt his authorship. Jonah apparently prophesied under Jeroboam II of Israel [781-753 B.C.] (II Kings 14:25). The book narrates Jonah's flight from his commission to Nineveh, taking a ship to Tarshish (1:1-3); the great tempest, the casting of lots finding Jonah as the cause, and casting him into the sea, where he is swallowed by a large fish (1:4-17); Jonah's prayer for deliverance and confession that salvation is of the Lord, followed by his deliverance (2); Jonah's recommissioning to Nineveh, giving it forty days to repent (3:1-4); Nineveh's repentance, which removes God's anger (3:5-10); Jonah's repining at the sparing of Nineveh (4:1-3); the Lord's gentle rebuke through the example of a shading plant which withers (4:4-11).

Micah

Tradition assigns this book to Micah of Morasthi in southern Judah, and there is no necessary reason to doubt his authorship. Micah prophesied under Jotham [739-731 B.C.], Ahaz [731-715 B.C.], and Hezekiah [715-

686 B.C.] (1:1). The book is divided into three sections introduced by the word, "Hear": "Hear all ye people" the message of destruction for Samaria (Israel) and Judah, ending with a word of hope (1-2); "Hear . . . O heads of Jacob" the message of denunciation upon the rulers and prophets, and the destruction of Jerusalem, ending with a description of the glories of the coming kingdom in the latter days (3-5); "Hear ye, O ye mountains" the message of the Lord's complaints and Israel's replies, ending with a description of future blessings for Israel (6-7).

Nahum

Tradition assigns this book to Nahum of Elkosha, possibly in Galilee, and there is no necessary reason to doubt his authorship. Nahum prophesied some time between the fall of Thebes [663 B.C.] and the fall of Nineveh [612 B.C.], for he declared the first was past and the second was yet to come (3:7-10). He may have prophesied under Josiah [640-609 B.C.], perhaps 622 B.C. The book begins with a declaration of praise for God's sovereign majesty and His angry vengeance on His enemies (1:1-14); the judgment of Nineveh is predicted (1:15-2:2); described and vindicated (2:3-3:19).

Habakkuk

Tradition assigns this book to Habakkuk, and there is no necessary reason to doubt his authorship. Habakkuk prophesied during the fall of Nineveh 612 B.C. His prophecy is divided in two. The first part is a dialogue where the prophet asks why God allows the wicked to continue (1:1-4); God responds by announcing the Babylonian captivity (1:5-11); then the prophet asks why God will use the wicked to punish Judah (1:12-2:1); God responds that He will eventually punish Babylon and deliver His people (2:2-20). The second part is a prayer that God would hasten His work (3:1-2); praise for the power and faithfulness of God (3:3-19).

Zephaniah

Tradition assigns this book to Zephaniah the son of Cushi, the son of Gedaliah, the son of Amariah, the son of Hezekiah (possibly the king of Judah), and there is no necessary reason to doubt his authorship. Zephaniah prophesied under Josiah [640-609 B.C.] (1:1), probably before Josiah's reforms in his eighteenth year 622 B.C., and possibly before Jeremiah began to prophesy 627 B.C. The book announces the day of the Lord when He will judge (1); repentance is the only escape (2:1-3); the judgment of Philistia, Moab, Ammon, Ethiopia, and Nineveh (2:4-15); the Jews will be taken captive by Babylon (3:1-7); a faithful remnant will be restored

and will prosper (3:8-20).

Haggai

Tradition assigns this book to Haggai of the time of Ezra (Ezra 5:1; 6:14), and there is no necessary reason to doubt his authorship. Haggai prophesied under Darius in Judea after the return from Babylon over a four-month period 520 B.C. (1:1; 2:20). With each of his prophecies he gives the exact date. His book records: a rebuke to the people for building their own houses while the Lord's house was left unfinished, resulting in the renewed efforts of the people (1); how Zerubbabel and Joshua begin the work with God's encouragement (2:1-9); an exhortation to purity and an encouragement that their faithfulness will bring fruit (2:10-19); a prophetic utterance about future glory of the Davidic line, using Zerubbabel as the figure (2:20-23).

Zechariah

Tradition assigns this book to Zechariah of the time of Ezra (Ezra 5:1; 6:14), and there is no necessary reason to doubt his authorship. Zechariah, the son of Berechiah, grandson of Iddo, and who was listed as a priest (Neh. 12:16), prophesied under Darius in Judea after the return from Babylon, from October 520 B.C. to November 518 B.C. (1:1; 7:1); he prophesied again, possibly many years later. His first prophecy includes: a call to repentance (1:1-6); visions of: horses and riders representing permission to build the temple (1:7-17); four horns and four craftsman indicating that the Samaritan opposition would not be permitted (1:18-21); a surveyor representing prosperity and protection in their work (2:1-13); Joshua the high priest and the rebuke of Satan representing future glory for The Branch (3); a golden lampstand and two olive trees representing the success of Joshua and Zerubbabel (4); a flying scroll representing judgment against robbery and perjury (5:1-4); a woman in a basket warning a second captivity if the Jews do not repent (5:5-11); four chariots representing the four empires of Babylon, Persia, Greece, and Rome (6:1-8); the symbolic gesture of crowning Joshua the priest representing the future glorious kingly priest, The Branch (6:9-15). His second prophecy concerns the fasting which they have begun on account of the destruction of Jerusalem; the Lord declares that they must obey the words of the Lord, encourages them to continue building, and releases them from fasting (7-8). Zechariah's final prophecies are divided into two burdens: first, a burden regarding nations – Alexander's conquest of Syria, Phoenicia, and Palestine (9:1-7); the Lord's continued protection of the temple (9:8); the coming King (9:9-10); the victories of the Jews (Maccabees) over Greece (9:11-17); the blessings of the Messiah (10); their rejection of the Messiah (11); second, a burden for Jerusalem – the preservation of Jerusalem (12:1-9); their grief for rejecting the Messiah (12:10-14); the crucifixion of the Messiah and the purging of the Jews (13); the day of the Lord's victory and the conversion of all nations (14).

Malachi

Tradition assigns this book to Malachi, and there is no necessary reason to doubt his authorship. Tradition holds that Malachi prophesied while Nehemiah was governor, and numerous points agree between Malachi and Nehemiah's second return (Neh. 13:6), including: the corruption of the priesthood (1:6-2:9 & Neh. 13: 7-9,28-30); neglect of paying tithes (3:8-10 & Neh. 13: 10-14); neglect of the ordinances (3:7,14 & Neh. 13: 15-22); neglect of marital prohibitions (2:10-16 & Neh. 13:23-27). So Malachi may have prophesied 420 B.C. In this prophecy, the Lord reminds Israel of His favor toward the sons of Jacob and not the sons of Esau (1:1-5); rebukes them for not reverencing God, which will bring about their rejection and the calling of the Gentiles (1: 6-11); rebukes the unfaithfulness of the priesthood in sacrifices (1:12-14), feasts (2:1-6), teaching (2:7-9), mixed marriage (2:10-12), divorce (2:13-16), and injustice (2: 17); announces that a messenger will come who will prepare the way for the Lord to come by purifying the people (3:1-6); rebukes them for neglecting the ordinances (3:7-15); identifies His jewels, those who fear the Lord (3:16-18); announces the coming of Elijah before the great and terrible day of God's judgment on Israel, the destruction of Jerusalem and the temple by the Romans in A.D. 70 (4).

The Greek Scriptures

❧ THE ORIGINAL ORDER ☙

Like the Hebrew Scriptures, the Greek Scriptures (which we call the New Testament) were originally arranged differently than in our common English versions.

> Whether [over 4,000 manuscript] copies contain the whole or a part of the sacred volume, the general *order* of the books is the following: Gospels, Acts, Catholic Epistles, Pauline Epistles, Apocalypse. (F.H.A. Scrivener, *A Plain Introduction to the Criticism of the New Testament*, London: George Bell and Sons, 1894, Volume I, p. 72)

We have listed the books below in their original order in the Greek canon.

1. Five books of historical narrative of the *Gospel*: Matthew, Mark, Luke, John, Acts of the Apostles
2. Twenty-one *Epistles*:
   a. Seven "general" epistles addressed to unspecified (possibly Hebrew) congregations: James, I Peter, II Peter, I John, II John, III John, Jude
   b. Fourteen epistles of Paul
   1) Nine epistles addressed to seven specified Gentile congregations: Romans, I Corinthians, II Corinthians, Galatians, Ephesians, Philippians, Colossians, I Thessalonians, II Thessalonians
   2) One epistle addressed to an unspecified (possibly Hebrew) congregation: Hebrews
   3) Four epistles addressed to three specified persons: I Timothy, II Timothy, Titus, Philemon
3. One *prophetic book*: Revelation

❧ THE WESTERN ORDER ☙

Our English versions follow the more common Latin or western arrangement of the Greek Scriptures, which places the fourteen epistles of Paul before the seven general epistles (thereby moving to the head the epistles to the Gentiles, and elevating Romans to first place among the epistles), and moves Hebrews to the end of Paul's epistles (next to the general epistles, so that all of the epistles possibly addressed to Hebrews are placed at the end).

A SURVEY OF ❧ THE GREEK SCRIPTURES ☙

Dates for each book are approximate, with a normal range of possible dates included in parentheses.

Matthew

Written c. A.D. 50 (40-60). Tradition assigns the writing to Matthew the Apostle (9:9; 10:3; Mark 3: 18), surnamed Levi (Mark 2:14; Luke 5:27), who had been a collector of Roman taxes, and internal evidence points the same direction. Of the four gospels, Matthew contains the most references to money, and to Hebrew history, custom, and social classes. Matthew's gospel addresses primarily a Hebrew audience with the message that Jesus is the son of David, Messiah, the King (1:1; 2: 2; 21:5; 25:31,34,40; 27:11,37), quoting and alluding to the fulfillment of Hebrew Scriptures much more than any other author in all the Scriptures. This gospel is arranged, not chronologically, but thematically, around five major discourses: the law of Christ's kingdom (the Sermon on the Mount), 5-7; the commissioning of the twelve apostles of Christ's kingdom, 10:5-42; the parables of the growth of Christ's kingdom, 13:3-52; the order for fellowship within Christ's kingdom, 18: 3-35; the emergence of Christ's kingdom (the Olivet Discourse), 24-25.

Mark

Written c. A.D. 64-67. Tradition assigns the writing to Mark the Evangelist, and internal evidence points the same direction. Mark is possibly the young man who fled capture in the garden (14:51-52), the son of a Christian widow named Mary (Acts 12:12), the cousin or nephew of Barnabas (Col. 4:10), and a traveler with Paul and Barnabas (Acts 12:25; 13:5); and though Paul at one time did not prefer his companionship (Acts 13: 13; 15:37-40), Mark was later associated with Paul (Col. 4:10; Philem. 24; II Tim. 4:11), but he was most closely associated with Peter, who called him "son" (I Pet. 5: 13) and from whom he probably received much of the information for his gospel. Mark is his Latin surname, and John is his Hebrew forename (Acts 12:12,25; 15:37). Mark's gospel addresses primarily Roman Christians with the message that Jesus is the Servant of the Lord (10:45). Tradition says that Mark was Peter's interpreter, and in agreement with this, Mark's gospel interprets Aramaic words (3:17; 5:41; 7:11,34; 15:22) and Hebrew customs and geography (7:2-4; 13:13; 14:12; 15:42), and includes several Latin words not found elsewhere (4:21; 6:27; 12:14,42; 15:15,16,39), and even follows the outline of Peter's short account of Christ's life at the household of the Roman Cornelius in Caesarea (Acts 10:36-43). There are fewer quotations and allusions to the Hebrew Scriptures in Mark than in the other gospels, while it records more miracles, and is written in a very action-oriented manner, describing many extra details.

Luke

Written c. A.D. 62-64. Tradition assigns the writing to Luke the Evangelist, a physician not "of the circumcision" (Col. 4:10-14) who accompanied the ailing Paul (Acts 16: 10-17; 20:5-16; 21:1-18; 27:1-28:16; Philem. 24) up to the time of Paul's death (II Tim. 4:11), and internal evidence points the same direction. Theophilus may have been a wealthy and well positioned patron who funded the circulation of this gospel. Luke was not an eyewitness of the events, but compiled them from eyewitnesses and servants of the Word (1:1-4), possibly acquiring information while he was in Jerusalem with Paul c. A.D. 58 (Acts 21:15ff), and while he visited Philip in Caesarea (Acts 21:8), besides what he learned by traveling with Paul elsewhere. Luke's gospel addresses Christians in general with the message that Jesus is the sinless and perfect Son of Man Who came to seek and to save the lost (19:10). Luke represents Jesus as the friend of the outcasts of society, recording more relationships, more prayer and praise, describing and detailing more medical conditions, economic conditions, family activities, nationalities, imperial offices, noting more the roles of women, and including more time references than the other gospels. Luke is written in well-educated Greek vocabulary and style, though it varies especially in Hebrew settings, possibly reflecting the sources Luke used for particular portions.

John

Written c. A.D. 85-95, from Ephesus. Tradition assigns the writing to John the Apostle, the son of Zebedee and Salome, younger brother of James the Apostle, and internal evidence points conclusively in the same direction, for the author was the disciple whom Jesus loved (13:23; 19:26; 20:2; 21:7,20,24) part of the inner circle of three – John, James, and Peter (Matt. 17: 1; Mark 5:37; 9:2; 14:33; Luke 8:51; 9:28) – but Peter is distinguished from the author (13:23-24; 20:2-10; 21: 20), and James was murdered c. A.D. 44, long before this was written (Acts 12:1-5), which leaves only John, who is never mentioned by name in the book. John 21: 24 may point to John's disciples writing the narrative at John's dictation, for 21:23 indicates the author had lived a long life. John's gospel assumes the details recorded in the other gospels, and fills in more of the reasoning, addressing a more philosophically minded audience with the message that Jesus is God the Son, the eternal Word (1:1,18,34,49; 3:18; 5:18; 6:46,49,69; 8:58; 10:30,33,36; 12:38-41; 13:3; 14:9; 19:7; 20:28,31), the "I am" (John 8:58; cf. 6:35,48,51; 8:12; 9:5; 10:7,9,11,14; 11:25; 14: 6,10,11,20; 15:1,5) come in human flesh (1:14).

Acts of the Apostles

Written c. A.D. 62-64. Tradition assigns the writing to Luke the Evangelist, and internal evidence points to it being authored by the same person who authored the gospel of Luke (cf. Luke 1:1-4 with Acts 1:1-1). By the process of elimination, the "we" passages (16:10-17; 20: 5-16; 21:1-18; 27:1-28:16) point directly to Luke. It is most likely that Luke wrote Acts while he attended to Paul under house arrest in Rome, for if it had been written later, he could not have failed to mention the outcome of Paul's trial, the burning of Rome and Nero's fierce persecution of Christians (A.D. 64), the deaths of Peter (A.D. 64) and Paul (A.D. 68), or the destruction of Jerusalem and the temple (A.D. 70). "Acts" means "accomplishments," and this book is addressed to Christians in general with a summary of the accomplishments of the Apostles by preaching Christ, accompanied by the witness of the Spirit, causing the spread of the invisible spiritual kingdom, and establishing visible local churches in Jerusalem (1-7), in Judea and Samaria and among devout Gentiles (8-12), and among idolatrous Gentiles throughout the empire (13-28). Luke's sources would have included Philip (Acts 21:8), James and others yet remaining in Jerusalem c. A.D. 58 (Acts 21:15ff), written documents (15:23; 23:26), and of course Paul and his companions. The books of Luke and Acts may have served as court documents in Paul's defense, recording the unfounded Jewish persecution of Paul along with the opinion of Roman officials throughout the empire that Paul's activities were not illegal. The historical accuracy of the book of Acts in every detail matched with its complete intermeshing with the epistles forms an impregnable testimony to the historicity of the ministry and the writings of the Apostles.

Romans

Written c. autumn A.D. 57 (57-58), from Corinth or Cenchrea. The author is expressly identified as Paul (1:1). It was written apparently after Paul had made his collection in Macedonia and Achaia and when he was about to sail toward Jerusalem to supply the poor (15:25-28; Acts 20:2-3,16). Since navigation in the Mediterranean Sea ceased for four months, beginning November 10 through March 10, this was written in early autumn. (However, a Jewish plot against him forced him to change his sailing plans, and he returned through Macedonia, Acts 20:3, and sailed from Philippi in the spring, Acts 20:6.) The book was originally addressed to the Christians in Rome, which included Hebrews and Gentiles, and may have begun as early as the day of Pentecost when Romans visited Jerusalem (Acts 20:10). The epistle features a full development of the doctrine of salvation, sometimes called "The Gospel According to Paul," including topics of sin and depravity (1:18-3:20), justification by faith (3:21-5:11), sanctification (5:12-8:39). election and predestination (9:1-11:36), spiritual gifts and graces (12:1-7), Christian behavior (12:9-13:14), the law of liberty (14:1-23), the need for unity and separation (15:1-13; 16:17-20).

I Corinthians

Written c. spring A.D. 56 (55-56), from Ephesus (16:8), where Paul stayed three years (Acts 19:8,10; 20:31). The author is expressly identified as Paul (1:1; 16:21). It was originally addressed to the church at Corinth, but its teachings were meant to extend to members of churches "everywhere" (1:2). Corinth was a center of commerce between Italy (east) and Asia (west), and of idolatry and sexual depravity devoted to Aphrodite, their goddess of love. Paul had initially visited Corinth c. autumn A.D. 52, and stayed about eighteen months (Acts 18:11). This epistle scolds the childish conduct of the Corinthians for the party spirit reported to him (1:11), coupled with a discussion of the difference between worldly wisdom and true spiritual wisdom, then it invokes discipline upon one member for the fornication reported to him (5:1), coupled with a statement about judging among brethren, then it addresses a long list of specific practical questions concerning: fornication (7:1), virgins (7:25), things being sacrificed to idols (8:1), customs (11:2,16), the Lord's Supper (11:17,20), the spiritual gifts (12:1), the gospel (15:1), collection for the saints (16:1), and Apollos (16:12).

II Corinthians

Written c. spring A.D. 57 (56-57), from Philippi of Macedonia, less than a year after writing the first epistle (8:10; 9:2, cf. I Cor. 16:1,2). The author is expressly identified as Paul (1:1; 10:1). It was originally addressed to the church at Corinth and the "saints" or members of churches "in all Achaia" (1:1). While the first epistle was primarily a response to certain reports and questions, this epistle is primarily a response to certain charges made by false teachers against Paul's authority to minister as an apostle. Paul defends his authority while addressing issues of comfort, discipline, and giving.

Galatians

Written c. A.D. 48 (48-58), from Antioch. The author is expressly identified as Paul (1:1; 5:2). It was probably written before the Jerusalem council of c. A.D. 49 (Acts 15). It was originally addressed to the churches of southern Galatia – which would include at least Iconium, Lystra, Derbe, and Antioch of Pisidia – which were founded on Paul's first missionary journey. Matthew and James alone have possible dates earlier than Galatians. This epistle refutes the arguments of the Judaizers who taught that justification and sanctification come by a fleshly obedience to the law of Moses – particularly with regard to circumcision (2:3-5; 5:1-6; 6:13-16; cf. Acts 15:1,5,24) – and who minimized Paul's authority as an apostle (1:11-2:14; 4:16-18). Paul defends what he regards as no less than "the truth of the gospel" (1:6-12; 2:5,14; 3:1; 4:16; 5:7; cf. Acts 15:2,7).

Ephesians

Written c. A.D. 61 (58-62), from Rome. The author is expressly identified as Paul (1:1; 3:1). Ephesus was a commercial center of the empire at the intersection of several trade routes. Paul had visited Ephesus at the end of his first missionary journey and stayed three years there during his third missionary journey, and it became a center for the spread of the gospel (Acts 19:10,20,26; I Cor. 16:8-9). Though the epistle is addressed to the "saints" or church-members at Ephesus, there is some evidence that it may have been circulated throughout Asia Minor, much like the circular epistles of Colossians 4:16 and Revelation 2-3. This epistle explains the mystery of the church as the temple, body, and bride of Christ, and includes many practical exhortations to live up to spiritual realities.

Philippians

Written c. A.D. 61 (58-62), from Rome. The author is expressly identified as Paul (1:1). Paul was in prison in proximity to the palace or Praetorian guard (1:13), and Caesar's household (4:22), in relative freedom (1:12-13), expecting a release soon (1:19,26; 2:24), all of which points to the time of his Roman imprisonment (Acts 28:16-31). Paul had worked to establish this as the first church in Europe (Acts 16:6-40). It was originally addressed to the "saints" or church-members at Philippi, and curiously adds "with the bishops and deacons," an expression which finds a distant parallel only in Acts 15:4,22,23. The theme of this epistle is joy in the Lord and fellowship in the gospel.

Colossians

Written c. A.D. 61 (58-62), from Rome. The author is expressly identified as Paul (1:1,23; 4:18). Like Ephesians, Philippians, and Philemon, it was written during Paul's Roman imprisonment (4:10). It was originally addressed to "saints" or church-members and "faithful brethren," possibly Christian visitors, at Colosse, consisting largely of uncircumcised Gentiles (2:13). This epistle is intertwined with Philemon, both listing virtually the same companions of Paul (1,2,10,23,24; cf. Col. 1:1; 4:9-14,17) with the exception of Justus. Onesimus, the slave of Philemon, traveled with Tychicus, the one who brought this epistle to Colosse. Though Ephesians and Colossians have different emphases, they cover much of the same material, and serve as complements to each other.

I Thessalonians

Written c. A.D. 50 (50-52), from Corinth. The author is expressly identified as Paul (1:1; 2:18). It was originally addressed to the church of Thessalonians, one of the four capitals of the region of Macedonia, and its largest and wealthiest city. Of all Paul's epistles, this or Galatians was the earliest. In it, Paul covers an array of basic Christian doctrine: election (1:4) the authority of the Word of God (1:5-6,8; 2:13,15; 4:15), the personality and power of the Holy Spirit (1:5,6; 4:8), the deity of Christ (1:1,3; 3:11-13; 5:28), the coming of Christ and the day of the Lord (1:10; 2:19; 3:13; 4:13-5:11,23), sanctification (4:1-12), and church leadership and conduct (5:12-22).

II Thessalonians

Written c. A.D. 51 (51-53), from Corinth. The author is expressly identified as Paul (1:1; 3:17). It was originally addressed to the same church as I Thessalonians, written shortly thereafter, perhaps within months, apparently to correct some misunderstandings or false teachings that the coming of the Christ had passed (2:1), explaining certain markers leading up to that event (2:1-16), and exhorting them to discourage idleness (3:6-15).

I Timothy

Written c. A.D. 63 (62-64), from Rome or Macedonia. The author is expressly identified as Paul (1:1). It was originally addressed to Timothy, a native of Lystra in Phrygia, whose father was a Greek (Acts 16:1). His mother Eunice and grandmother Lois were God-fearing, possibly Hebrews (II Tim. 1:5), and he was raised in a God-fearing manner (II Tim. 3:14-15), though uncircumcised as a child (Acts 16:3). Timothy may have been converted under Paul's earlier ministry in Lystra (Acts 14:6-20). Timothy became Paul's companion and assistant during Paul's second missionary journey (Acts 16:1-3) and was associated with him ever afterwards (Acts 17:14-15; 18:5; 19:22; 20:4). He co-authored six epistles with Paul and is mentioned in five other epistles of Paul. Paul called him "servant of Christ," "workfellow," "dearly beloved son," and "my own son." Paul expected to be acquitted and released from Roman imprisonment (Phil. 1:19), and this epistle was possibly written soon thereafter. It establishes in writing the order of eldership being practiced in the churches, along with "how thou oughtest to behave thyself in the house of God, which is the church of the living God" (3:15), and specifically addresses an early form of gnostic heresy (4:1-11), charging Timothy to remain faithful (1:18-19; 4:9-16; 5:21; 6:11-14).

II Timothy

Written c. A.D. 67 (64-68), from Rome. The author is expressly identified as Paul (1:1). It was originally addressed to Timothy, while Paul was in his second imprisonment (1:8) in Rome (1:16-17) not long before Paul's death by execution (4:6-9) under Nero, who blamed the Christians for starting the fire which burned Rome in A.D. 64. Paul did not want to depart this life without, if possible, seeing Timothy one final time, or at least communicating to him through this epistle. These are Paul's final instructions.

Titus

Written c. A.D. 63 (62-64), from Rome or Macedonia, about the same time as I Timothy. The author is expressly identified as Paul (1:1). It was originally addressed to Titus, whom Paul calls "my brother," "partner," and "fellowhelper," who was a Gentile, having never been circumcised (Gal. 2:1-3). Apparently, Titus accompanied Paul to the Jerusalem conference (Acts 15:2). It appears that after Paul's release from Roman imprisonment, he helped to plant a church on Crete, and left Titus behind to "set in order the things that are wanting, and ordain elders in every city" (1:5). The epistle is a concise summary of church order and of zeal for good works (2:14).

Philemon

Written c. A.D. 61 (60-62), from Rome. The author is expressly identified as Paul (1,9,19). This epistle was written during Paul's Roman imprisonment (1,23). It was originally addressed primarily to Philemon (1), but also to Apphia (possibly Philemon's wife), Archippus (possibly an elder, or son, or both), and the church in Philemon's house (2) in Colosse (see Colossians above). Philemon, a Christian, was the owner of the slave Onesimus, who had run away, and had also converted to faith in Christ. In that day, Roman slaves far outnumbered Roman citizens, so their control was very important to the empire. Christian faith did not require the immediate dissolution of slavery, but had a policy of attrition which, if consistently practiced, would eventually eliminate slavery: those who could free slaves or slaves who could be freed should pursue that course, but nobody was to enslave another or to enter slavery himself (I Cor. 7:21,23). Thus Paul was enforcing this policy by sending Onesimus back to secure his freedom from Philemon, and exhorting Philemon to free Onesimus, and to lay any charges to Paul's account, reminding Philemon that, in a ministerial way, he owed his very "life" and spiritual freedom to Paul.

Hebrews

Written c. A.D. 67 (64-68), from Rome. Though the original readers apparently knew the author (13:18-19,22-23), the epistle itself does not name its author nor its audience. Authorship is traditionally ascribed to Paul, and the form and content resemble Paul's other writings. However, the vocabulary and style more closely resemble Luke's writings, and it is not unlikely that someone such as Luke may have assisted Paul in composing what may have been one of his final epistles. Timothy (13:23) is frequently identified as Paul's amanuensis, and Paul had asked Timothy to bring the Scriptures to him (II Tim. 4:13), which would have been useful in composing this quotation-filled epistle. It was originally addressed to Hebrew Christians, for it everywhere assumes the audience has particular knowledge of Hebrew ceremonial law. The extensive use of the Septuagint Greek in Old Testament quotations may indicate that it was addressed to Hebrews outside of Jerusalem or Judea, who had "not yet resisted unto blood, striving against sin" (12:4). The reference to "those from Italy salute you" (13:24) most likely indicates that it was written in Italy, possibly Rome, though it might indicate Italians away from home sending greetings back home. All of these factors agree with the theory that this may be Paul's first and final written exhortation to his fellow Hebrews. The epistle exhorts Hebrew Christians to go on to completion in Christ (6:1; 12:1,2), displaying the superiority and finality of Christ in all things, and the better and heavenly New Covenant's total displacement of the earthly Old Covenant. It quite possibly refers to the imminent destruction of the temple in Jerusalem by fire (12:26-29) according to Christ's promise. The epistle closes with a customary blessing not unlike Paul's (13:25; cf. II Thess. 3:17-18).

James

Written c. A.D. 46 (40-50), from Jerusalem, before the Jerusalem conference. The author is expressly identified as James (1:1). Some have suggested the Apostle James, brother of John, as the author, but this has no traditional support, and the Apostle James was martyred c. A.D. 44, which may be before this epistle was written. Tradition assigns this book to James, son of Joseph and Mary, half-brother of Jesus (Matt. 12:46-47; Mark 3:31-32; Luke 8:19-20; John 2:12; 7:3,5,10; Acts 1:14; I Cor. 9:5; Gal. 1:9), brother of Joses, Simon, and Judas (Matt. 13:

55; 27:56; Mark 6:3; 15:40; Jude 1:1), a prophet and elder at Jerusalem (Acts 12:17; 15:13; 21:18; Gal. 2:9,12). The absence of any reference to the Jerusalem council of c. A.D. 49 (Acts 15), and the use of the Hebrew term for a gathering (συναγωγή 2:2) as equivalent to the Greek term for "church" (ἐκκλησία 5:14) may suggest a very early date. It was originally addressed to "the twelve tribes which are scattered abroad," possibly the believing Hebrews who "were scattered abroad upon the persecution that arose about Stephen" c. A.D. 34 (Acts 11:19; cf. 8:1,4), and after the death of the Apostle James and the imprisonment of Peter c. A.D. 38 (Acts 12:1-19); and it may have circulated widely among Hebrew Christians. This epistle is the Proverbs of the Greek Scriptures, instructing in practical ethics, the works which genuine faith necessarily produces, and containing many allusions to the Sermon on the Mount (Matt. 5-7).

I Peter

Written c. A.D. 65 (64-66), possibly from Rome under the figure of Babylon (5:13; cf. Rev. 14:8; 16:19; 17:5; 18: 2,10,21). The author is expressly identified as "Peter, an apostle of Jesus Christ" (1:1). It was originally addressed "to the strangers [/pilgrims] scattered throughout Pontus, Galatia, Cappadocia, Asia, and Bithynia, elect . . ." (1: 1,2), provinces of Asia Minor, an area already evangelized by Paul. The recipients are described as formerly fashioned according to ignorant lusts (1:14), walking in "vain conversation received by tradition" from their fathers (1:18), and were therefore "not a people," but had now been "called out of darkness" (2:9,10) and had "wrought the will of the Gentiles" (4:3) – all of which would more likely be applied to Gentiles, though there is a sense in which it could also be applied to Hebrews. Assuming Peter is in Rome, and since Paul made no mention of Peter while in Rome, this was likely written after Paul had been released c. A.D. 62 and before he had been re-imprisoned c. A.D. 67, probably before Nero's persecution c. A.D. 64. Peter emphasizes that Christians can expect suffering for the kingdom (1: 6-7; 2:19-25; 3:14-22; 4:12-19), stresses sanctification of spirit and submission to lawful authority (1:13-3:13; 4:1-11), and lays out in writing the order of elders in the church (5:1-11).

II Peter

Written c. A.D. 66 (65-68), possibly from Rome shortly before Peter's death, presumably just before the destruction of Jerusalem. The author is expressly identified as "Simon Peter, a servant and an apostle of Jesus Christ" (1:1). It was originally addressed to those who "have obtained like precious faith with us" (1:1) which is very general, though it specifies this is a second epistle written to them (3:1), suggesting the same audience as the first epistle. This epistle anticipates the imminent death of Peter (1:13,14), and some tradition suggests that he died in Rome under Nero's persecution, which began c. A.D. 64. There are many parallels between II Peter and Jude (see under Jude). In this epistle, Peter stresses sanctification motivated by the imminent return of Christ.

I John

Written c. A.D. 90 (85-95), possibly from Ephesus, by John the Apostle, who does not identify himself by name in this epistle, but describes himself as among the apostles who heard, saw, handled, and testified to Christ, the Word of life (1:1-10; 4:14). It was probably written before the persecution under Domitian c. A.D. 95. There is no identifiable place of origin or destination, but tradition assigns the origin to Ephesus and the destination to Asia Minor. This epistle focuses on the doctrine of unity and fellowship in Christ, and assurance of faith. It is marked by comparisons and contrasts: light and darkness, love and hate, life and death, God and the devil. Many portions appear to be addressing incipient forms of gnostic philosophy and the denial of Christ's human incarnation, which may have been infecting churches in Asia Minor.

II John

Written c. A.D. 90 (85-95), presumably from Ephesus, by John, who calls himself "the Elder" (1; cf. Philem. 9; I Pet. 5:1), probably the Apostle John referring to his advanced age. He addresses "the elect lady and her children" with greetings from "the children of your elect sister." This may be a figurative expression for a church and its individual members (1,13), because the church is elsewhere referred to as a woman (II Cor. 11:2; Eph. 5:25-27,31,32; I Pet. 5:13; Rev. 21:2,9; 22:17), the plural pronouns (6,8,10,12) imply a plural audience, and the letter addresses problems faced by a church. This epistle was probably written after I John, for it assumes the readers understand the expression "antichrist" (7; cf. I John 2:18,22; 4:3). This epistle contains a commendation for walking in the truth (4); a plea to walk in love according to Christ's commandments (5-6); a warning not to receive deceivers such as those who deny Christ's incarnation (7-10).

III John

Written c. A.D. 90 (85-95), presumably from Ephesus,

by John the Apostle, who calls himself "the Elder" (1) to Gaius. This epistle contains a commendation for walking in the truth (2-4); a commendation for receiving brethren in love (5-8); a warning about Diotrephes who loves preeminence among the church and does not receive the Apostle John and his entourage (9-11).

Jude

Written c. A.D. 69 (60-69). The author is expressly identified as Jude, brother of James (1). It was not written by an apostle (17), which leaves the Lord's half-brother as the only other likely possibility, and tradition agrees. II Peter 2:1-3:4 is very similar to Jude 4-18. While II Peter anticipates false teachers (2:1-2; 3:3), Jude refers to them in the past tense (4,11-12,17-18), and Jude 18 directly quotes II Peter 3:3, calling it "the words which were spoken before by the apostles," which facts suggest that Jude followed II Peter. Jude is intensely concerned that his readers should "earnestly contend for the faith which was once delivered unto the saints" (3), describing false teachers and their eventual judgment, with illustrations from Hebrew history.

Revelation

Written c. A.D. 68 (68-70), while the author was on the island of Patmos (1:9,19; 10:4; 14:13; 19:9; 21:5). The visions were seen on "the Lord's day" (1:9). Though this expression came to be used in the second century to refer to the first day of the week, there is no evidence that it was so used in the first century. If John follows the regular (though not universal) pattern of Hebrew prophets for dating the present time of their prophecy (e.g. Isa. 1:1; Jer. 1:2-3; Ezek. 1:1-3; Dan. 1:1; Hos. 1:1; Amos 1:1; Mic. 1:1; Zeph. 1:1; Hag. 1:1; Zech. 1:1), then "the Lord's day" refers not to what day of the week (which would have no prophetic significance here), but to the specific time of the prophecy, "the day of the Lord" (Isa. 2:12; 13:6,9; 34:8; 61:2; 63:4; Jer. 46:10; 51:6; Lam. 2:22; Ezek. 13:5; 30:3; Joel 1:15; 2:1,11,31; 3:14; Amos 5:18,20; Obad. 1:15; Zeph. 1:7,8,14,18; 2:2,3; Zech. 14:1; Mal. 4:5; Luke 21:22; Phil. 1:6,10; 2:16; I Thess. 5:2; II Thess. 2:2; II Pet. 2:9; 3:7,10), which in this case would be the time of the destruction of Jerusalem by the Roman armies under Vespasian and Titus. (In Greek, "the Lord's day" places emphasis on the *day*, while the synonymous and interchangeable expression "the day of the Lord" places emphasis on the *Lord*.) Jerusalem had not yet been destroyed when Revelation was written (11:2). The book itself describes "things which must shortly come to pass . . . the time is at hand" (1:1,3) and "things which must shortly be done. . . . Seal not the

sayings of the prophecy of this book: for the time is at hand" (22:6,10; contrast Dan. 8:26; 12:4,9). Those who believe the book does not predictively describe the fall of Jerusalem prefer to assign a later date c. A.D. 95-96. The author is expressly identified as John (1:1,4,9; 21:2; 22:8). Some have questioned whether the gospel of John and the book of Revelation could have been written by the same author. Though there are observable differences in grammar, vocabulary, and style, these differences may be accounted for by observing that John himself, apparently while in a visionary state, wrote Revelation almost at dictation as an urgent prophetic discourse, whereas John's gospel, an historical narrative sharing the reflections of a lifetime, was likely written thirty years later, more or less at leisure, with the aid of others (John 21:24). One might wonder that there aren't greater differences. Yet there are many expressions common only to the gospel, epistles, and Revelation of John. Here are just a few: the Word of God referring to Jesus (John 1:1; I John 1:1; Rev. 19:13); He Who Conquers (John 16:33; I John 2:13,14 etc.; Rev. 2:7,11 etc.); the Lamb of God (John 1:19,36; Rev. 5:6,8,12,13 etc.); the Water of Life (John 7:37; Rev. 22:17); cleansing blood (I John 1:7; Rev. 1:5); piercing of Christ (John 19:37; Rev 1:7); emphasis on truth (John 1:9 etc.; I John 2:8 etc.; Rev. 3:7 etc.); emphasis on testimony (John 19:35; Rev. 1:2); it is peculiar to John to state his proposition affirmatively, rather than to deny their contrasts (e.g. John 1:20; 1 John 1:5,6; Rev 2:3,13; 3:5,8,9,18). The book contains a symbolic seven-fold vision of the glorified Lord Jesus as the Ancient of Days (1); seven epistles of promise and warning sent by Jesus to the churches of Asia Minor (2-3); the judgment of "Sodom and Egypt" (4:1-11:15) – including the seven attendants to God's throne (4:1-5:7), seven seals (5:8-8:1), and seven trumpets (8:2-11:15); the judgment of "Babylon" (11:15-19:10) – including seven signs (11:15-15:1), seven bowls (15:2-16:21), and seven dirges (17:1-19:10); the seven destinies of sinners (19:11-20:10); the seven adornments of saints (20:11-22:5); closing admonitions. Various methods of interpreting these visions include: Idealist – they depict broad principles which operate in history; Historical – they depict the progress of church history; Futurist – they depict events which are still future to us; Preterist – they depict the judgment of God on Jerusalem and on Rome in the first century.

Literature of Egypt

Here is a select list of literature from Egypt. We have chosen those works commonly considered to be culturally important, yet not inappropriate for students ages twelve and up.

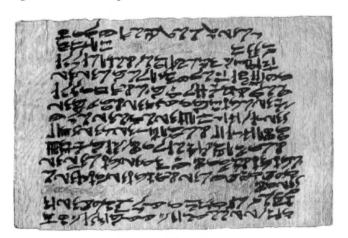

Writings of Ptah-Hotep

Egyptian Precepts (also called *The Instruction of Ptah-Hotep*)

Considered the oldest book in the world; thought to have been written c. 2450 B.C. and ascribed to Ptah-Hotep (a vizier of a king of the fifth dynasty); written on papyrus (now in the National Library in Paris); inscribed on tombs. It is a compilation of wise sayings.

Letter of Pepi II

Harkhuf received a letter from the Egyptian pharaoh Pepi II (ruled c. 2161-c. 2067 B.C.) concerning a dwarf.

The Edwin Smith Surgical Papyrus

The earliest known scientific document; written by someone who lived in the Old Kingdom. It is a treatise on surgery, in which the author draws conclusions from observed facts.

Epitaph of Beka

Inscription on a funeral pillar now in the Museum of Turin. Beka, the person who died, was the great steward of the Public Granary.

Foreign captives making bricks at Thebes

The Laboring Classes

From a papyrus in the British Museum written in the twelfth dynasty or earlier. This document compares the different occupations and their hardships with the easy occupation of a scribe.

Story of Sinuhe

Considered to be the oldest form of the novel. It is the story of an Egyptian official who goes into exile after the death of Pharaoh Amenemhat I (ruled c. 1796-1767 B.C.), but returns to Egypt some years later. It is not known if this is fictional or biographical. It is considered to be the most accomplished piece of prose literature of this time period.

The Shipwrecked Sailor

Dates from the Middle Kingdom. A man tells of his fantastic adventure.

Products of Arabia

Inscription on the inner wall of an Egyptian temple, giving an account of the conquest of Arabia during the time of Thutmose III (ruled c. 1138-c. 1085 B.C.).

Pharaoh Amenhotep II as a Sportsman

Inscription found on a stele describing Egyptian Pharaoh Amenhotep II (ruled c. 1085-1059 B.C.) as a great sportsman.

Pharaoh Akhenaten

Tablets of Tel El-Amarna

Letters from the Egyptian Governor of Palestine to Pharaoh Akhenaten (ruled c. 1022-1006 B.C.), announcing a revolt. Palestine is under Egyptian rule, and the governor tells pharaoh of a general revolt of the natives.

Ramesses II, Son and Second Self of the God Ptah-Totunen

Inscription which glorifies the Pharaoh Ramesses II (ruled c. 940-873 B.C.) as the son and incarnation of the chief deity.

Ramesses II

Ramesses at Kadesh

Poem recording the battle between Pharaoh Ramesses II (ruled c. 940-873 B.C.) and the Hittite King Muwatallis II.

Treaty between Ramesses II and the Hittite King Hattusilis III after the battle of Kadesh

Hattusilis was the brother of Muwatallis II. The oldest existing treaty between two nations. Ramesses II ruled Egypt from c. 940-873 B.C.

Apology of Hattusilis III

One of the major Hittite historical texts. This text mentions the treaty between Ramesses II and Hattusilis III; and the battle between Ramesses II and Muwatallis II.

The Israel Stela of Merneptah

The earliest known document, outside of the Bible, to mention the name of Israel. The document records a military campaign of Merneptah, son of Ramesses II.

Spoliation of Tombs

Extract from a longer document from the time of Ramesses IX (ruled c. 835-816 B.C.), showing that tomb robbery was common even during ancient times.

Book of the Dead

Collection of Egyptian magic spells, rubrics, prayers to the gods, poems, songs, and religious documents. It is believed by some that parts of this work were in general use before the rule of the pharaohs of the First Dynasty.

The Hymn to Aton

A song/prayer to the god Aton.

The Hymn to the Nile

A song/prayer praising and recognizing the wonders of the Nile.

Literature of the Hebrew People

Although there are some important works in Greek, Aramaic, and Arabic, the literature of the Hebrew people has mainly developed in the Hebrew language. Only a few of the many significant excerpts from these works have been noted here.

The Hebrew Scriptures

See section on The Bible.

Apocrypha

A collection of early writings produced by Alexandrian Jews, written in the Greek language, but in a Hebrew style. The Hebrews exclude them from the canon of the Hebrew Scriptures. The Greek Orthodox Church and the Roman Catholic Church include them in their Old Testament canon, while the Protestants exclude them.

I Esdras

Written first century B.C.; chiefly contains selections from II Chronicles and Ezra-Nehemiah; gives an account of the return of the Hebrews from Babylonian captivity, the building of the temple, and the establishment of divine worship.

II Esdras

Written during Domitian's reign c. A.D. 81-96; contains Hebrew apocalyptic prophecies.

Tobit

Written second century B.C.; relates the history of Tobit and his family, whom Shalmaneser took captive to Nineveh.

Judith

Written in the Maccabean age; relates how Judith helps the Hebrews defeat the Assyrians.

Additions to Esther

Written first or second century B.C.; provides a preface and conclusion, and expands the narrative to the Biblical book of Esther, giving it a more religious character.

Wisdom of Solomon

Written shortly before the Christian era; teachings on immortality and wisdom; also contains a descriptive commentary on the Exodus.

Ecclesiasticus, or the Wisdom of the Son of Sirach

Written shortly before the Maccabean persecution. The first part is a textbook of morals; the second part is a prose-hymn called "The Praise of Famous Men."

Baruch

Written first century B.C.; contains several minor unconnected writings resembling the prophetic utterances of the Old Testament. The last chapter is called "The Letter of Jeremiah."

The Song of the Three Young Men

An addition to the book of Daniel; a prayer supposedly spoken by Azarias (Abed-Nego) and a song which the three Hebrew youths supposedly sang in the midst of the fiery furnace.

The History of Susanna

An additional thirteenth chapter of Daniel; the story of how Susanna is wrongfully accused of adultery, but Daniel discovers the truth.

Bel and the Dragon

An additional fourteenth chapter of Daniel which takes place during the time of Cyrus. Daniel exposes the dishonesty of the priests of Bel and slays the dragon god.

I Maccabees

Written during the first or second decade of the first century B.C.; a history of the Hebrews from the beginning of the reign of Antiochus Epiphanes to the death of Simon (175-134 B.C.). It describes the oppression and persecution of the Hebrew people at the hands of the Seleucid kings and the peoples who paid them homage.

II Maccabees

Written during the first century B.C.; an abridgment of a larger history of the Maccabees in five volumes written by Jason of Cyrene.

The Prayer of Manasseh

Purportedly the penitential prayer of Manasseh, King of Judah, mentioned in II Chronicles 33:18-19

❧ SIGNIFICANT EXCERPTS ❧

I Esdras 3-4 – Three young courtiers debate the question, "What is the strongest thing in the world?"

Judith 8.1-8 – Description of Judith.

Judith 13.1-10 – Judith cuts off the head of her enemy.

Wisdom of Solomon 7.1-14 – The gift of wisdom.

Ecclesiasticus 27.11-21 – The discourse of a godly man.

Ecclesiasticus 37.7-12 – Seeking counsel of godly men.

I Maccabees 1.1-9 – The person and conquests of Alexander the Great, his death, and the breakup of his kingdom.

I Maccabees 1.10-64 – The rise of Antiochus Epiphanes and how he persecuted the Hebrews and desecrated the Temple at Jerusalem.

I Maccabees 1.11-15 – Unfaithful Hebrews compromise with the pagan Greeks and build a gymnasium in Jerusalem according to the Gentile religion.

I Maccabees 4.1-25 – Battle against Gorgias.

I Maccabees 4.36-59 – Institution of the feast of Hanukkah in 164 B.C.

I Maccabees 6.1-16 – Defeat and death of Antiochus IV in 164 B.C.

I Maccabees 8.1-32 – Judas and the Hebrews make a treaty with the Romans to protect them from the Greeks.

I Maccabees 9.11-22 – Death of Judas in 160 B.C.

I Maccabees 9.28-31 – Judas's brother Jonathan chosen as the leader of Israel.

I Maccabees 10.1-89 – Jonathan and the Hebrews side with Alexander Epiphanes (son of Antiochus) and not with Demetrius, and Alexander makes Jonathan High Priest.

I Maccabees 11.1-74 – Ptolemy, the king of Egypt, plots with Demetrius against Alexander. Ptolemy enters Antioch and crowns himself King of Egypt and Asia. Alexander is beheaded by an Arabian, Ptolemy dies, and Demetrius reigns. Jonathan makes a treaty with Demetrius, but later makes war on Demetrius and is victorious.

I Maccabees 12.1-53 – Jonathan renews his treaty with the Romans. Trypho captures Jonathan.

I Maccabees 13.1-53 – Simon is appointed by the Hebrews to succeed Jonathan. Simon makes a treaty with Demetrius.

I Maccabees 15.33-35 – Simon's answer to Antiochus, defending the right of the Hebrews to possess Judea.

I Maccabees 16.1-3 – Simon makes his two sons, John and Judas, rulers over the Hebrews.

I Maccabees 16.16-17 – Simon and Judas are killed, and John alone rules.

Pseudepigrapha

A collection of early Hebrew and some Hebrew-Christian writings composed between c. 200 B.C. and c. A.D. 200, not found in the Bible or in rabbinic writings. Most of the works are anonymous.

Includes: Apocalypse of Abraham, Apocalypse of Adam, Testament of Adam, 2 Baruch, 3 Baruch, Apocalypse of Daniel, Apocalypse of Elijah, 1 Enoch, 2

Enoch, 3 Enoch, Apocryphon of Ezekiel, Fourth Book of Ezra, Greek Apocalypse of Ezra, Questions of Ezra, Revelation of Ezra, Vision of Ezra, Testament of Job, Testament of Moses, Apocalypse of Sedrach, Treatise of Shem, Sibylline Oracles, Testament of Solomon, Testaments of the Three Patriarchs, Testaments of the Twelve Patriarchs, an Apocalypse of Zephaniah, Life of Adam and Eve, Ahiqar, Letter of Aristeas, Aristeas the Exegete, Aristobulus, Artapanus, 4 Baruch, Cleodemus Malchus, More Psalms of David, Demetrius the Chronographer, Eldad and Modad, Eupolemus, Pseudo-Eupolemus, Ezekiel the Tragedian, Fragments of Pseudo-Greek Poets, Pseudo-Hecataeus, Hellenistic Synagogal Prayers, Martyrdom and Ascension of Isaiah, Ladder of Jacob, Prayer of Jacob, Jannes and Jambres, Joseph and Aseneth, History of Joseph, Prayer of Joseph, Jubilees, 3 Maccabees, 4 Maccabees, Prayer of Manasseh, Syriac Menander, Orphica, Philo the Epic Poet, Pseudo-Philo, Pseudo-Phocylides, The Lives of the Prophets, History of the Rechabites, Odes of Solomon, Psalms of Solomon, and Theodotus.

Ancient Jewish book

Talmud

During the second through the sixth centuries A.D., rabbis compiled, edited, and interpreted the religious and civil law of the Hebrews, called the Talmud. The Talmud (meaning *doctrine* or *learning*) consists of two general parts: the *Mishna* or text, and the *Gemara* or commentary.

The Mishna (meaning *repetition*), consisting of six books or Orders (Sedarim), divided into 63 treatises (Massektoth). It is a collection of various oral traditions of the Jews and of expositions of texts of Scripture, written in Hebrew, which supposedly were delivered to Moses while he remained on Mount Sinai; and through Aaron, Eleazar, and Joshua they were supposedly transmitted to the prophets, who handed them down to the Great Sanhedrin, who passed them on to Simeon, Gamaliel, and ultimately at the end of the second century A.D., to Rabbi Jehuda ha-Nasi, who labored for forty years to collect and preserve them in writing. From this time, they have been carefully preserved through the generations and are esteemed by many to be higher than the written law of Moses itself.

There are two Gemaras or commentaries on the Mishna, written in Aramaic. The *Gemara of Jerusalem* was compiled in the third (some say the fifth) century A.D., and is held in little esteem by the Jews. The *Gemara of Babylon* was compiled in the sixth century A.D.. The Jews call these commentaries *Gemara* (meaning *perfection*) because they consider them to be the final explanation of the whole law to which nothing more can be added. When the Mishna is accompanied by the Jerusalem Gemara, this is called the *Jerusalem Talmud*; and when the Mishna is accompanied the Babylon Gemara, this is called the *Babylonian Talmud*. The Babylonian Talmud is longer and more comprehensive and sophisticated and is held in much higher esteem by the Jews than the Jerusalem Talmud. The Jews consider it a sure and authoritative guide in all difficult questions.

The Talmud touches on a wide range of subjects, offering information and comment on astronomy, geography, historical lore, domestic relations, and folklore.

Midrash

Midrash (meaning *to examine, to investigate*) is an interpretation of the Hebrew Scriptures, consisting of exegesis and homily following the order of the text.

Midrash halakah deals with the legal portions of Scripture.

Midrash haggada deals with Biblical lore or poetical digressions which use parables, legends, allegories, tales, and anecdotes to illustrate and apply religious and ethical principles.

Midrashic exposition of both kinds appears throughout the Talmud. Individual midrashic commentaries, mostly haggada, were composed by rabbis after the second century A.D. The Midrash Rabbah is a collection of commentaries on the Torah and the Five Scrolls (the Song of Songs, Esther, Ruth, Lamentations, Ecclesiastes), and the Pesikta Midrashim is concerned with the festivals.

Targum

When the Jews of Palestine and Babylon could no longer speak Hebrew so that the people could understand, it became customary during synagogue services to accompany the reading of the Hebrew Scriptures with a translation and explanation in the Aramaic language. These oral paraphrases were eventually written down under the name *Targum*, which is Aramaic for *translation*. The Targum is an Aramaic paraphrase of the Hebrew Scriptures.

Written Targums may have existed from an early date. The last saying of Christ Jesus on the Cross (Matt. 27: 46) is the Aramaic form of Psalm 21:2, which suggests that an Aramaic translation of the Psalms may have been current among the people. A Targum of the Book of Job is mentioned in the mid-first century A.D. No Targum manuscript has been preserved from further back than the fifth century A.D. There are Targums for all the books of the Hebrew Scriptures except Daniel, Ezra, and Nehemiah. Some books have more than one Targum. In the fourth century the Targums to the Pentateuch and to the Prophets were finished.

As regards age and linguistic character they may be divided into three classes: (1) Targum of Onkelos and Targum of Jonathan; (2) Jerusalem Targums; (3) Targum on the Hagiographa.

One of the best-known Targums extant is the Targum Onkelos.

Dead Sea Scrolls

These ancient leather and papyrus scrolls were first discovered in 1947 in caves on the northwest shore of the Dead Sea. A Hebrew sect known as Essenes, which came into existence in the mid-second century B.C., hid a library of scrolls in caves near its settlement at Qumran. The settlement was destroyed c. A.D. 68, but the scrolls have survived. Most of the scrolls date from between the first century B.C. and the first half of the first century A.D. They are of three types: 1) copies of books of the Hebrew Scriptures, including two almost complete scrolls of Isaiah; 2) copies of books now collected in the Old Testament Apocrypha and Pseudepigrapha, including Tobit, 1 Enoch, and Jubilees; and 3) documents composed by Qumran Essenes expressing their distinctive theology, including The Manual of Discipline (community rules), The War of the Sons of Light with the Sons of Darkness (an allegorical account of the community), The Thanksgiving Psalms (devotional poems), a commentary on the Book of Habakkuk, and the Temple Scroll, an extensive work containing ritual law.

Other texts have been found in the area around the Dead Sea – manuscripts of Sirach and the Songs of the Sabbath Sacrifice were found near Masada. In the caves at Wadi Murabbaat, many documents concerning Bar Kokba's army were found, as well as more Biblical manuscripts. In caves south of En Gedi, other documents from the Bar Kokba era were discovered, including Biblical fragments, psalms, various legal documents, and a lost Greek translation of the minor prophets. At a site north of Jericho were found the oldest documents, left there by Samaritans who were massacred by Alexander the Great in 331 B.C.

Literature of Mesopotamia

Sumer, Accad, Babylonia, Assyria, and Persia

Here is a select list of literature from Sumer, Accad, Babylonia, Assyria, and Persia. We have chosen those works commonly considered to be culturally important, yet not inappropriate for students ages twelve and up.

The Babylonian-Assyrian Story of the Creation

Long epic poem inscribed on a series of tablets, first found in Nineveh (now located in the British Museum). This poem is the Babylonian-Assyrian version of the story of the creation, and it dates from c. 650 B.C., although the narrative itself is much older.

Gilgamesh Tablet

Babylonian-Assyrian Epic of Gilgamesh Flood Story

The Epic of Gilgamesh is inscribed on twelve tablets (now in the British Museum). This is a long epic poem (thought to have been first recorded c. 1200 B.C., but the story was in existence long before), which tells, in narrative form, the deeds of real or mythical heroes. In the beginning of the story, there is conflict between Gilgamesh (who is two-thirds god and one-third man) and the rulers of Uruk, who claim that Gilgamesh is acting like a tyrant. The nobles ask the gods for help, and Aruru, the mother goddess, creates Enkidu to try to stop Gilgamesh's tyranny. Gilgamesh sends a harlot to tame Enkidu before he is brought to Uruk. At Uruk, the two heroes fight, then become friends. They leave Uruk together and face many dangerous events. They slay the monster Huwawa (who guards the Cedar Forest for the storm-god Enlil). This insults the goddess Ishtar, who falls in love with Gilgamesh and tries to seduce him. Gilgamesh and Enkidu destroy the bull of Heaven sent by Ishtar to kill Gilgamesh. Enkidu eventually dies, and Gilgamesh is sad. He now wants to find everlasting life, so he searches and finds Utnapishtim (the Babylonian "Noah"), the man to whom the gods have granted immortality, in order to learn from him how to obtain eternal life. The rest of the epic incorporates the story of a great flood similar to the flood account in Genesis. Utnapishtim tells how he obtained eternal life as a reward for the deeds he performed at the time of the Flood. Gilgamesh's long search for immortality is a failure. The flood account portion of this epic (recorded on the eleventh of the twelve tablets) is useful to compare with that of the Genesis account. The remainder is rather profane and should be pre-read by the parent.

Chronicle of the Reign of Sargon

Tablet (now in the British Museum) composed after c. 606 B.C. but known to be a summary of an earlier narrative. This tablet provides details on Sargon of Accad.

Achievements of Hammurabi

Babylonian inscription of the deeds of the Babylonian King Hammurabi (c. 1565 B.C.).

Hammurabi on Throne

Code of Hammurabi

Tablet containing the law code of Hammurabi, king of Babylonia (c. 1565 B.C.).

Inscription of Tiglath-Pileser I King of Assyria

Record of the victories of Tiglath-Pileser (ruled c. 1120-1100), inscribed on four octagonal cylinders of clay originally buried under the foundation of a temple in Assur (but now in the British Museum). This describes the deeds of the first notable Assyrian conqueror.

Moabite Stone

Moabite Stone

Inscription to commemorate the victory of Mesha, King of Moab, over his Israelite enemy, King Omri.

Sargon's Capture of Samaria

Records the capture of Samaria c. 721 B.C. by Sargon II of Assyria (ruled c. 721-705 B.C.).

Captive Israelites before Sennacherib

Annals of Sennacherib

Story of Sennacherib's (king of Assyria who ruled c. 705-681 B.C.) siege of Jerusalem, written in cuneiform on a prism, as told by Sennacherib himself. Compare the Bible version in II Kings 18 and 19.

Sennacherib: The Capture and Destruction of Babylon

Rock inscription detailing Sennacherib's military conquest of Babylon c. 689 B.C.

Letter of an Assyrian Physician Reporting Upon a Patient

Letter addressed to an Assyrian king written by a physician.

The Black Stone of Esarhaddon

Tells how Esarhaddon of Assyria (ruled c. 681-668 B.C.), the son of Sennacherib of Assyria (ruled c. 705-681 B.C.), rebuilt the holy city of Babylon which his father had destroyed.

An Inscription of Nebuchadnezzar

Nebuchadnezzar (ruled c. 605-562 B.C.) boasting of his glory and mighty deeds.

A Babylonian Lawsuit

Inscription on a tablet describing Babylonian legal practices and documents during the time of Nebuchadnezzar (ruled c. 605-562 B.C.). A Jew, who had been carried to Babylon as captive after the destruction of Jerusalem, sues in order to recover his original status.

How Cyrus Took Babylon

Cylinder inscription. Cyrus the Persian (ruled c.

559-529 B.C.) took Babylon c. 538 B.C.

Behistan Inscription

The Behistan Inscription of King Darius

Isolated rock near the western border of Iran. In c.

516 B.C., Darius the king (ruled c. 522-485 B.C.) had his artists smooth a large area more than 300 feet above the ground, where they sculpted scenes from his religious and military life, along with a chronicle of his deeds. This inscription is in Old Persian, Elamite, and Accadian, and served as the starting point for the recovery of the lost languages and the history of Mesopotamia.

Letter of Darius

Personal letter from Darius (ruled c. 522-485 B.C.) to one of his satraps or district governors, instructing him not to require the sacred gardeners of Apollo to dig profane ground and plant fruit trees.

Literature of Greece and Rome

Including Early Literature of Christians

Here is a select list of authors and literature from Greece and Rome. All the major authors are listed alphabetically in this index, along with their extant works and numerous significant excerpts.

Accius

C. 170-86 B.C.
Lucius Accius

Accius is considered the best of the Roman tragedians. His plays were based on Greek legends, and were translations and adaptations of the Greek plays. There are forty-five titles which have come down to us today.

❧ EXTANT WORKS INCLUDE ❧

Achilles

Alcimeo

Andromeda

Bacchae

Aeschines

C. 389-314 B.C.

Aeschines was an Athenian orator, a political opponent of Demosthenes, and a friend of Philip and Alexander of Macedon. Demosthenes accused him of taking bribes from Philip. In his speeches, Aeschines is critical of the immorality in Athens, which he describes. His speeches help us to understand the political situation in Athens at this time.

❧ EXTANT WORKS ❧

Against Ctesiphon – Aeschines attempts to convince the Athenians not to honor Demosthenes with a golden crown; written 330 B.C.

Against Timarchus – Aeschines brings an indictment against Timarchus, charging that in his earlier life he had been addicted to immorality and therefore should be excluded from the Athenian assembly; written 345 B.C.

On the Embassy – Aeschines defends himself against charges by Demosthenes that he was working for Philip against Athens; written 343 B.C.

❧ SIGNIFICANT EXCERPTS ❧

Against Ctesiphon

On the Embassy

Aeschylus

C. 525-455 B.C.

Aeschylus is considered one of the three great Athenian tragedians, along with Sophocles and Euripides. Aeschylus wrote approximately ninety plays, but only seven survive. His plays center around the ancient myths and legends popular in his day. He took part in the Persian War and fought in the battles of Marathon and Salamis.

EXTANT WORKS

The Suppliants – The fifty daughters of Danaus, betrothed by Aegyptus (their father's brother) to his fifty sons, flee with Danaus to Argos to escape the marriage; written c. 490 B.C.

The Persians – Presents in dramatic form the invasion of Xerxes and his overthrow at Salamis. It is the only extant Greek historical tragedy. It is a piece of contemporaneous history, since Aeschylus actually was present at the battle of Salamis; written 472 B.C.

The Seven Against Thebes – Two rival princes (the two sons of Oedipus) fight against each other, and both are killed. They are buried by their two sisters, who are the only ones left of the royal house; written 467 B.C.

Prometheus Bound – Prometheus is bound to the top of a mountain in punishment for giving mankind the gift of fire without the consent of the gods; written 460 B.C.

The Oresteia trilogy (*Agamemnon*, *The Choephore*, and *The Eumenides*) – The tale of the House of Atreus; considered Aeschylus' best work; written 458 B.C.

SIGNIFICANT EXCERPTS

The Persians

Aesop
C. 620-560 B.C.

Aesop was the semi-legendary Greek writer and/or collector of 350 fables. He was a slave from Phrygia, or Lydia, and he served on the island of Samos before being freed.

EXTANT WORKS

Aesop's Fables

SIGNIFICANT EXCERPTS

Aesop's Fables

Ambrose
C. A.D. 339-397
Ambrosius

Ambrose was brought up in a Christian home in Gaul, and educated in Rome. He first became a government official, and later a bishop of Milan. He was reputedly involved in the conversion of Augustine. He wrote many commentaries on the Bible, dogmatic works, books on the sacraments and the duties of the clergy, and writings on monastic and moral life. He was a great orator and preacher, and some consider him to have been the first to write Christian hymns with rhyme and meter.

EXTANT WORKS INCLUDE

On the Duties of the Clergy – A manual of Christian morality.

On the Christian Faith

On Virginity

On the Holy Spirit

On the Mystery of the Lord's Incarnation

On the Mysteries

On Penitence

On Widows

91 *Letters*

SIGNIFICANT EXCERPTS

Letters

22 – To his sister, describing the discovery of the bodies of two saints.

57 – To Emperor Eugenius the Usurper, telling him he is excommunicated from the Church because of his donations to the upkeep of pagan temples.

63 – To the Church at Vercelli refuting Epicureanism.

69 – To Irenaeus, explaining why women should wear women's clothes and men should wear men's clothes.

Ammianus
C. A.D. 330-391
Ammianus Marcellinus

Ammianus was a Roman historian who wrote in Latin, though he was born in Greece to Greek parents. He served for a time in the Roman army, and later settled in Rome to write his history of the Roman empire, continuing the work of Tacitus. His history was divided into thirty-one books, of which the first thirteen are lost. The surviving eighteen books describe history from A.D. 353 to 378. This history is a clear and understandable account of events as told by someone who was actually living during that time period. He greatly admired the emperor Julian.

❧ EXTANT WORKS ❧

The History

❧ SIGNIFICANT EXCERPTS ❧

The History

- 14.6 – Vices of the Senate and Roman people.

- 15.12 – Characterization of the Gauls.

- 17.7 – Earthquake in Nicomedia in A.D. 358.

- 20.3 – Eclipse of the sun.

- 20.11.26-30 – Digression on rainbows.

- 22.4 – Julian expels all the eunuchs, barbers, and cooks from the palace; corruption of military discipline.

- 25.4.4-26 – Julian's good and bad characteristics; reference to Christians.

- 31.2-4 – Description of the Huns and the movements of the Goths.

- 31.12-14 – Battle of Adrianople in A.D. 378.

Anaxagoras
C. 500-427 B.C.

Anaxagoras was a pre-Socratic Greek philosopher, the teacher of Pericles, Thucydides, Euripides, and possibly Socrates. Only fragments of his work remain.

❧ SIGNIFICANT EXCERPTS ❧

FROM OTHERS WRITING ABOUT ANAXAGORAS OR INCLUDING HIS WRITINGS IN THEIR WORKS:

Diogenes Laertius – *Lives of the Philosophers*, Anaxagoras

Anaximander
C. 611-547 B.C.

Anaximander was a pre-Socratic Greek philosopher and a friend and pupil of Thales. Only a few fragments of his writings remain.

❧ SIGNIFICANT EXCERPTS ❧

FROM OTHERS WRITING ABOUT ANAXIMANDER OR INCLUDING HIS WRITINGS IN THEIR WORKS

Diogenes Laertius – *Lives of the Philosophers*, Anaximander

Antiphon
C. 480-411 B.C.

Antiphon was the earliest of the ten Attic orators. He was largely responsible for the establishment of the Four Hundred in 411 B.C., and when the democracy was restored, he was accused of treason and condemned to death. He was a professional speechwriter for other litigants, and never addressed the people himself, except when he defended his policy at his trial. It is believed that Antiphon began the practice of writing out entire speeches for clients to memorize and to deliver as their own. Six of his speeches are extant: three are school exercises, divided into tetralogies, each consisting of two speeches for prosecution and two for defense; three refer to actual legal processes; all deal with cases of homicide; some are rather profane and not suitable for children to read.

❧ EXTANT WORKS INCLUDE ❧

First Tetralogy – A man and his servant are killed.

Second Tetralogy – The javelin-throwing case.

Third Tetralogy – An old man, who has been assaulted by

a young man, dies of his wounds.

On the Murder of Herodes – A man is accused of murdering his companion during a sea voyage.

On the Chorus Boy – A man accidentally causes the death of a chorus boy by giving him a drug to improve his voice.

Against the Stepmother for Poisoning – A stepmother is accused of hiring a slave to poison her husband.

SIGNIFICANT EXCERPTS

First Tetralogy

Second Tetralogy

On the Murder of Herodes

On the Chorus Boy

Appian of Alexandria
C. A.D. 90-160

Appian was a Greek who was born in Egypt and came to Rome during the reign of Hadrian. He became an advocate in the courts of the emperors until they appointed him procurator. His history of the Roman conquests begins at the founding of Rome and extends to the reign of Trajan. Although strongly biased in favor of Roman imperialism, and often criticized for lack of accuracy in details, this history has preserved for us many documents and sources which otherwise would have been lost. Of the twenty-four books, written in Greek, only Books 6-7 and Books 11-17 have been fully preserved. We have only fragments of the other books. Appian's writing is very easy to understand.

EXTANT WORKS

The Roman History (We use one of two different systems available for enumerating Appian's work.)

Book 1 – Rome under the kings; contains the exploits and doings of the seven kings; fragments.

Book 2 – Italian Roman history; embraces all of Italy except along the Adriatic gulf; fragments.

Book 3 – Samnite Roman history; includes the war of the Romans against the Samnites – a great nation and one hard to conquer. The Romans waged war with them eighty years, and with difficulty subjugated them and the nations allied with them; fragments.

Book 4 – Gallic Roman history; contains the wars of the Romans against the Gauls; fragments.

Book 5 – Of Sicily and the other islands; fragments.

Book 6 – Wars in Spain.

Book 7 – Hannibalic War; the war of the Romans against Hannibal the Carthaginian.

Book 8 – Punic Wars; African, Carthaginian, and Numidian; fragments.

Book 9 – Macedonian Affairs; fragments.

Book 10 – Illyrian Wars; fragments.

Book 11 – Syrian Wars.

Book 12 – Mithridatic Wars.

Book 13 – Civil Wars; Marius and Sulla.

Book 14 – Civil Wars; Pompey and Julius Caesar.

Book 15 – Civil Wars; Antony and Octavius Caesar.

Book 16 – Civil Wars; Triumvirate.

Book 17 – Civil Wars; Antony and Octavius.

Books 18-24 – Only fragments remain.

SIGNIFICANT EXCERPTS

The Roman History

6.6-13 – Causes of the Second Punic War.

7.1-4 – Hannibal crosses the Alps.

8.3-4 – Story of Regulus in 256 B.C.

8.132-135 – Destruction of Carthage in 146 B.C.

13.7-12 – Condition of the farmers of Italy before Tiberius Gracchus.

13.61 – Gaius Marius.

13.76-84, 95-106 – Sulla.

13.108, 114-119 – Pompey.

14.2-3, 7 – Catiline.

14.19 – Death of Caesar's daughter; shocking state of Roman political life.

14.83-87 – Pompey sails for Egypt, where he is assassinated; retreat of the Pompeians to Africa.

14.106-117 – Caesar.

14.120 – Picture of the corruption of Roman society at that time and of its incapacity for self-government.

14.136-148 – Piso calls for the reading of Caesar's will; Brutus addresses the people; his speech applauded; the reading of Caesar's will; Antony's funeral oration; the populace roused to fury; the murderers flee from the city.

14.149-154 – Comparison of Caesar with Alexander.

15.15-20 – Conversation between Octavius and Antony.

16.1-4 – Reconciliation of Octavius and Antony; the new Triumvirate of Octavius, Antony, and Lepidus; fearful prodigies at Rome.

16.89-101 – Brutus and Cassius arrive at the Gulf of Melas; speech of Cassius to the Republican army, after which they move against the enemy.

Archimedes of Syracuse
c. 287-212 B.C.

Archimedes was a Greek mathematician, physicist, astronomer, and inventor, born in Syracuse, Sicily. We know almost nothing about his life. It is likely that, when he was a young man, Archimedes studied with the successors of Euclid in Alexandria. Other than in the prefaces to his works, information about Archimedes comes to us from several sources such as in stories from Plutarch, Livy, and others. Archimedes considered most significant his accomplishments concerning a cylinder circumscribing a sphere, and he asked for a representation of this, together with his result on the ratio of the two, to be inscribed on his tomb.

❧ EXTANT WORKS INCLUDE ❧

On Plane Equilibriums (two books) – Concerned with establishing the centers of gravity of various rectilinear plane figures and segments of conics.

Quadrature of the Parabola – Demonstrates that the area of any segment of a parabola is 4/3 of the area of the triangle having the same base and height as that segment.

On the Sphere and Cylinder (two books) – The surface area of any sphere is four times that of its greatest circle and that the volume of a sphere is two-thirds that of the cylinder in which it is inscribed.

On Spirals – Develops many properties of tangents to the spiral of Archimedes.

On Conoids and Spheroids – Deals with determining the volumes of the segments of solids formed by the revolution of a conic section about its axis.

On Floating Bodies (two books) – The first known work in hydrostatics. Its purpose is to determine the positions that various solids will assume when floating in a fluid, according to their forms and the variations in their specific gravities.

Measurement of a Circle – Pi, the ratio of the circumference to the diameter of a circle, is shown to lie between the limits of 3 1/7 and 3 10/71.

The Sand-Reckoner – A small treatise written for the common man which describes a system for expressing in language very large numbers – the number of grains of sand that it would take to fill the whole of the universe. This work also gives the most detailed surviving description of the heliocentric system of Aristarchus of Samos and explains how Archimedes determined the sun's apparent diameter by observation with an instrument.

The Method Concerning Mechanical Theorems – Describes the process of discovery in mathematics. It is the sole surviving work from antiquity, and one of the few from any period, which deals with this topic. Archimedes tells how he used a mechanical method to arrive at some of his key discoveries, including the area of a parabolic segment and the surface area and volume of a sphere.

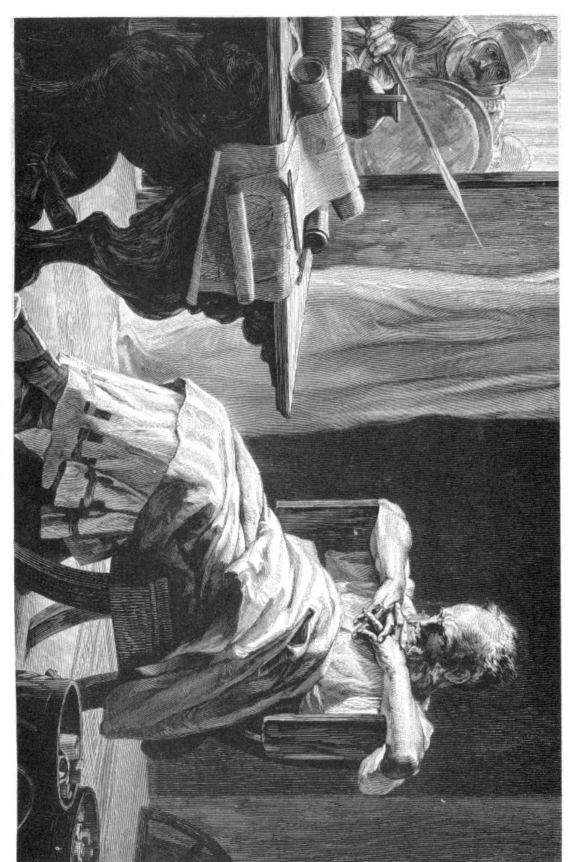

Death of Archimedes

❧ SIGNIFICANT EXCERPTS ❧

The Method

Introduction – Mechanical method on geometry.

On Floating Bodies

2.318-336 – Hydrostatics.

The Sand-Reckoner

3 – System for expressing large numbers.

❧ SIGNIFICANT EXCERPTS ❧

FROM OTHERS WRITING ABOUT ARCHIMEDES OR
INCLUDING HIS WRITINGS IN THEIR WORKS

Plutarch – *The Lives of the Noble Grecians and Romans,* Marcellus 14-19

Polybius – *The Histories* 8.5.3-5

Livy – *The Early History of Rome* 24.34

Diodorus Siculus – *Historical Library* 1.34.2; 5.37.3

Aristarchus of Samos
C. 310-230 B.C.

Aristarchus was a great astronomer of the Hellenistic age. In the third century B.C., he made a fairly accurate computation of the size of the sun and of the moon and of their distance from the earth. Later, he became convinced that the sun was the center around which the earth and the planets revolved.

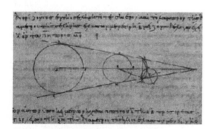

Drawing by Aristarchus

❧ EXTANT WORKS ❧

On the Sizes and Distances of the Sun and Moon

He is also quoted by Archimedes in *The Sand-Reckoner.*

Aristides
FL. C. SECOND CENTURY A.D.

Aristides was a Christian apologist who wrote the oldest complete apologetical text existing today. It is a defense of Christianity and, according to Eusebius and Jerome, this apology was presented to the Emperor Hadrian in response to the emperor's persecution of the local Christians in A.D. 126.

❧ EXTANT WORKS ❧

To the Emperor Hadrian Caesar from the Athenian Philosopher Aristides – Examines the beliefs of the four classes of men who comprise humanity: barbarians, Greeks, Jews, and Christians. Shows that only Christians have the true conception of God and that the gods of the nations fall short. "God is the selfsame being Who first established and now controls the universe." The mythology of the Greeks and barbarians is absurd and contradictory.

❧ SIGNIFICANT EXCERPTS ❧

To the Emperor Hadrian Caesar from the Athenian Philosopher Aristides

1-2, 4, 13, 15-16 – The absurdity of Greek mythology.

Aristophanes
C. 445-380 B.C.

Aristophanes was a Greek who wrote more than forty comedy plays, eleven of which have survived in their entirety. His plays are on many topics which were dear to the hearts of his Greek audience: politics, religion, famous writers of the day, women, etc. The plays of Aristophanes may be described as a cross between an R-rated stand-up comedy routine and a television soap opera. The author seemed to enjoy writing about perverse topics (of the very worst), and his audience seemed to enjoy being entertained in this manner. His plays often received the highest prizes. Even Plutarch, who himself held to a morality which even unbelievers today would question, criticized Aristophanes in his essay, "The Summary of a Comparison between Aristophanes and Menander." Plutarch found the characteristics of knocking down and ridiculing man's behavior in the plays of Aristophanes to be disgusting and degrading: "But the witticisms of Aristophanes are bitter and rough and possess a sharpness which wounds and bites. And I do not know wherein his vaunted cleverness resides, whether in his words or his characters. Certainly even whatever he imitates he makes worse; for with him roguishness is not urbane but malicious, rusticity not simple but silly, facetiousness not playful but ridiculous, and love not joyous but licentious (Moral Essays, X.4.471-73). Plutarch believed that Aristophanes' writing would appeal only to the uneducated or to emotionally immature young people. "[I]n his diction there are tragic, comic, pompous, and prosaic elements, obscurity, vagueness, dignity, and elevation, loquacity and sickening nonsense. And with all these differences and dissimilarities, his use of words does not give to each kind its fitting and appropriate use. . . ." (Moral Essays, X.1.467).

❧ EXTANT WORKS ❧

The Acharnians – 425 B.C.

The Knights – 424 B.C.

The Clouds – 423 B.C.

The Wasps – 422 B.C.

The Peace – 421 B.C.

The Birds – 414 B.C.

The Lysistrata – 411 B.C.

The Thesmophoriazusae – 411 B.C.

The Frogs – 405 B.C.

The Ecclesiazusae – 393 B.C.

The Plutus – 388 B.C.

Aristotle
384-322 B.C.

Aristotle was a Greek philosopher, logician, political thinker, biologist, and literary critic. His father was a court physician and friend of the father of Philip the Great. At the age of eighteen, Aristotle was sent to Athens, where he attended and was otherwise associated with the Academy of Plato for the next twenty years. It is believed that Aristotle was the tutor of Alexander the Great from 343 to 340 B.C.. The next twelve years, Aristotle devoted to the establishment of a school called the Lyceum.

❧ EXTANT WORKS ❧

The works of Aristotle fall under three headings:

1. Dialogues and other works of a popular character, modeled on those of Plato. These are now lost except for fragments. Written 367-347 B.C.

2. Collections of facts and material from scientific treatment: The works in this second group include 200 titles, mostly in fragments, collected by Aristotle's school and used as research. Some may have been done at the time of Aristotle's successor Theophrastus. Included in this group are 158 constitutions of Greek states, including:

   The Athenian Constitution (sketch of the political and constitutional history of Athens from before the time of Draco down to the fourth century B.C.). A very valuable piece of literature.

3. Systematic works or treatises: These works were not, in most cases, published by Aristotle himself or during his lifetime, but were edited after his death from unfinished manuscripts. They are dated 335-322 B.C. These systematic treatises may be grouped in several divisions:

Logic:

1. *Categories* – Ten classifications of terms.

2. *On Interpretation* – Propositions, truth, modality.

3. *Prior Analytics* – Syllogistic logic.

4. *Posterior Analytics* – Scientific method and syllogism.

5. *Topics* – Rules for effective arguments and debate.

6. *On Sophistical Refutations* – Informal fallacies.

Physical Works:

1. *Physics* – Explains change, motion, void, time.

2. *On the Heavens* – Structure of heaven, earth, ele-

ments.

3. *On Generation* – Through combining material constituents.

4. *Meteorologics* – Origin of comets, weather, disasters.

Psychological Works:

1. *On the Soul* – Explains faculties, senses, mind, imagination.

2. *On Memory, Reminiscence, Dreams, and Prophesying.*

Works on Natural History:

1. *History of Animals* – A detailed, descriptive account of the appearance, habits, and characteristics of the more than five hundred animals which he knew, divided into genera and species, beginning with the lowest types of marine creatures, hardly more than plants, and going on through insects, fish, birds, and land beasts, up to man.

2. *On the Parts of Animals* – An anatomical study, made in his school at Athens, of the animal body in general as an organism composed of parts, with an attempt to assign to each part its particular function. (Use this work as a primary source in biology.)

3. *On the Movements of Animals.*

4. *On the Progression of Animals* – Animal locomotion.

5. *On the Generation of Animals.*

6. *Minor treatises.*

7. *Problems* – Questions and answers about why things are the way they are.

Philosophical Works:

1. *Metaphysics* – Reviews the theories of all the leading Greek philosophers down to his own day, including those of Plato and other contemporaries. For one reason or another, he rejects them all. None is sufficiently analytical. All overlook points which should be considered and problems which should be solved. This work is his study of the meaning and nature of being in the broadest sense.

2. *Nicomachean Ethics* – On the soul, happiness, virtue, and friendship. His most popular and influential work. This work is divided into ten books: 1, The good for man; 2-5, Moral virtues; 6, Intellectual virtue; 7, Continence and incontinence, pleasure;

8-9, Friendship; 10, Pleasure and happiness.

3. *Eudemian Ethics.*

4. *Magna Moralia.*

5. *Politics* – Deals with the best states, utopias, constitutions, and revolutions. This work is a general application of the theories presented in *Nicomachean Ethics*:

Book 1 – The family.
Book 2 – The best constitutions known.
Book 3 – The nature of the state.
Book 4 – Existing constitutions.
Book 5 – Revolutions, their causes and their prevention.
Book 6 – Democracy and oligarchy; offices of government.
Book 7-8 – The best constitution, external conditions, population, education.

6. *Rhetoric* – A speaker's manual, composed of elements of forensic and political debate.

7. *Poetics* – An essay in the field of art, including tragedy and epic poetry. Aristotle's observations on fifth century drama, and on drama of his own era. Aristotle was the first professional literary critic.

❧ SIGNIFICANT EXCERPTS ❧

The Athenian Constitution

Chapters 2-3 – The change from kingship to republic; the constitution before Draco.

Chapter 4 – The constitution of Draco; the first code of laws.

Chapters 5-12 – The constitution of Solon; Solon's political poetry.

Chapters 13-19 – The tyranny of Peisistratus and his sons.

Chapter 20-22 – The reforms of Cleisthenes; creation of democracy.

Chapter 23-24 – Aristeides and Themistocles; founding of the Delian confederacy.

Chapter 25-27 – Democracy restored by Ephialtes and extended under Pericles.

Chapter 29-30 – Revolution of the Four Hundred; Athens forced to abandon democracy; citizenship limited to Five Thousand.

Chapter 31 – The Council of Four Hundred.

Chapter 32-34 – Democracy restored, then Sparta defeats Athens and sets up the Thirty.

Chapter 35-38 – Rule of the Thirty and their defeat by Thrasybulus.

Chapter 39-40 – Democracy restored.

Chapters 42-69 – The constitution of the fourth century B.C.

Politics

1.1-2 – The definition and origin of the State, the family, and the village; slavery.

1.11 – Thales.

3.4-7 – Constitutions classified; the true object of the state; varieties of authority in private life; the three forms of government and the three perverted forms; evolution of government.

4.10 – The different species of tyrannies, their principles, and their causes.

4.11-12 – The best constitution for the average state and for the particular person.

7.4-5 – The population and territory of the ideal city-state should be limited.

7.11 – The situation of the ideal city-state and the arrangement of houses in streets.

8.1-3 – Education in the ideal state.

History of Animals

1.1 – Differences exhibited by animals.

On the Parts of Animals

2.4 – Blood.

2.5 – Lard and suet.

2.7 – The brain.

2.9 – Bones.

2.10 – The source of sensation is the heart.

2.17 – The tongue.

3.1 – Teeth.

On the Progression of Animals

8 – The reason why snakes have no legs.

11 – The movement of man compared with birds; winged human beings are impossible.

Problems

15.3 – Why do all men count in tens?

18.2 – Why are discussions good training for the mind?

18.5 – Why do we regard the philosopher as a better man than the orator?

Nicomachean Ethics

4.3 – The great man.

9.8 – Self-love.

10.6-8 – The happy man.

Poetics

15 – The four points to consider when forming the characters of a play.

17 – Aristotle's description of the story of the *Odyssey*.

18 – The four varieties of tragedies.

20-22 – The subject of diction.

23-24 – How an epic differs from tragedy; how to tell a lie by using a fallacy.

25 – Problems (difficult passages or expressions) in poetry and their solutions.

Metaphysics

983b. 20-28 – Thales.

On the Soul

405a. 20-22; 411a. 7-8 – Thales.

On the Heavens

294a. 28-66 – Thales.

Arrian

C. A.D. 96-180
Flavius Arrianus

Arrian was a Greek, born in Nicomedia. Emperor Hadrian appointed him Governor of Cappadocia from A.D. 131 to 137, and he saw some military service. Arrian is considered the prime historian of Alexander the Great, but since he was not alive during Alexander's reign, his history would not be considered a primary source. For source material, Arrian consulted two of Alexander's generals as main authorities: Ptolemy and Aristobulus. In the Preface to *Anabasis of Alexander* Arrian states, "Wherever Ptolemy son of Lagus and Aristobulus son of Aristobulus have agreed in their histories of Alexander son of Philip, I record their story as quite accurate; where they disagree, I have chosen what I feel to be more likely and also better worth the narrating. Others have given various accounts of Alexander, in fact there is no one over whom historians have been more numerous and less harmonious. My own view is that Ptolemy and Aristobulus are more trustworthy narrators, for Aristobulus took the field with King Alexander; Ptolemy not only did the same, but, as he was a king himself, falsehood would have been more shameful to him than to anyone else. Besides, since Alexander was dead when they both wrote their histories, there lay on them neither any constraint nor any hope of gain in writing other than plain fact. . . ." Arrian was a pupil of Epictetus, and is considered an important authority on his teaching.

❧ EXTANT WORKS ❧

Anabasis of Alexander (7 books) – Describes the campaigns of Alexander the Great.

Indica – An account of the voyage of Alexander's general Nearchus to India.

❧ SIGNIFICANT EXCERPTS ❧

Anabasis of Alexander

1.6 – How Alexander drew up his phalanx.

1.11-16 – Alexander defeats the Persians in the Battle of Granicus.

2.4 – Alexander falls ill.

2.6-14 – Battle of Issus; Alexander defeats Darius.

3.1 – The founding of Alexandria by Alexander the Great.

3.3-4 – Arrian's account of Alexander's visit to the Oracle of Zeus-Ammon.

3.7-16 – Battle of Gaugamela; Alexander again defeats Darius in 331 B.C.

4.8-14 – The death of Cleitus, and what happened to Alexander after it.

4.22-30 – Alexander in India.

5.1-29 – Alexander in India.

5.19 – Alexander's horse Bucephalas dies.

6.1-28 – Alexander in India.

6.10-14 – Alexander is wounded.

6.24-26 – The march through the desert.

6.29 – The Tomb of Cyrus.

7.1 – Alexander's aspirations.

7.9 – Alexander's tribute to the transformation which Philip accomplished in Macedonia.

7.24-30 – Character and death of Alexander.

Athanasius
C. A.D. 295-373

Athanasius was born of Christian parents. He became a bishop of Alexandria, and defended Christ's divinity during the Arian controversy. He is considered by some to be the most important theologian of the fourth century. Much of his life was spent in exile.

❧ EXTANT WORKS ❧

Four Orations against the Arians

Letters

On the Incarnation of the Word – Defense of the doctrine that God assumed human nature in the person of Jesus Christ.

Life of Antony of Egypt

❧ SIGNIFICANT EXCERPTS ❧

On the Incarnation of the Word

2 – Athanasius refutes Plato and the Epicureans concerning origins.

54 – God became man in the form of Jesus Christ.

Life of Antony of Egypt

1-12, 44-47, 49-51, 54-55, 67, 69, 72-74, 77-79, 86, 89-94 – An apology for the monastic life.

Alexander discovers the dead body of Darius

Augustine
A.D. 354-430
Aurelius Augustinus

Augustine was born in Roman North Africa, and converted from paganism to Christianity as an adult. He became bishop of Hippo in 395. During his lifetime, Rome fell before the Goths and Vandals as they invaded Italy. Augustine wrote extensively, including sermons, letters, poems, theological works, commentaries on the Scriptures, defenses of Christianity, and philosophical and rhetorical essays. His writings are considered by many to be among the most outstanding in the history of Christianity.

EXTANT WORKS INCLUDE

Against Faustus, the Manichee

Sermons

The Trinity – This is considered his greatest dogmatic work.

Letters

Handbook on Faith, Hope, and Love – A short work on the grace of God.

Commentary on the First Letter of John

Augustine's Rule

City of God – Augustine contrasts the city (or, the state) of this world with the ideal city of God; an answer to the pagans who accused the Christians of causing the downfall of the Roman Empire.

Confessions – Considered to be the first and greatest ancient autobiography.

On Christian Doctrine – A work on scriptural interpretation, in four books.

SIGNIFICANT EXCERPTS

Confessions

1.8 – Description of his childhood.

1.9, 13-14, 19 – Miseries of the schoolboy.

5.8; 5.12 – The sorrows of a schoolmaster.

8.6-7 – Asceticism.

9.8-9 – Augustine describes his mother and father.

City of God

Preface – Augustine explains why he is writing this work.

1.1 – Of the adversaries of the name of Christ, whom the barbarians for Christ's sake spared when they stormed the city.

2.6 – The pagan gods are immoral.

8.1-2 – The early philosophers.

8.3 – Augustine on Socrates.

8.4-8 – Augustine on Plato.

8.9 – The philosophy that is closest to Christianity.

8.10-16 – More on Plato.

12.11 – According to Scripture, man has been on the earth less than 6,000 years.

12.12 – The different theories of origins which the philosophers hold.

14.24 – Strange occurrences of the power of the will over the body.

15.1 – Augustine defines this work; the two lines of descent of the human race.

15.10-11 – Augustine discusses the discrepancy between the Hebrew version of Scriptures and the Latin translation of the Greek Septuagint.

15.27 – Noah's Flood.

16.3 – The lines of descent from Noah's three sons.

21.4 – Augustine is intrigued by a magnet.

Augustus
63 B.C.-A.D. 14
Gaius Julius Caesar Octavianus

Augustus was Emperor of the Roman Empire from 30 B.C. to A.D. 14. This is the emperor who ruled when Jesus was born.

❧ EXTANT WORKS ☙

The Acts of Augustus as Recorded on the Monumentum Ancyranum – An account of his deeds engraved on bronze tablets and fastened to his tomb. This is Augustus's own account of his life, his political measures, and his military activity.

❧ SIGNIFICANT EXCERPTS ☙

The Acts of Augustus as Recorded on the Monumentum Ancyranum

Avianus
FL. C. A.D. 400

Avianus wrote fables in Latin which were found in standard schoolbooks throughout the Middle Ages. Forty-two of his fables survive.

❧ EXTANT WORKS ☙

Forty-two *Fables*

❧ SIGNIFICANT EXCERPTS ☙

Fables

Caesar
C. 102-44 B.C.
Gaius Julius Caesar

Caesar was an Emperor of Rome who claimed to be of divine descent. He is considered to be one of the greatest figures of the ancient world, both as a general and ass a statesman. Cicero considered Caesar's literary works to be accurate.

❧ EXTANT WORKS ☙

Commentaries on the Gallic War (7 books) – covers 58-52 B.C.; concerns his campaign in Gaul and Britain.

Commentaries on the Civil War (3 books) – covers 49-48 B.C.; concerns the war between himself and Pompey.

❧ SIGNIFICANT EXCERPTS ☙

Gallic War

> 2.16-28 – (57 B.C.) Sudden attack on Caesar's army by the Nervii; the Nervii's defeat.

> 4.20-36 – (55 B.C.) Caesar's first expedition to Britain.

> 5.44 – (53 B.C.) Rivalry of Pullo and Vorenus.

> 6.13-14 – The Druids in Gaul.

> 6.19 – Families of Gaul; funerals in Gaul.

> 6.21-23 – Life and manners of the Gauls.

> 7.69-89 – Siege of Alesia.

Civil War

> 1.1-11 – Describes the outbreak of the Civil War.

> 3.47 – (48 B.C.) Scarcity in Caesar's army; abundance in Pompey's army.

Caesar crossing the Rubicon

3.88 – Description of the battle of Pharsalus, the most important fight of Caesar's career.

Cato the Elder
234-149 B.C.
Marcus Porcius Cato

Cato was a politician and was considered the "Father of Latin Prose." He was active in public affairs throughout his life. Rome originally attempted to keep out Greek influence, and Cato was a leader in the struggle against Greek learning. He was critical of the weaknesses in Hellenism. He wrote much, and was the first Roman who published speeches on a large scale. Most of his writing has been lost or is in fragments.

EXTANT WORKS

On Agriculture – Oldest extant prose work in Latin, and the earliest comprehensive treatment of agricultural practices in ancient Rome. This is a collection of agricultural precepts based upon the author's own experience on his farm.

SIGNIFICANT EXCERPTS

On Agriculture

1 – Things to consider when buying a farm.

2 – How an owner of a farm should deal with his overseer.

4 – Relationship with neighbors.

5 – Duties of an overseer.

6 – What you should plant and in what places.

10 – Equipping an olive plantation.

49 – How to transplant an old vine.

56-59 – Food, wine, and clothes for the slaves.

98 – Directions for the prevention of moths.

111 – Directions for detecting diluted wine.

120 – Directions for keeping grape juice throughout the year.

123 – Remedy for hip-gout.

143 – Duties for the overseer's wife.

Catullus
C. 84-54 B.C.
Gaius Valerius Catullus

Catullus was a Roman poet who wrote love poems which represented the pleasure-loving sensuality of the age.

EXTANT WORKS

Book of Poems

Celsus
C. 25 B.C.-A.D. 50
Aulus Cornelius Celsus

Celsus was considered to be the most important Roman medical writer, "the Hippocrates of the Romans." During the reign of Tiberius, Celsus wrote a book on medicine.

EXTANT WORKS

On Medicine (8 books)

Preface – A history of medical progress from the days of Homer to his own time.

Books 1-2 – Diet and hygiene.

Book 3 – Treatment of disease, including fevers, insanity, heart problems, lethargy, dropsy, tuberculosis, jaundice, palsy; signs of inflammation.

Book 4 – Internal diseases, including diseases of the throat, thorax, abdomen, and other organs.

Book 5 – Drugs and their uses; wounds and their

treatment.

Book 6 – Skin diseases, diseases of the eye, ear, nose, teeth, and tonsils; venereal diseases.

Book 7 – Operating procedures.

Book 8 – Treatment of fractures and dislocations.

❧ SIGNIFICANT EXCERPTS ❧

On Medicine

2.1-2 – How weather affects health; signs of sickness.

2.6.1-6 – Signs of impending death.

5.27.1-2 – Wounds which are caused by a bite.

7.5.3-4 – Wounds which are caused by weapons.

Chrysostom
C. A.D. 347-407
John Chrysostom

Chrysostom was born at Antioch to a Christian mother. He became a Christian theologian, writer, preacher, and overseer of Constantinople. He wrote exegetical works, letters, liturgical works, sermons, and treatises. Many of his writings are extant.

❧ EXTANT WORKS INCLUDE ❧

The Homilies on the Statues

The Priesthood

Instructions to Catechumens

Letters

❧ SIGNIFICANT EXCERPTS ❧

Letter to Olympias – The role of women in the Church.

Cicero
106-43 B.C.
Marcus Tullius Cicero

Cicero was a Roman statesman, the greatest of the Roman orators, and a Stoic philosopher, and is considered the greatest literary figure of his day. His ideas were influenced by the study of Plato, Aristotle, and other early philosophers and political figures. He held many public offices and he took part in all of the intrigues and wars of his day. He was responsible for suppressing the Catilinarian conspiracy, was exiled twice from Rome, and was involved in the personal rivalries of Caesar, Pompey, and the Roman Senate. Mark Antony had Cicero executed after Caesar was assassinated.

❧ EXTANT WORKS ❧

57 speeches including:

Against Caecilius

In Defense of Cluentius

In Defense of the Manilian Law

In Defense of Murena

In Defense of Flaccus

On the Consular Provinces

In Defense of Plancius

Philippics (14 speeches against Antony)

Against Catiline

In Defense of Archias

In Defense of Sestius

Against Verres

In Defense of Milo

Collections of correspondence

Letters to Friends (16 books) – Letters to his friends and family.

Letters to Atticus (16 books) – Letters addressed to Titus Pomponius Atticus, his most intimate friend.

Letters to His Brother Quintus (3 books)

Letters to Brutus (2 books)

Works on Rhetoric

On Invention

On the Best Kind of Orator – A sketch of the ideal orator and the pattern of perfect eloquence.

Methods of Drawing Conclusions (Topica)

The Making of an Orator – Discusses oratory and the degree of intellectual culture required by the perfect orator; invention, wit and humor, arrangement, and memory; rules of elegant diction, of delivery and gesture; written 55 B.C.

On Fate

Paradoxes of the Stoics

Classification of Oratory

Brutus – A review of the history of Greek oratory; an account of the orators of Rome.

[*Treatise on Rhetoric*] – This work has been attributed to Cicero but is not by him.

Philosophical Works

On the State (Republic) – Concerns the best form of government and the ideal citizen; written 54 B.C.

On the Laws – The origin and nature of law; the state of law at Rome; what the laws would be like in the best form of government; follows Plato's work; written 46 B.C.

On the Supreme Good and Evil – Explains the Epicurean, Stoic, Academy, and Peripatetic schools of thought.

Discussions at Tusculum – Discusses the troubles which beset human happiness; the nature of death and endurance of pain; wisdom triumphing over sorrow and mental distress; virtue sufficient to secure happiness.

On the Nature of the Gods – Sets out the doctrines of Epicurus and the Stoics.

Academics – Survey of the history of philosophy with special reference to the doctrines of the New Academy.

Cato the Elder, On Old Age – Praises old age.

Laelius, On Friendship – Expounds the theory of friendship.

Moral Duties – For his son, Cicero discusses honor; written in 44 B.C.

On Virtues

❧ SIGNIFICANT EXCERPTS ❧

Letters to Atticus

4.1 – Cicero returns from his exile.

4.4 – Letter describing his library.

7.1 – Cicero is in trouble because he is friends with both Julius Caesar and Pompey.

7.20 – Letter asking for advice and guidance concerning Caesar.

13.52 – Cicero entertains Caesar in 45 B.C.; Caesar was cold, but polite.

Letters to Friends

4.5 – Letter from Servius Sulpicius to Cicero upon the death of Cicero's daughter.

5.7 – Letter from Cicero to Gnaeus Pompey.

7.1 – Letter to M. Marius describing a festival at Rome in 55 B.C.

7.5 – Letter from Cicero to Caesar in Gaul.

8.14 – Letter from Caelius Rufus to Cicero in 50 B.C. showing the relations between Caesar and Pompey.

10.28 – Letter from Cicero to Gaius Trebonius concerning the conspiracy which resulted in the assassination of Caesar.

14.1-2 – Letter from Cicero to his wife and children.

14.14 – Letter from Cicero to his wife in Rome after he left Rome following news that Caesar had crossed the Rubicon.

16.21 – Letter to Tiro, Cicero's secretary, from Cicero's son while he was at college.

Letters to His Brother Quintus

1.1.8-35 – Description of the duties and challenges of a provincial governor.

2.15 – Letter asking Quintus what Caesar thought of Cicero's book.

Letters to Brutus

1.16 – Letter from Brutus giving his point of view of Caesar's assassination.

On the State

1.35-71 – The three forms of government.

2.5-17 – Sketch of the reign of Romulus.

2.30 – The beginning of the Republic.

2.32 – The senate and the consuls.

2.34 – The growth of plebeian rights.

The Making of an Orator

1.16 – The orator needs a wide education.

1.25 – The requirements of the orator; natural gifts are essential.

1.43-44 – The importance of the youth learning the Law of the Twelve Tables so that they would understand Roman law and institutions.

1.61 – The important thing is practice.

2.12-15 – On the writing of history.

2.86 – Memory, the pigeonhole method.

3.11 – Pronunciation.

Second Philippic

1, 25-30, 84, 112-114, 116-119 – An attack on Mark Antony.

Laelius, On Friendship

6-9 – Definition of friendship.

Moral Duties

1.150-151 – Discusses trades and means of livelihood.

The First Oration Against Catiline 1

Discussions at Tusculum

5.56 – Concerning Gaius Marius.

In Defense of Sestius

96-100, 102-103,136-139 – The two classes of men in the State.

Against Verres

Clement of Alexandria
C. A.D. 150-215
Titus Flavius Clemens

Clement was a Greek who studied philosophy under numerous pagan teachers before he became a Christian theologian and writer. He was a great admirer of Plato.

EXTANT WORKS INCLUDE

Exhortation to the Greeks – Clement tries to win pagans to the Christian faith. He scorns the mysteries and says the legends and myths are worthless and debasing. The gods, with their human needs and passions, are ridiculous and immoral. He defends the philosophers, especially Plato, as clearly teaching the unity, supremacy and goodness of God.

The Tutor (3 books) – Written to help the ordinary Christian live a disciplined life.

Miscellanies (7 books) – A loosely related series of remarks covering the importance of philosophy for the pursuit of Christian knowledge; God's truth is to be found in revelation and Greek philosophy.

Who Is the Rich Man That Shall Be Saved

SIGNIFICANT EXCERPTS

Exhortation to the Greeks

5-6 – The opinions of the philosophers concerning the gods.

Miscellanies

1.5 – Clement's view on the place of ancient philosophy in Christianity; the Jews were prepared for Christ by the law and the Gentiles were prepared by philosophy.

6.13; 7.10 – Shows Clement's relation to the Gnostics and his conception of the ideal Christian character.

7.16 – Misuse of Scriptures by heretics.

Who Is the Rich Man That Shall Be Saved

42 – The story of St. John and the robber.

Clement of Rome
FIRST CENTURY A.D.

Clement was a Christian writer. We only have one of his works today.

❧ EXTANT WORKS ❧

Epistle to the Corinthians (also called *I Clement*) – Other than the New Testament, this is the earliest Christian document we possess; written A.D. 96 or 97. This letter addresses the problems of the church at Corinth.

❧ SIGNIFICANT EXCERPTS ❧

Epistle to the Corinthians

  5.1-7 – Refers to the persecution of the Christians during the reigns of Domitian and Nero; contains the earliest reference to the deaths of Peter and Paul; seems to imply that Paul traveled to countries beyond Rome.

Commodianus
C. A.D. 249

Commodianus was a Roman and the first Christian poet.

❧ EXTANT WORKS ❧

Carmen Apologeticum – A long poem in defense of Christianity and against paganism.

Instructions – A collection of eighty short poems of instruction in favor of Christian discipline against the gods of the heathens.

❧ SIGNIFICANT EXCERPTS ❧

Instructions

  3 – The worship of demons.

  17 – Of the images of the gods.

  22 – The dullness of the age.

  63 – The daily war.

  74 – Of funeral pomp.

Cyprian
C. A.D. 200-258
Thascius Caecilius Cyprianus

Cyprian was born into a wealthy pagan family in Africa, and was a prominent trial lawyer and teacher of rhetoric. He was converted to Christianity in middle age, and in A.D. 248 he became bishop of Carthage.

❧ EXTANT WORKS INCLUDE ❧

81 *Letters*

To Donatus – The grace of God allows the converted to conquer sin.

On the Unity – The importance of unity among Christians; the role of the bishops in guaranteeing that unity.

The Lapsed – Discusses what should be done with those Christians who had denied the faith under the persecution of Decius in 249.

The Dress of Virgins

❧ SIGNIFICANT EXCERPTS ❧

Letters

  55.9 – The sudden death of Decius.

  55.14 – The opinion of the Church as to the libellatici.

  58 – God has warned that more persecution is coming.

  80 – The persecution under Valerian.

The Lapsed

  1-3 – Joy at the return of peace for the Church.

  4-6 – The condition of those who denied the faith during the persecution of Decius.

  7-9 – God's commands were forgotten; men even dragged others down in their haste to get to the sacrifice.

  10-12 – They could have escaped the persecution but they didn't want to leave their possessions.

  13-14 – The tortures are no excuse.

  15-17 – The lapsed need to do penance.

27-28 – Those known as libellatici, who did not actually sacrifice in the tests which were applied to Christians, but, by bribery, had procured certificates that they had sacrificed.

Demosthenes
384-322 B.C.

Demosthenes was considered to be the greatest of the Greek orators. The speeches he wrote give us a picture of the public and private life in the Athens of his time. As a young man, Demosthenes became a professional writer of speeches for private suits of every kind, sometimes speaking in place of his clients. Even later in his life, when he was involved in politics (or more correctly, statesmanship), it appears this is how he made his living. Demosthenes wrote over sixty speeches which have been handed down to us today, including political speeches, and law-court speeches composed for private cases and for political cases. At age thirty, when Demosthenes first entered upon his career as public orator and statesman, Philip of Macedon was on good terms with Athens, and Demosthenes' first public speeches did not even mention any danger with Philip, but were more concerned with the balance of power among the Greek states. Slowly, Demosthenes came to recognize the danger of the growing power of Philip, which caused Demosthenes to encourage a policy of a united defense of the city-states against a military autocracy. His great speeches relating to Philip, – the *First, Second,* and *Third Philippics* and the three *Olynthiacs, On the Peace, On the Embassy,* and *On the Chersonese,* – show Demosthenes becoming more and more concerned with the dangers of Philip.

﹌ EXTANT WORKS INCLUDE ﹏

The First Philippic

On the Peace

On the Chersonese

The Third Philippic

On the Crown

On the False Legation

Third Olynthiac

Against Aristocrates

On the Embassy

﹌ SIGNIFICANT EXCERPTS ﹏

The First Philippic

2-12, 40-41, 47-51 – Delivered early in 351 B.C. before the Athenian Assembly. It is the first of Demosthenes' series of attacks on Athenian political apathy and indifference to the plots of Philip of Macedon.

On the Embassy

255 – Delivered in 343 B.C. Demosthenes was prosecuting his political opponent, Aeschines, for being a traitor when a member of the embassy sent to Macedonia in 346 B.C. This excerpt is a poem written by Solon in 594 B.C. and quoted by Demosthenes; Solon is trying to bring order into Athenian society.

The Third Philippic

1-5, 36-40, 67-76 – This is the most eloquent and most effective of his attacks on Philip, delivered before the Athenian Assembly in the early summer of 341 B.C.

On the Crown

1-8, 42-51, 66-72, 95-101, 168-179, 188-194, 199-210, 232-235, 321-324 – Delivered in August, 330 B.C. before a jury of Athenian citizens, in defense of Ctesiphon, who had proposed six years earlier that Demosthenes should receive a golden crown for his services to Athens. The prosecutor, who was an enemy of Demosthenes', was attempting to prove that Demosthenes' whole political career had been disloyal and dangerous to Athens. Demosthenes defends himself.

Dio Cassius
C. A.D. 150-235
Cassius Dio Cocceianus

Dio Cassius was a Roman historian who wrote in Greek. He held various offices in the government, so he had access to official documents and opportunities for historical investigation. His history originally included eighty books, but we only have books 34-60, 78, and part of 79, plus a few fragments of others. We have knowledge of the lost portions of Dio's work from the excerpts and epitomes of others.

EXTANT WORKS

Roman History

Fragments of Books 1-11, covers 753-250 B.C.

Fragments of Books 12-35, covers 250-85 B.C.

Books 36-40, covers 69-50 B.C.

Books 41-45, covers 49-43 B.C.

Books 46-50, covers 43-31 B.C.

Books 51-55, covers 31 B.C.-A.D. 8

Books and Fragments 56-60, covers A.D. 9-46

Epitome of Books 61-70, covers A.D. 47-138

Epitome and Fragments of Books 71-80, covers A.D. 161-229

SIGNIFICANT EXCERPTS

Roman History

7.19 – Growth of the Roman constitution and the institution of consular tribunes.

8.21-22 – Causes of the Second Punic War.

37.15-19 – The Jews.

43.10-13 – How Cato killed himself.

44.12-22 – Julius Caesar is killed.

51.9-14 – Antony and Cleopatra die.

52.14-19, 23, 27-30, 34, 36, 39; 53.11-12, 16-22, 30-32 – The "democracy" of the Roman Empire under Augustus; Dio Cassius believed that Augustus's attempt to restore the republic was only pretense.

55.13 – How Augustus adopted Tiberius.

55.14-21 – How Livia convinced Augustus to rule more mercifully.

62.16-18 – The great fire at Rome in the days of Nero.

67.14 ff. – The persecution under Domitian in A.D. 95.

Dio Chrysostom
C. A.D. 40-115

Dio Chrysostom was a Greek sophist and orator. He favored the philosophy of the Cynics and Stoics.

EXTANT WORKS

80 *Orations* on literary, political and philosophical subjects.

SIGNIFICANT EXCERPTS

Orations

7.34ff – The depopulation of Euboea (said to be one of the causes of the fall of the Roman Empire).

14.18 – Defines freedom and slavery: freedom is knowledge of what is allowable and what is forbidden, and slavery is ignorance of what is allowed and what is not.

16.1-11 – Teaches the Stoic belief that since there are so many things in life to hurt us, we should fortify our spirits so as to be insensible to them.

17.1-22 – Covetousness is evil and contentment is blessed.

18.1-21 – On training for public speaking.

41.11-14 – The benefits of friendship.

Diodorus Siculus
90-21 B.C.

Diodorus was a Sicilian historian who wrote in Greek. He wrote a world history in forty books, covering Egyptian, Mesopotamian, Indian, Scythian, Arabian, and North African history and parts of Greek and Roman history, ending with Caesar's Gallic Wars. Books 1-5 and 11-20 are fully preserved, and large fragments remain of the other 25 books. The history, which is a compilation of other sources, is often repetitive and contradictory, and there are differing opinions as to the reliability of Diodorus. It is valuable, however, as a source for the lost works of earlier authors, from whom he borrowed, and for his chronological lists of famous people. His *Historical Library* follows the history of the entire world from creation up until Diodorus's own days, ending with Caesar's consulate in 60 B.C.

EXTANT WORKS

Historical Library

Book 1 – The myths, kings and customs of Egypt prior to the Trojan War. This is the fullest literary account of the history and customs of that country after Herodotus.

Book 2 – History of Assyria, description of India, Scythia, Arabia, and the islands of the Ocean prior to the Trojan War. Much mythological material.

Book 3 – Ethiopia, the Amazons of Africa, the inhabitants of Atlantis and the origins of the first gods prior to the Trojan War. Much mythological material.

Book 4 – The principal Greek gods, the Argonauts, Theseus, the Seven against Thebes. Much mythological material.

Book 5 – The islands and the peoples of the West, Rhodes and Crete prior to the Trojan War. Much mythological material.

Books 6-10 – Fragments, from the Trojan War to 480 B.C.

Book 11 – Mediterranean history 480-451 B.C. This is the only consecutive literary account for the chronology of this period.

Book 12 – Mediterranean history 450-416 B.C. This is the only consecutive literary account for the chronology of the period to 430 B.C.

Book 13 – Mediterranean history 415-405 B.C.

Book 14 – Mediterranean history 404-387 B.C.

Book 15 – Mediterranean history 386-361 B.C.

Book 16 – Mediterranean history 360-336 B.C. This is the only consecutive literary account for the chronology of this period.

Book 17 – Mediterranean history 335-324 B.C. This is the only consecutive literary account for the chronology of this period.

Book 18 – Mediterranean history 323-318 B.C. This is the only consecutive literary account for the chronology of this period.

Book 19 – Mediterranean history 317-311 B.C. This is the only consecutive literary account for the chronology of this period.

Book 20 – Mediterranean history 310-302 B.C. This is the only consecutive literary account for the chronology of this period.

Books 21-40 – Fragments, years 301-60 B.C.

SIGNIFICANT EXCERPTS

Historical Library

1.6-8 – The beginning of time.

1.34.2 – Archimedes.

1.63-64 – Construction of the pyramids.

2.7-9 – Founding of Babylon and an account of its building.

2.10-12 – The hanging garden and other marvelous things in Babylon.

2.29-31 – The Chaldaeans and their observation of the stars.

3.12-14 – The gold mines on the farthest borders of Egypt and the working of the gold.

4.79 – Minos.

5.21-23 – The island of Britain and the island called Basileia, where amber is found.

5.25-31 – Gaul, its inhabitants, and its customs.

5.35-38 – How the Iberians work the silver mines.

5.37.3 – Archimedes.

5.78, 84 – The kingdom, legislation, and naval power of Minos.

9.1, 3-4, 17, 20, 26-27 – Solon.

9.17, 20, 37 – Peisistratus.

10.3-11 – Pythagoras.

12.38-40 – The causes of the Peloponnesian War.

14.41-43 – Preparations for war with Carthage; the manufacture of arms.

15.48-50 – The earthquake and the comet in the Peloponnesus.

16.1-3 – How Philip succeeded to the Macedonian throne.

16.14 – Philip defeats the Greeks at Chaeroneia.

17.1-7 – How Alexander, having succeeded to the throne, disposed the affairs of his kingdom.

17.20-22 – Alexander the Great and the destruction of Persepolis.

17.49-51 – Diodorus's account of Alexander's visit to the Oracle of Zeus-Ammon.

17.70-72 – The sack of Persepolis by Alexander.

17.84-107 – Alexander in India.

20.36 – The Appian Aqueduct and the Appian Way.

34.2 – A slave rebellion which began in Sicily in 135 B.C. and lasted until 132 B.C.

Diogenes Laertius
C. A.D. 222-250

Diogenes wrote a book of biographical sketches of the Greek philosophers. He is the chief source for the continuous history of Greek philosophy, though the information in Diogenes cannot be accepted on his authority alone, but must be tested against texts and fragments of each philosopher himself. For each philosopher, he describes the following:

1. Origin.
2. Education, philosophical training, travels.
3. Founding of a school, or place within a school's succession.
4. Character and temperament, illustrated by anecdotes and sayings (costume, physical characteristics, temperament, moral character, love affairs, eating habits and daily routine, literary appraisal, etc.).
5. Important events of his life.
6. Anecdotes about his death, epigrams.
7. Chronological data.
8. Works.
9. Doctrines.
10. Documents (last will, letters).
11. Other men of the same name.
12. Miscellaneous notes, such as lists of followers, jibes in comic or satiric poets, inventions, political activity.

❧ EXTANT WORKS ☙

Lives of the Philosophers

Book I – Prologue, Thales, Solon, Chilon, Pittacus, Bias, Cleobulus, Periander, Anacharsis, Myson, Epimenides, Pherecydes

Book II – Anaximander, Anaximenes, Anaxagoras, Archelaus, Socrates, Xenophon, Aeschines, Aristippus, Phaedo, Euclides, Stilpo, Crito, Simon, Glaucon, Simmias, Cebes, Menedemus

Book III – Plato

Book IV – Speusippus, Xenocrates, Polemo, Crates, Crantor, Arcesilaus, Bion, Lacydes, Carneades, Clitomachus

Book V – Aristotle, Theophrastus, Strato, Lyco, Demetrius, Heraclides

Book VI – Antisthenes, Diogenes, Monimus, Onesicritus, Crates, Metrocles, Hipparchia, Menippus, Menedemus

Book VII – Zeno, Ariston, Herillus, Dionysius, Cleanthes, Sphaerus, Chrysippus

Book VIII – Pythagoras, Empedocles, Epicharmus, Archytas, Alcmaeon, Hippasus, Philolaus, Eudoxus

Book IX – Heraclitus, Xenophanes, Parmenides, Melissus, Zeno of Elea, Leucippus, Democritus, Protagoras, Diogenes of Apollonia, Anaxarchus, Pyrrho, Timon

Book X – Epicurus

❧ SIGNIFICANT EXCERPTS ☙

Lives of the Philosophers

Dionysius of Halicarnassus
C. 55-7 B.C.

Dionysius was a Greek rhetorician and historian who wrote in Greek. He taught at Rome, spending twenty-two years learning the language and literature of the Romans, and was considered an important critic of his day. *The Roman Antiquities* is his longest work, although we have only books 1-10, most of book 11, and fragments of the remaining 9 books. He covers the history of Rome from its origins to the First Punic War. (He tried to prove that Rome's founders were of Greek origin.) Though it is biased toward the Roman standpoint, it is nevertheless carefully researched, and when combined with Livy's *The Early History of Rome*, it is considered by some to be the most valuable source for early Roman history. Dionysius was first a rhetorician, then an historian, so the form of his work was sometimes considered more important than the facts. He borrowed from the works of Demosthenes, Thucydides, and Xenophon, and it is believed by some that many of the speeches included in his history were invented. (From Book 3 onward the speeches occupy nearly one-third of the total text.) He frequently refers to divine providence, looks down on the atheists, and says the Greek myths are shameful. Dionysius's other works concern literary criticism and are in the form of letters addressed to a literary friend.

❧ EXTANT WORKS ❧

The Roman Antiquities

Book 1.1-1.22 – A brief survey of the empires of the past, from the Assyrian to the Macedonian, including some Greek history. Dionysius tells the ancient history of Rome and proves his idea that Rome's founders were of Greek origin, and, thereby, he hoped to reconcile his fellow Greeks to Roman rule.

Book 1.23-1.63 – Covers 1242-1183 B.C.

Book 1.64-1.66 – Covers 1182-1151 B.C.

Book 1.67-1.74 – Covers 1150-751 B.C. (to the founding of Rome).

Book 1.75-2.56 – Romulus rules 751-715 B.C.

Book 2.57-2.76 – Numa rules 715-670 B.C.

Book 3.1-3.35 – Tullus Hostilius rules 670-638 B.C.

Book 3.36-3.45 – Ancus Marcius rules 638-614 B.C.

Book 3.46-3.73 – Lucius Tarquinius rules 614-576 B.C.

Book 4.1-4.40 – Servius Tullius rules 576-532 B.C.

Book 4.41-4.53 – Tarquinus Superbus II rules 532-509 B.C.

Book 4.54-4.85 – Tarquins ousted; constitutional discussions leading to establishment of the republic in 509 B.C.

Book 5 – Republic established and consuls rule Rome 509 B.C.

Books 6-20 – Covers 509-264 B.C. (to the beginning of the First Punic War).

Rhetorical Works:

First Letter to Ammaeus
On the Arrangement of Works
On the Ancient Orators
On the Style of Demosthenes
On Imitation
Letter to Cn. Pompeius
On Dinarchus
On Thucydides
Second Letter to Ammaeus

❧ SIGNIFICANT EXCERPTS ❧

The Roman Antiquities

1.3, 74-75 – The date of the founding of Rome.

1.72-73 – The founders of Rome.

1.88 – Romulus.

2.7-14, 16, 18-21, 26-27 – Romulus is praised for rejecting such of the myths as attributed any unseemly conduct to the gods; achievements of Romulus.

3.13-22 – The combat between the Horatii and the Curiatii.

5.5-8 – The Tarquins try to return to power; how the conspiracy was subdued by Brutus; Brutus is forced to kill his own sons to subdue the conspiracy.

5.75 – The dictators.

6.95.1-2 – Provisions of a treaty with the Latin League in 493 B.C.

9.41 – The comitia tributa instituted.

11.45 – Further growth of plebeian rights.

11.53-63 – Growth of the Roman constitution; the institution of consular tribunes.

Ennius
239-169 B.C.
Quintus Ennius

Ennius was the first great epic poet at Rome. He applied the idea of Pythagorean transmigration to himself, believing that the spirit of Homer, once incarnate in a peacock, and again in the philosopher Pythagoras, had entered his own body. He was an Epicurean. He also wrote tragedies which were translations and adaptions of the works of the Greek tragedians into Latin. His favorite model for writing was Euripides. We have fragments of twenty-two tragedies, two comedies, and one epic.

EXTANT WORKS INCLUDE

Andromeda

Hecuba

Iphigenia

Medea Exul

Melanippa

Telephus

Alexander

Andromacha Aechmalotis

Annales – Epic tale of the history of the Romans in 18 books; only fragments survive.

Thyestes

Epictetus
C. A.D. 60-135

Epictetus was a Greek philosopher who was heavily influenced by Stoic philosophy. He was originally a slave. He wrote nothing, but most of his teaching was written down in A.D. 104-107 by his pupil, the historian Arrian, in two works written in Greek – *The Discourses of Epictetus* and *The Manual*.

EXTANT WORKS

OF OTHERS WHO HAVE WRITTEN ABOUT EPICTETUS OR RECORDED HIS WORKS

The Discourses of Epictetus as Reported by Arrian

The Manual as Reported by Arrian – A summary of the philosophy of Epictetus.

SIGNIFICANT EXCERPTS

The Discourses of Epictetus

1.1 – An example of how a Stoic reacted to calamity.

1.9 – All men are brothers.

1.14 – Examples of Stoic teachings on how all things are under the divine inspection.

The Manual

33 – Examples of Stoic teachings; how a person should behave.

41 – It is a mark of want of intellect to spend much time in things relating to the body.

42 – When a person speaks ill of you . . .

43 – When your brother acts unjustly toward you . . .

45 – Do not pretend to understand the motives of others.

Epicurus
C. 341-270 B.C.

Epicurus was a Greek who founded a school and a system of philosophy, styled Epicureanism.

EXTANT WORKS

Letter to Herodotus – He summarizes his key doctrines. Epicurus says he is of the atomistic/materialistic tradition of Democritus. He explains mental function in terms of the movements of specialized neural atoms and suggests that the universe is filled with other worlds where extraterrestrial life is possible. Another important theme of this letter is the role of physical knowledge in promoting human happiness and negating skepticism and superstition.

Letter to Menoeceus – This is a summary of his ethical theories; addressed to his pupil, but meant for the general reader. After a brief statement of the nature of the gods and of death, the goal of life is defined as pleasure, and the limitations on this definition are stated.

Letter to Pythocles – Epicurus's beliefs on meteorology and astronomy.

Principle Doctrines – Forty ethical aphorisms.

Sententiae Vaticanae – Eighty ethical aphorisms.

SIGNIFICANT EXCERPTS

Letter to Menoeceus

SIGNIFICANT EXCERPTS

FROM OTHERS WRITING ABOUT EPICURUS OR INCLUDING HIS WRITINGS IN THEIR WORKS

Diogenes Laertius – *Lives of the Philosophers*, Epicurus.

Eratosthenes
C. 276-195 B.C.

Eratosthenes was a Greek scientist. He was librarian at Alexandria, and was interested in astronomy and geography. Although it was a well-known fact in his day that the earth was round, its exact size had not been determined. Eratosthenes made the closest calculation to his date. He also calculated the distances of the sun and moon from the earth, and the size of the sun. He was the first person to attempt a scientific chronology from the siege of Troy, and he wrote a geographical work in three books. His writings only survive through others.

SIGNIFICANT EXCERPTS

FROM OTHERS WRITING ABOUT ERATOSTHENES OR INCLUDING HIS WRITINGS IN THEIR WORKS

Cleomedes – *Concerning the Circular Motion of the Heavenly Bodies*, 1.10.52 – A description of Eratosthenes' computation of the size of the earth.

Strabo – *Ancient Geography* 1.4.1-9 – Critique of Eratosthenes.

Euclid
C. 330-275 B.C.

Euclid was a Greek mathematician who probably received his early mathematical training at Athens from the pupils of Plato. We know nothing for certain of his life except that he taught and founded a school at Alexandria in the time of Ptolemy I, who reigned from 306 to 283 B.C. Proclus tells the story of Euclid's reply to King Ptolemy, who asked whether there was any shorter way in geometry than that of the *Elements* – "There is no royal road to geometry." Another story relates that a pupil, after learning the very first proposition in geometry, wanted to know what he would get by learning these things, so Euclid called his slave and said, "Give him threepence since he must needs make gain by what he learns."

Elements

EXTANT WORKS

Elements of Geometry– This work is divided into thirteen books:

Books 1-2 – On the geometry of the straight line.

Books 3-4 – On the circle.

Books 5-6 – On the theory of proportion.

Books 7-9 – On the theory of numbers and proof that the number of primes is infinite.

Book 10 – On incommensurable magnitudes, or irrational lines.

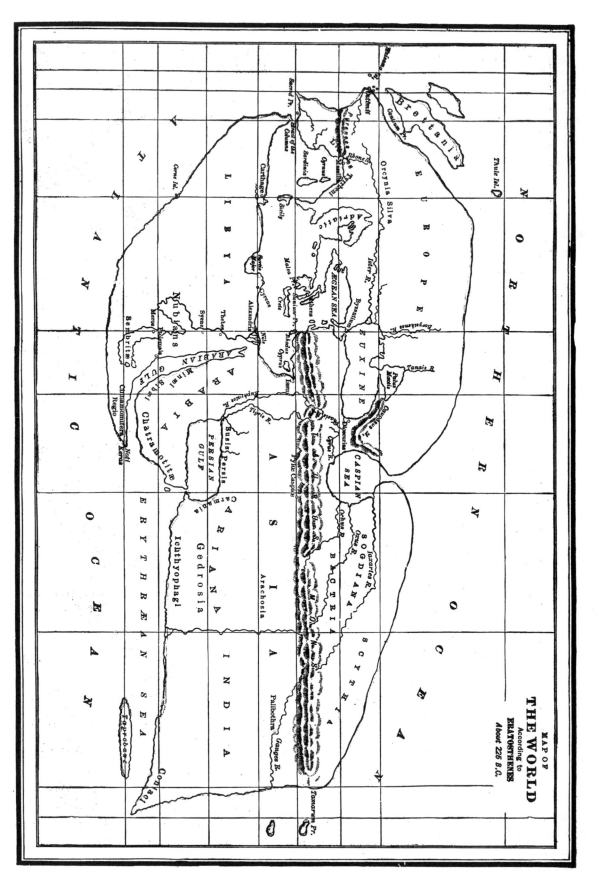

Map of the world according to Eratosthenes

Books 11-13 – On solid geometry.

Elements of Geometry

Book 7 – Prefix – Definitions

Euripides
C. 480-406 B.C.

Euripides was a Greek tragedian. He composed many plays during his life, but only seventeen tragedies and one satyr play survive. Because he was too unconventional for the Greeks, he was not as popular during his lifetime as was Sophocles. He enlivened the ancient myths, which formed the basis of his plays, by altering their plots and adding more credible dimensions. He portrayed life as it really was, and made the stage a living representation of the Athens of his day. The Greeks of his day didn't like this, but the Greeks of later centuries did. He is considered "the most tragic of poets."

🌿 EXTANT WORKS 🌿

Cyclops – A play based on Homer's story of Odysseus's escape from the Cyclops' cave; written 443 B.C.

Alcestis – When his day of death comes, Admetus has been granted the right to escape, if he can find a willing substitute. His old parents refuse to die for him; his young wife consents and dies; written 438 B.C.

Medea – Jason, with Medea and their two children, has escaped to Corinth, which is ruled by an old king, Creon, with a daughter but no son to succeed him. Creon wants Jason to marry his daughter, if only he will be rid of Medea. Jason consents, and Medea is ordered to exile. Medea gets revenge by killing the bride, Creon, and Jason's two children; written 431 B.C.

Hippolytus – The wife falls in love with the chaste youth, and, when rejected, slanders him. The wife hangs herself and the youth dies; written 428 B.C.

Hecuba – Hecuba's daughter Polyxena is sacrificed on Achilles' tomb to satisfy a superstitious mob. Her other daughter has been taken for Agamemnon's slave. Her son Polydorus has been murdered for his gold. Hecuba kills the murderer's children and blinds the murderer. Hecuba, maddened by the suffering, is transformed into a devil; written 425 B.C.

Andromache – Neoptolemus, son of Achilles, who had taken Andromache, the widow of Hector, as his mistress, has put her away in order to marry Hermione, daughter of Helen, but he still likes and trusts Andromache. Hermione is childless and suspects Andromache of bewitching her. Her old betrothed, Orestes, still loves her, and her father, Menelaus is in league with him. Murder and deceit and all manner of wickedness follow.

The Heraclidae

The Suppliant

Heracles

Ion

The Trojan Women

Iphigenia in Tauris

Helena

Electra

Orestes

The Phoenissae

The Bacchae

Iphigenia in Aulis

Eusebius
C. A.D. 260-339

Eusebius was a Christian writer and was considered the "Father of Church History." He was a friend and confidant of Constantine, and one of the leaders at the Council of Nicaea. Only fifteen of his forty-six works have come down to us intact. He was born in Caesarea, and he wrote in Greek.

❧ EXTANT WORKS INCLUDE ❧

The Martyrs of Palestine – An account of martyrdoms which took place over a period of eight years.

The Life of Constantine – Important (though biased) historical account of the Council of Nicaea.

The Chronological Tables – A summary of events in various countries, arranged side by side in dated sequence.

The History of the Church – Eusebius's most important work, this history is made up of nine books:

Book 1 – The nature and work of Christ; His contemporaries; His choice of followers; correspondence with Abgar.

Book 2 – Tiberius to Nero; the work of the apostles from the choice of Matthias to the deaths of Paul and Peter.

Book 3 – Vespasian to Trajan; the distribution and writings of the apostles and their successors; enemies within the Church; persecutions.

Book 4 – Trajan to Marcus Aurelius; the succession of bishops; their writings and martyrdoms.

Book 5 – Marcus Aurelius to Severus; the succession of bishops; their refutation of Marcion and Montanus; their settlement of the date of the Easter festival.

Book 6 – Severus to Decius; the work of Origen and his contemporaries; widespread persecution.

Book 7 – Gallus to Gallienus; the work of Cyprian and Dionysius; the heresies of Sabillius, Novatus, Nepos, Paul, and the Manichees.

Book 8 – Diocletian to Maximian; persecutions; the imperial recantation.

Book 9 – Maximian's renewed attacks on the Church; the end of persecution.

Book 10 – Peace and recovery of the Church; victory of Constantine.

❧ SIGNIFICANT EXCERPTS ❧

The History of the Church

2.25 – This is the earliest explicit statement that Peter and Paul suffered martyrdom at the same time, and that Peter was ever in Italy.

3.18 – The persecution under Domitian.

3.31 – The last days of the Apostle John.

3.36 – The story of Ignatius.

4.15 – Martyrdom of Polycarp in A.D. 155.

4.23 – Reproduction of the "Epistle to the Roman Church" by Dionysius of Corinth – Dionysius discusses how some false teachers have been falsifying his letters along with other Scriptures.

5.1 – An account of the persecution in Gaul in the days of Marcus Aurelius (A.D. 177).

5.10 – The gospel has been taken to India.

6.1 – Persecutions under Severus.

6.18 – Origen's conception of a good education.

6.34 – It is reported that Emperor Philip (A.D. 244-249) is a Christian.

6.39 – Decius persecutes the Church.

7.13 – Edict from Emperor Gallienus in A.D. 261 allowing Christians to worship freely.

8.2, 6 – Descriptions of the edicts of Diocletian against the Christians in A.D. 303.

8.7 – Eusebius describes the execution of a Christian which he witnessed in A.D. 303.

10.5 – Edict of Milan in 313; letters from Constantine.

10.6-7 – Letters from Constantine.

Life of Constantine

1.24 ff. – How Constantine overthrew Maxentius and favored Christianity.

3.25 ff. – How Constantine ordered the erection of a church at Jerusalem.

Eutropius
FL. FOURTH CENTURY A.D.
Flavius Eutropius

Eutropius was a Roman historian. His work is a summary of Roman history from the foundation of the city to the accession of Valens.

EXTANT WORKS

A Concise History of Rome

SIGNIFICANT EXCERPTS

A Concise History of Rome

  1.1-20 – The founding of Rome; the kings of Rome
  and the early Republic.

  8.12-14 – The reign of Marcus Aurelius.

Frontinus
C. A.D. 40-103
Sextus Julius Frontinus

Frontinus was a Roman soldier and author. He served
as governor of Britain and later as superintendent of the
aqueducts at Rome.

EXTANT WORKS

On Water (2 books) – A history and description of the
  water supply of Rome; laws concerning the use of
  water.

The Stratagems – The rules of military science.

SIGNIFICANT EXCERPTS

On Water

  2.74-76 – Description of the water supply and water
  thieves in first century A.D. Rome.

  2.119-124 – Maintenance of the water system.

Galen
C. A.D.129-199
Claudius Galen

Galen was a Greek physician who wrote about medical
practice. During his life, he wrote, lectured, gave public
demonstrations, and had a successful private practice. He
wrote 500 to 600 papers, which have been reported to
comprise approximately two and one half million words.
Only about 100 of his works remain today.

EXTANT WORKS INCLUDE

On the Natural Faculties – He explains the physiological or
  biological powers of the living organism. He believed
  living organisms were governed by a Physis or Nature,
  and this Nature was the biological principle upon
  which he based his medical teaching. This work is
  a combination of philosophy and medicine – mostly
  philosophy.

On the Nature of Man

Exhortation to Study the Arts

On Diagnosis from Dreams

On the Elements, According to Hippocrates

The Best Doctor Is Also a Philosopher

Is Healthiness a Part of Medicine or of Gymnastics

The Affections and Errors of the Soul

The Construction of the Embryo

The Thinning Diet

On the Use of the Parts of the Human Body

The Soul's Dependence on the Body

The Best Constitution of our Bodies

Good Condition

The Exercise with the Small Ball

The Pulse for Beginners

The Art of Medicine

Regimen in Acute Diseases in Accordance with the Theories of Hippocrates

Cohesive Causes

The Parts of Medicine

❧ SIGNIFICANT EXCERPTS ❧

On the Use of the Parts of the Human Body

   I, 2-3 – The purpose of the human hand.

On the Natural Faculties

   1.2 – Definition of terms

   1.5 – Birth, growth, and nutrition.

Gellius
C. A.D. 123-169
Aulus Gellius

Gellius was a Roman author and grammarian. His only work is the *Attic Nights*, which is a collection of entertaining essays on grammar, geometry, philosophy, history, biography, law, and nearly every other branch of knowledge. Gellius has preserved numerous extracts from Greek and Roman writers whose works are now lost. *Attic Nights* is easy to read, and most of this work is extant.

❧ EXTANT WORKS ❧

Attic Nights

❧ SIGNIFICANT EXCERPTS ❧

Attic Nights

   2.7 – On the obedience of children to their parents.

   3.13 – Why Demosthenes deserted Plato and became a follower of Callistratus.

   4.13 – How it is said that gout can be cured by playing the flute.

   5.2 – A story about Alexander the Great and his horse Bucephalas.

   5.14 – Androclus and the lion.

   5.16 – How the eye functions.

   7.3 – An account of the killing of a serpent of great length.

   7.17 – Who was the first to establish a public library; how many books were in the public libraries in Athens before the Persian War.

   9.3.21 – The birth of Alexander.

   10.7 – The three largest rivers in the world.

   11.18 – Comparing the laws of Draco, Solon, and the Twelve Tables, concerning theft.

   12.1 – Mothers should nurse their own children instead of giving them up to other nurses; the importance of nursing your baby so you will develop bonds with the child.

   13.5 – How Aristotle chose his successor using graceful tact.

   13.18 – The meaning of Marcus Cato's phrase "betwixt mouth and morsel."

   14.3 – A discussion on whether or not Plato and Xenophon were at odds with each other.

   16.13 – The meaning of the terms municipium and colonia; what Hadrian said in the Senate about the name and rights of municipes.

   20.4 – That devotion and love paid to play-actors was disgraceful, with a quotation of the words of the philosopher Aristotle on the subject.

Herodian
C. A.D. 170-240

Herodian was a Greek historian. His historical work deals with the fifty-eight years between the death of Marcus Aurelius (A.D. 180) and the accession of Gordianus III (A.D. 238). Herodian claimed to have "written a history of the events following the death of Marcus which I heard and saw in my lifetime."

❧ EXTANT WORKS ❧

History of the Emperors

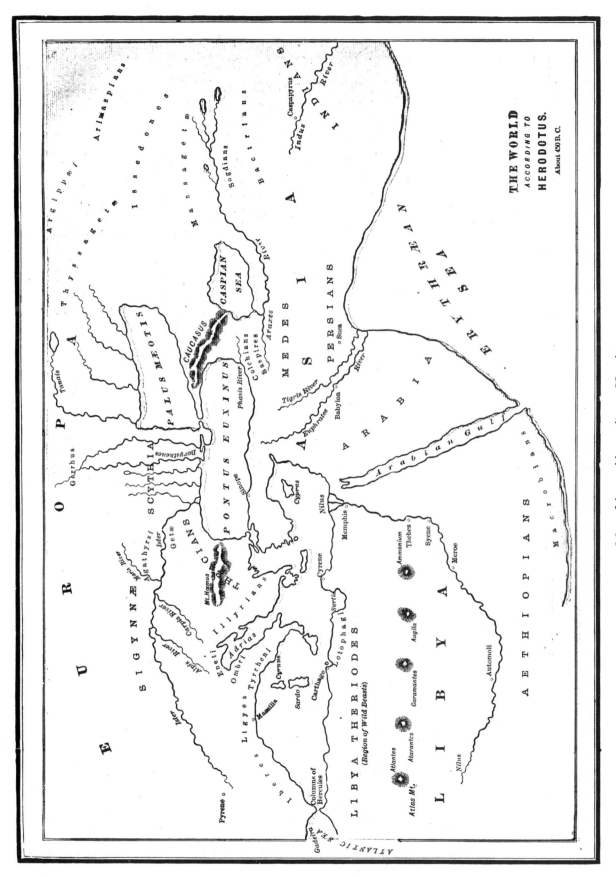

Map of the world according to Herodotus

❧ SIGNIFICANT EXCERPTS ❧

History of the Emperors

2.1-5 – Pertinax rules for a brief period (193) and is then killed by the Praetorian Guard.

2.6 – After the murder of Pertinax, the guards "sell" the empire to the highest bidder, Didius Julianus.

4.2 – The deification of Septimius Severus in 211.

Herodotus
c. 484-425 B.C.

Herodotus was a Greek historian. He wrote the earliest surviving Greek history, *The History of the Persian Wars,* consisting of nine books. Herodotus states two reasons for writing his History: 1) ". . .to preserve the memory of the past by putting on record the astonishing achievements both of our own [Greek] and of the Asiatic [Persian, Egyptian, etc. – barbarian] peoples;" and 2)". . . to show how the two races came into conflict." Herodotus isn't always accurate in his narrative, although he is objective in his observations and is free of national prejudice and racial bias.

❧ EXTANT WORKS ❧

The History of the Persian Wars (also called *The History*)

Book 1– The rise of the Persian Empire through the downfall of the Lydian Empire; covers the middle of the 700s B.C. until the death of Cyrus in 529 B.C.

Book 2 – The history, geography, and customs of Egypt up to 529 B.C.; the succession of Cyrus's son Cambyses; a history of the Egyptian kings; Amasis is king of Egypt when Cambyses decides to invade Egypt.

Book 3 – The establishment of the Persian Empire under the reigns of Cambyses, Smerdis, and Darius.

Book 4 – The conflict of Persia against Scythia and Libya.

Book 5 – The developing struggle between Persia and Athens.

Book 6 – The growth of the Hellenic spirit in Ionia and Greece; the battle of Marathon.

Book 7 – Xerxes' march against Greece.

Book 8 – The battle of Salamis.

Book 9 – The battles of Plataea and Mycale; the failure of the Persian invasion.

❧ SIGNIFICANT EXCERPTS ❧

The History of the Persian Wars

1.29-33 – How Solon visited Croesus at Sardis.

1.74-75 – Thales.

1.95-106 – Early history of Persia.

1.107-130 – Birth and rise of Cyrus.

1.131-140 – Customs of the Persians.

1.171 – The Carians (former subjects of King Minos).

1.190-191 – The taking of Babylon.

1.195 – Description of Babylonian clothing.

2.2-5 – The antiquity of Egypt.

2.14 – Farm labor in Egypt is easy because of the Nile.

2.19-28 – The Nile flood.

2.35-38 – Manners and customs of the Egyptians.

2.68-76 – Egyptian crocodile and the hippopotamus.

2.86-88 – How the Egyptians embalm their dead.

2.95 – Egyptian mosquitoes.

2.124-128 – The building of the pyramids by Cheops.

3.39-43 – The ring of Polycrates.

3.80-97 – The Persians reject democracy; Darius' state.

3.122 – The Carians (former subjects of King Minos).

4.196 – Phoenician trade with Libya.

5.49-51 – Aristagoras at Sparta.

5.58 – The Phoenicians gave the alphabet to Greece.

5.66-77 – How Athens was given a democratic organization by Cleisthenes and triumphed over her neighbors.

5.97, 99-101 – Aristagoras at Athens and what came of it.

5.102-106 – How the Persians came to Marathon.

6.56-58 – The two kings of Sparta: their privileges in war and peace, their dinner, jurisdiction and funeral.

6.102-117, 120 – The battle of Marathon.

7.1-7 – Darius dies; ascension of Xerxes.

7.22-24 – Mt. Athos.

7.33-56 – Bridging of Hellespont.

7.60-83 – The contingents and nations in Xerxes' army.

7.100-105 – Dialogue between Xerxes and Demaratus.

7.118-120 – How the Greek towns were forced to entertain Xerxes' army.

7.138-144 – How Athens resolved to face the Persians, and how Themistocles interpreted the adverse oracles.

7.145-147 – How Xerxes dealt with the Greek spies.

7.175-177 – The Greeks decide to take a stand at Thermopylae by land and at Artemisium by sea.

7.196-234 – Battle of Thermopylae.

8.40-43 – The evacuation of Attica and the mustering of the Greek fleet.

8.74-86, 96-99 – Salamis.

8.118 – The Persians' devotion to Xerxes.

8.143 – The answer the Athenians gave the Persian envoy before the battle of Plataea.

9.52-70 – The battle of Plataea.

9.82 – Persian magnificence and Greek simplicity.

Hesiod
FL. EIGHTH CENTURY B.C.

Hesiod was a near contemporary of Homer. He wrote a genealogical account of the origin of the Greek gods. His epic poems were meant to instruct the common man in the ordinary pursuits of life. His compilation of myths, legends, and stories of deities provided later writers and artists the material upon which they built their own works.

❧ EXTANT WORKS ☙

Works and Days – Wise sayings and practical advice for farmers and other ordinary people. The theme is the presence of evil in the world and the escape from it through industry and toil. There are four parts to this work: an exhortation to Hesiod's younger brother Perses; a collection of rules for farming and navigation; ethical and religious precepts; and a calendar of lucky and unlucky days.

Theogony – An epic of the origins and dynasties of the gods.

❧ SIGNIFICANT EXCERPTS ☙

Works and Days

Lines 342-345 – Neighbors and kinfolk.

Lines 571-581 – The best time to work.

Lines 618 ff. – The perils of the sea.

Hippocrates
c. 460-377 B.C.

Hippocrates is the most famous of the Greek physicians. He lived and taught on the island of Cos, near Asia Minor. He based his medical practice on observations of the human body. He believed that illness had a physical and a rational explanation; and he rejected the current view of his time that illness was caused by superstitions, by possession of evil spirits, and by disfavor of the gods. We have fifty-two works ascribed to him, of which only a few are probably genuine. Most of the works attributed to him were probably written by his pupils and successors.

EXTANT WORKS

On Ancient Medicine – Hippocrates' view of what causes illnesses; he doesn't mix medicine with philosophy, although he conserves what he considers valuable from the past.

The Book of Prognostics – A general description of the concept of disease as applied to all the disorders of the animal frame; contrasts the healthy with the sick.

The Aphorisms – This is his most famous work. He collected together all the conclusions he had come to concerning all of his studies on medicine. It is a general review of all the results of his preceding inquiries.

The Epidemics

The Regimen in Acute Diseases – Discusses the proper distinction of diseases from one another and the rules for treating acute diseases.

On Airs, Waters, and Places

On the Articulations – Treating dislocations at the shoulder-joint and other parts of the body.

On Fractures – Discusses the general principle in treating fractures and dislocations.

The Instruments of Reduction – How to treat fractures and dislocations.

The Physician's Establishment, or Surgery – Concerns the treatment of fractures and similar injuries, including the rules for the management of this part of surgical practice.

On the Injuries of the Head – Begins with a description of the bones of the head; describes the various kinds of injury which the different sorts of weapons are most likely to inflict; how the different injuries should be treated; operations on the skull.

The Oath of Medical Ethics – An oath taken by physicians today as they begin their medical practice.

The Law – Describes the perfect physician.

On the Sacred Disease – Shows that epilepsy is connected with the brain and exposes the quacks who try to treat it; he writes against the idea that epilepsy was a result of divine possession.

On Ulcers – How ulcers are treated.

On Fistulae – A continuation of the work *On Ulcers.*

On Hemorrhoids – A continuation of the work *On Fistulae.*

[*The Physician*] – Probably not written by Hippocrates.

SIGNIFICANT EXCERPTS

On Ancient Medicine

> 1-7 – The methods and origins of medicine; medicine is a corollary to dietetics.
>
> 13 – Remarks in refutation of the hypothesis of cold, heat, moist, and dry.
>
> 16 – Remarks on the effects of the cold bath.
>
> 19 – Observations on rheums or defluxions.
>
> 20 – Philosophy is not so necessary to medicine as medicine is to philosophy.

The Oath of Medical Ethics

On Airs, Waters and Places

> 1-16 – How the seasons, geographic location, and customs affect the health of people.

On the Sacred Disease

The Epidemics

Map of the world according to Homer

I, 1-3 – An epidemic resulting from a particular type of weather.

I – Fourteen cases of disease.

The Instruments of Reduction

1 – Brief description of the bones of the human body.

2 – A fractured nose.

The Physician

1 – Qualities of a good doctor.

Homer
C. EIGHTH CENTURY B.C.

Homer wrote two epic poems concerning the Trojan War which some believe to have occurred about 1200 B.C. This war raged for ten years between the Trojans and the Greeks. According to the mythological accounts, the war began when Paris, son of the king of Troy, was called upon to judge a beauty contest between the goddesses Aphrodite, Hera, and Athena. All the goddesses tried to bribe Paris, but Aphrodite won after she promised to give to Paris the beautiful Helen, wife of Spartan king Menelaus. Paris abducted Helen, and thus began the Trojan War. Nothing is known about Homer's life. He probably wrote *The Iliad* and *The Odyssey* about 750 B.C.

❧ EXTANT WORKS ☙

The Iliad – Epic poem set in the ninth year of the Trojan War. This is a tale of heroes and heroines and gods and goddesses. The great Greek hero Achilles has been awarded a slave girl, but the Greek leader Agamemnon takes her from Achilles, and Achilles is offended. Achilles prays to his mother Thetis, a goddess, to turn the tide of the battle against the Greeks. The gods give him his request and Achilles leaves the battle only to return when his best friend is killed by the great Trojan hero, Hector. Achilles kills Hector and drags Hector's body around the walls of Troy.

The Odyssey – Occurs ten years after the siege, when the great Greek hero Odysseus is trying to return home from the Trojan War to his wife. His homecoming has been delayed for ten years because of the anger of the gods. For most of those ten years, Odysseus has been living on an island with the goddess Kalypso, who is in love with him.

Horace
65-8 B.C.
Quintus Horatius Flaccus

Horace was a Roman lyric poet of Epicurean persuasion. His poems are imitations of the poetry of the Greek lyrists and their followers. He was a friend of Augustus.

❧ EXTANT WORKS ☙

Epodes – Collection of seventeen short lyrical pieces which imitate and translate the Greek poets Sappho and Alcaeus.

Satires – Informal conversations, phrased in everyday language, describing life in his time.

Odes – Love poems similar to Sappho and Alcaeus.

Epistles – Letters similar to the Satires.

❧ SIGNIFICANT EXCERPTS ☙
SPECIAL CAUTION ADVISED

Odes

3.5 – On Regulus's departure for Carthage in 250 B.C.

Satires

1.1 – On greed.

1.6.65-88 – Horace's debt to his father.

2.6.78-115 – The country mouse and the city mouse.

Ignatius of Antioch
C. A.D. 50-117

Ignatius was one of the earliest Church theologians. Having been condemned to death, and expecting to be thrown to the wild animals in the theater, he wrote seven letters on his way from Antioch to Rome. These letters have been the most controversial of all the early

Church writings, as they contain numerous statements on topics which divide Christians.

EXTANT WORKS

7 *Letters* – To Ephesus, To Magnesia, To Tralles, To Rome, To Philadelphia, To Smyrna, To Polycarp

SIGNIFICANT EXCERPTS

7 *Letters*

Irenaeus of Lyons
C. A.D. 130-200

After his conversion to Christianity, Irenaeus became a missionary and Church leader. He is considered by some to be the most important theologian of the second century. He was the first person to give reasons for admitting or rejecting books into the canon of the New Testament. He wrote in Greek.

EXTANT WORKS

Against All Heresies (5 books) – An attack on Gnosticism and an apologetic for the deity of Christ.

Proof of the Apostolic Preaching – A work on Christian doctrine.

SIGNIFICANT EXCERPTS

Against All Heresies

1.10.3 – Describes how far Christianity has extended geographically.

2.22.5; 3.3.4 – Information about the last days of the Apostle John.

3.11.8 – His opinion on the canon of the New Testament.

Isocrates
436-338 B.C.

Isocrates was born in Athens shortly before the Peloponnesian War. His family was wealthy, but Isocrates lost his inherited wealth during the war, so he began to earn money by writing speeches for others to use in the courts (similar to Demosthenes). This was the usual beginning to a career as an orator. Unfortunately, Isocrates did not have the voice or self-confidence necessary for a public speaker. His writings were political pamphlets in the form of imaginary speeches. He is also known for his school, where he trained pupils in the art of rhetoric. He attracted students from all over the Greek-speaking world, many of whom went on to become important leaders of their day. Isocrates led a politically active life until his death, and through his speeches he promoted his political ideas of Pan-hellenism (unifying all of Greece under one rule, and attacking Asia). Twenty-one of these speeches exist today; they all concern the politics of ancient Greece. Isocrates looked for some leader who would unify and lead Greece, and believed that Philip of Macedon would best fit that role. In the opinion of Demosthenes, Philip was a barbarian. We also have nine of Isocrates' letters which address a wide variety of topics, including education, rhetoric, and beauty.

EXTANT WORKS INCLUDE

Against the Sophists – Explains his opposition to the rhetoric taught by his school's rival, Plato's Academy, and to the oversimplified rhetorical techniques advanced by contemporary sophists.

Antidosis – Explains his beliefs in the ethical obligation of rhetors and the factors imperative for effective rhetoric.

Panegyricus – Composed in 380 B.C.; designed to be recited; published at a time when the power and influence of Athens were at a low ebb and when the Greek world was in a sorry state. The crowning shame of this condition of affairs was the so-called Peace of Antalcidas, under which terms the Greeks submitted themselves formally, for the first time in history, to the rule of the Persian king. This speech advocates the unification of Greek city-states against the Persian army. Considered to be Isocrates' masterpiece.

On Peace – Advocates a policy of equality and alliance between Athens and the subject cities of the empire; written in 355 B.C.

On the Areopagiticus – Mourns the moral degeneracy of the republic; written in 354 B.C.

Philip of Macedonia

To Philip – An appeal to the king of Macedon to assume that initiative in the war on Persia which Isocrates had stopped expecting from any Greek city; written in 346 B.C.

Aegineticus

Archidamus

Busiris

Against Callimachus

Against Euthynus

Evagoras

Helen

Letters

Against Lochites

Nicocles, or The Cyprians

Panathenaicus

Plataicus

On the Team of Horses

To Demonicus

To Nicocles

Trapeziticus

❧ SIGNIFICANT EXCERPTS ❧

Panegyricus

> 110-122 – Isocrates calls for a crusade against Persia which would unite Greece once more.

On the Areopagiticus

> 1-28, 76-84 – The present power of Athens may lead to disaster; Isocrates calls for a return to the good old days of that ancient Athenian court.

To Philip

14-16, 30-41, 68-71, 154

Jerome
C. A.D. 347-420
Eusebius Sophronius Hieronymus

Jerome was born of Christian parents and led the life of an ascetic. He is known for his Latin translation of the Bible (the Vulgate) and for his commentaries. He was considered to be the most educated of the Latin Fathers.

❧ EXTANT WORKS INCLUDE ❧

The Vulgate

On the Lives of Illustrious Men

Commentary on Galatians

Commentary on Ezekiel

126 *Letters*

❧ SIGNIFICANT EXCERPTS ❧

Commentary on Galatians 26.462 – Information about the last days of the Apostle John.

Commentary on Ezekiel, Preface – Jerome's account of the capture of Rome by Alaric in 410.

Letters

> 1 – Earliest letter of Jerome; relates the story of a miracle.

> 60.16-18 – Calamities brought on by the invaders; Jerome believes that Rome was falling.

> 107 – Letter to Laeta regarding the Christian education of girls.

> 125 – Advice to a young monk.

> 127 – Experiences of Principia and Marcella, two Christian women, in the sack of Rome by the Goths.

> 128 – Feminine training.

Josephus
C. A.D. 37-100
Flavius Josephus

Josephus was a Jewish priest, a soldier, and a scholar. He was born in Jerusalem a few years after the days of Jesus' earthly ministry, during the time of the Roman occupation of Israel. He was an eyewitness of the war between the Jews and Rome, and of the destruction of Jerusalem and the Holy Temple in A.D. 70. Josephus is our primary source for reconstructing history in the late second temple period, the time of Jesus, and the first century A.D.

❧ EXTANT WORKS ❧

War of the Jews – The history of the Jewish revolt against the Roman Empire in the years A.D. 66-74, as experienced by Josephus himself; published in A.D. 78.

Preface to the *War of the Jews*

Book 1 – From the taking of Jerusalem by Antiochus Epiphanes to the death of Herod the Great.

Book 2 – From the death of Herod until Vespasian was sent to subdue the Jews by Nero.

Book 3 – From Vespasian's coming to subdue the Jews to the taking of Gamala.

Book 4 – From the siege of Gamala to the coming of Titus to besiege Jerusalem.

Book 5 – From the coming of Titus to besiege Jerusalem to the great extremity to which the Jews were reduced.

Book 6 – From the great extremity to which the Jews were reduced to the taking of Jerusalem by Titus.

Book 7 – From the taking of Jerusalem by Titus to the sedition of the Jews at Cyrene.

Antiquities of the Jews – The history of the Jews prior to the revolt; based on the Bible, other Jewish writings, and the works of previous historians. Published in A.D. 93.

Preface to the *Antiquities of the Jews.*

Book 1 – From creation to the death of Isaac.

Book 2 – From the death of Isaac to the Exodus out of Egypt.

Book 3 – From the Exodus out of Egypt to the rejection of that generation.

Book 4 – From the rejection of that generation to the death of Moses.

Book 5 – From the death of Moses to the death of Eli.

Book 6 – From the death of Eli to the death of Saul.

Book 7 – From the death of Saul to the death of David.

Book 8 – From the death of David to the death of Ahab.

Book 9 – From the death of Ahab to the captivity of the Ten Tribes.

Book 10 – From the captivity of the Ten Tribes to the first year of Cyrus.

Book 11 – From the first year of Cyrus to the death of Alexander the Great.

Book 12 – From the death of Alexander the Great to the death of Judas Maccabeus.

Book 13 – From the death of Judas Maccabeus to the death of Queen Alexandra.

Book 14 – From the death of Queen Alexandra to the death of Antigonus.

Book 15 – From the death of Antigonus to the finishing of the temple by Herod.

Book 16 – From the finishing of the temple by Herod to the deaths of Alexander and Aristobulus.

Book 17 – From the deaths of Alexander and Aristobulus to the banishment of Archelaus.

Book 18 – From the banishment of Archelaus to the departure of the Jews from Babylon.

Book 19 – From the departure of the Jews from Babylon to Fadus the Roman Procurator.

Book 20 – From Fadus the Procurator to Florus.

The Life of Flavius Josephus – Josephus's autobiography,

written shortly after A.D. 100.

Josephus's Discourse to the Greeks Concerning Hades

Flavius Josephus Against Apion – A defense of Judaism, answering an attack by a Roman author.

❧ SIGNIFICANT EXCERPTS ❧

The War of the Jews

Preface; 1-4 – Josephus tells us that he is going to be impartial in this history and that it was the tyrants among the Jews who brought the Roman power upon Jerusalem.

2.17.1 – The seditious temper of the leading Jews.

2.18.2 – The magnitude of the calamities and slaughters which came upon the Jews.

4.5.2 – Reference to crucifixion.

5.2.1 – Titus marched to Jerusalem with ensigns.

5.3.1 – The number of people within the city during the siege.

Siege of a city

5.6.3 – Stones of 100 pounds thrown upon the city.

5.6.5 – Reference to crucifixion.

5.10.2 – Intolerable things those who stayed in Jerusalem suffered by famine.

5.11.1 – Reference to crucifixion.

5.13.7 – An account of the miseries in Jerusalem.

6.3.3 – More accounts of the calamities in Jerusalem.

6.3.4 – Accounts of infanticide and cannibalism in Jerusalem.

6.4.1-8 – The temple is burned; Titus is not at fault.

6.5.3 – Signs which preceded the destruction of Jerusalem and the temple.

6.9.3 – Number of captives and dead.

6.10.1 – Seventh sacking of Jerusalem.

7.1.1 – Entire city of Jerusalem destroyed.

Antiquities of the Jews

1.5 – The Tower of Babel.

10.8.1-7 – Nebuchadnezzar took Jerusalem and burnt the temple.

11.1.1-3 – How Cyrus, king of the Persians, delivered the Jews out of Babylon and allowed them to return to their own country, and to build their temple.

11.8.1-7 – Philip, king of Macedon, is killed, and his son Alexander rules; what benefits he bestowed on the Jews.

12.2.1-15 – How Ptolemy procured the laws of the Jews to be translated into the Greek tongue.

12.5.3-4 – Antiochus made an expedition against Jerusalem, emptied the temple and sacrificed a pig on the altar of God; reference to crucifixion.

17.8.1 – When compared with Luke and Matthew, this passage gives us the year of Jesus' birth and also confirms Matthew 2:22.

18.1.2-6 – The four philosophies of Judiasm.

18.3.3 – Reference to Jesus Christ.

18.5.2 – Reference to John the Baptist.

19.8.2 – Account of the death of Herod Agrippa I.

20.6.1 – Samaritans and Luke 9.51.

20.8.5 – Josephus tells why God had Jerusalem and the temple destroyed.

20.9.1 – Reference to James, brother of Jesus.

Against Apion

1.2 – Thales.

Julian the Apostate
C. A.D. 331-363
Flavius Claudius Julianus

Julian was Emperor of Rome from A.D. 360-363. He tried to repress Christian privileges and to restore Rome's ancient pagan culture. Julian wrote prolifically (in Greek), leaving behind eight orations and eighty letters.

EXTANT WORKS

8 *Orations*

80 *Letters*

SIGNIFICANT EXCERPTS

Letters

23, 38 – Julian wants the Christian books destroyed.

36 – Edict against Christian teachers reading the pagan authors with their pupils, which meant that they must cease to teach, since all education was based on reading the classics.

37, 39, 40, 41 – Julian's attitude toward the Christians.

49 – Letter to a pagan high priest.

56 – Edict against Christians on funerals – no daytime funerals.

Justin
FL. SECOND CENTURY A.D.
Marcus Junianus Justinus

Justin was a Roman historian. He rewrote a work of history written by a man named Pompeius Trogus.

EXTANT WORKS

Epitome of the Philippic Histories – History of the Macedonian monarchy.

SIGNIFICANT EXCERPTS

Epitome of the Philippic Histories

7.5 – How Philip began his reign.

9.3-5 – Philip gains control of Greece.

9.8 – Philip's character.

50.100 – Philip contrasted with Alexander.

Justin Martyr
C. A.D. 100-165

Justin Martyr was a Gentile Stoic and Platonist philosopher born in Palestine; he became an apologist for Christianity. He is the first Christian writer to try to reconcile ancient philosophy (especially Platonism) with Christianity.

EXTANT WORKS

First Apology – A work which asks the Roman Emperor, Antonius Pius, for justice on behalf of the Christians, who are being persecuted; an exposition and demonstration of Christianity.

Second Apology – Why God permits evil.

The Dialogue with Trypho, the Jew – The story of Justin's philosophic education and conversion; on the law and on Christ; on the Christians.

Discourse to the Greeks

Exhortation to the Greeks

The Monarchy or Rule of God

❧ SIGNIFICANT EXCERPTS ❧

First Apology

> 1.31, 53 – Defense of Christianity.
>
> 1.5, 14, 46 – The place of ancient philosophy in Christianity; his view of Socrates.
>
> 1.61-67 – Describes Christian worship in the second century.
>
> 1.68 – Copy of a letter by Emperor Hadrian concerning Christians.

Second Apology

> 2.2 – The attitude of the Roman government toward Christians.
>
> 2.10, 13 – The place of ancient philosophy in Christianity; his view of Socrates.

The Dialogue with Trypho, the Jew

> 17 – How the Jews persecute the Christians.
>
> 117 – The extension of Christianity during the first half of the second century.

Juvenal
C. A.D. 55-135
Decimus Iunius Iuvenalis

Juvenal is the harshest and most violent of the Roman satirists. He depicts the vulgar life of Rome in a lurid light with repulsive and coarse detail. He attacks the evils of the day.

❧ EXTANT WORKS ❧

Satires (5 books)

Lactantius
C. A.D. 250-330
Lucius Caecilius Firmianus Lactantius

Lactantius was born a pagan in Africa, but later converted to Christianity. He obtained some local fame as a teacher of rhetoric, and he was appointed by Diocletian to be professor of rhetoric in his new capital of Nicomedia. Lactantius lost this position during the Diocletian persecution. Afterward, he was tutor to the son of Constantine. He was considered "the Christian Cicero."

❧ EXTANT WORKS ❧

On the Craftsmanship of God – The human body shows the existence of a wise and beneficent Creator.

Divine Institutes (7 books) – Arguments against paganism; a full and eloquent statement of what Christian doctrine is.

The Anger of God – Directed primarily against the Epicureans and Stoics; discusses in what sense anger can be attributed to a perfect Being.

On the Deaths of the Persecutors – Describes God's judgments on the persecutors of the Church from Nero to Diocletian.

❧ SIGNIFICANT EXCERPTS ❧

Divine Institutes

> 3.13-15 – Of the immortality of the soul; of wisdom, philosophy, and eloquence; that Lucretius and others and Cicero himself have erred in fixing the origin of wisdom; the error of Seneca in philosophy; how the speech of philosophers is at variance with their lives.
>
> 3.18-19 – The Pythagoreans and Stoics, while they hold the immortality of the soul, foolishly persuade persons to suicide; Cicero and others of the wisest men teach the immortality of the soul, but in an unbelieving manner; a good or an evil death must be weighed from the earlier life.

On the Deaths of the Persecutors

> 2 – The death and resurrection of Jesus.
>
> 3 – Domitian.

4 – The Decius persecution in A.D. 249-251.

7-14 – The persecution of the Christians by Diocletian.

33-35 – Edict of toleration of Christianity in A.D. 311 issued by Galerius on his deathbed.

44 – The battle of the Milvian Bridge.

48 – The Edict of Milan in A.D. 313 issued by Constantine which granted toleration to the Christians.

Livy
59 B.C. - A.D. 17
Titus Livius

Livy was a great Roman prose writer of the Augustan period, and a friend of Augustus. Of all of his writings, only his history has survived to today, and even most of it has been lost. Of the 142 books of this history, we have only 35 (Books 1-10 and 21-45). Although Livy's history is not always the most accurate, all historians after Livy draw their information from his work. *The Early History of Rome* begins with the story of Aeneas, who left Troy on its capture by the Greeks and settled in Italy in 753 B.C., and ends with the death of Drusus, stepson of Augustus, in 9 B.C.

❦ EXTANT WORKS ❧

The Early History of Rome

Book 1 – The earliest legends and history of Rome from 753 to 509 B.C. (expulsion of the kings).

Book 2 – The early years of the republic.

Book 3 – The decemvirate.

Book 4 – The growing power of the plebs.

Book 5 – The veii and the destruction of Rome by the Gauls.

Book 6 – (389-366 B.C.) The reconciliation of the orders.

Book 7 – (366-341 B.C.) Frontier wars.

Book 8 – (341-321 B.C.) First Samnite war and settlement of Latium.

Book 9 – (321-304 B.C.) The second Samnite war.

Book 10 – (303-293 B.C.) The third Samnite war.

Book 21 – From Saguntum to the Trebia.

Book 22 – The disaster of Cannae.

Book 23 – Hannibal at Capua.

Book 24 – The revolution in Syracuse.

Book 25 – The fall of Syracuse.

Books 26-30 – Records history to the end of the second Punic War.

Books 31-45 – Records history from the end of the second Punic War to the defeat of Macedon in 167 B.C. (34 years).

❦ SIGNIFICANT EXCERPTS ❧

The Early History of Rome

1.1-7 – The foundation of Rome (mythology).

1.19-20 – Numa Pompilius.

1.32 – The ancient Roman form of declaring war.

1.43-44 – Servius Tullius.

2.1 – The consuls.

2.2 – The king of the sacrifices.

2.5 – Brutus condemns his own sons to death (509 B.C.).

2.9-10 – How Horatius held the bridge and saved Rome from the Etruscans in 508 B.C.

2.18 – The dictators.

2.23-24, 32-33 – The secession of the plebeians and the first tribunes.

3.26-29 – How Cincinnatus saved a Roman army.

3.33-34 – The law of the twelve tables (451 B.C.).

4.1-2, 4-6, 8, 35, 42 – Further growth of the plebeian rights.

5.39-43, 47-49 – The Gallic sack of Rome in 390 B.C.

6.34-42 – How the plebeians won the consulship (376-367 B.C.).

8.8 – The reformed army.

8.14 – Municipia and colonies.

9.17-19 – What would it have been like if Alexander the Great had been alive at the time of the Roman

Empire?

21.1 – Before the Second Punic War.

21.3-4 – Hannibal.

21.10 – The speech of Hanno, who wished to deliver Hannibal into the hands of the Romans.

21.18 – How the Second Punic War was declared in 219 B.C.

21.30-38 – The march across the Alps by Hannibal and his army.

22.4-6 – The battle of Lake Trasimene and the greatness of Hannibal.

22.44-49 – The Battle of Cannae.

23.17 – The Carthaginians in Capua.

24.34 – Archimedes.

Hannibal

26.7, 9-11 – Hannibal at the gates.

27.45 – (207 B.C.) Nero marches to join his brother Consul against Hasdrubal.

28.27 – (206 B.C.) Scipio addresses his mutinous army.

30.32-35, 44-45 – The battle of Zama in 202 B.C. and the end of the Second Punic War.

33.11-12, 30-33 – Rome defeats Macedonia; their foreign policy toward Greece.

34.2 – (195 B.C.) Cato argues for the continuation of a law against feminine extravagance.

37.39 ff. – The defeat of Antiochus at Magnesia.

38.51 – (187 B.C.) The end of Scipio's greatness.

39.40 – (184 B.C.) The character of Cato.

39.51 – The death of Hannibal.

Lucan
A.D. 39-65
Marcus Annaeus Lucanus

Lucan was a Latin poet who wrote a variety of works in prose and poetry. Only one poem remains today – an epic in ten books.

❧ EXTANT WORKS ☙

The Civil War – The story of the civil war between Julius Caesar and Pompey, with bias towards Pompey.

❧ SIGNIFICANT EXCERPTS ☙

The Civil War

1.120-157 – Caesar vs. Pompey.

Lucian
C. A.D. 120-180
Lucian of Samosata

Lucian was a Greek humorist and satirist, nicknamed "the blasphemer" because in his writings he asserts that everything told about the gods is ridiculous. His writings are often obscene.

❧ EXTANT WORKS INCLUDE ☙

Dialogues of the Gods

Dialogues of the Dead

Banquet of Philosophers

The Way to Write History

The True History

The Sale of Creeds

Life of Peregrinus – An account of the life and death of a Cynic philosopher who, for a short time in his early life, followed Christianity. In this work, Lucian attacks Christianity.

🌿 SIGNIFICANT EXCERPTS 🍃

SPECIAL CAUTION ADVISED

Life of Peregrinus

11-16 – Lucian treats Christianity as an object of derision. Important to read.

Lucilius
C. 180-103 B.C.
Gaius Lucilius

Lucilius is regarded as the most original of all Roman poets. He was considered to be the inventor of satires, and wrote his satires in the form of poems which were sharp attacks upon persons, institutions, and customs of his day; full of humorous and sexually perverse remarks about the failings of his neighbors. This kind of poetry is not an imitation of anything Greek. We have only fragments of all his work left to us today – 1,300 lines in all.

🌿 EXTANT WORKS 🍃

Satires – 30 books on numerous subjects, in fragments.

Lucretius
C. 99-55 B.C.
Titus Lucretius Carus

Lucretius was a Roman Epicurean poet. Many believed that he had periods of insanity. He was a missionary for the system of Epicurus, and his poem *On the Nature of Things* is the first systematic presentation of the Epicurean doctrines. He was the first to write a Latin poem on Greek philosophy.

🌿 EXTANT WORKS 🍃

On the Nature of Things (6 books) – An artistic presentation of the philosophy of Epicureanism: pleasure is the main reason for living; is found by gaining peace of mind; and is secured by refined enjoyments, the simple life, and an avoidance of excessive passions and of political entanglements. This philosophy is based in materialism and avoids public duties. Lucretius deifies Epicurus. Of the six books, two are on the atomic theory, two on psychic processes, two on the evolution of nature and the causes of the most impressive natural phenomena.

🌿 SIGNIFICANT EXCERPTS 🍃

On the Nature of Things

3.894-977 – We shouldn't fear death; death is of less concern to us than sleep.

Lysias
C. 459-380 B.C.

Lysias was an Attic orator who was involved in politics and who wrote speeches for others to deliver in the law courts. He was a supporter of absolute democracy, and he adds to our knowledge of the ordinary life of the ancient Greeks. Thirty-five speeches (three fragmentary) under the name of Lysias have come down to us today.

🌿 EXTANT WORKS INCLUDE 🍃

Against Eratosthenes, Who Had Been One of the Thirty – A picture of the reign of terror which the Thirty established at Athens; a firsthand account (Lysias and his brother were victims of this reign); his greatest speech; written 403 B.C.

Against Agoratus: In Pursuance of a Writ – A picture of the reign of terror under the Thirty and a source for our historical information on Athens during the months following the defeat at Aegospotame; written 398 B.C.

Olympic Oration – Expresses the spirit of the festival at Olympia; calls Greeks to unite against their common enemies – Dionysius, tyrant of Syracuse, and Artaxerxes, King of Persia; criticizes the harsh policy of Sparta; written 388 B.C.

Plea for the Constitution – The well-being of Athens depends on maintaining democratic principles; written 403 B.C.

Before the Council: In Defense of Mantitheus at His Scrutiny – An Athenian makes a defense of his honor against the charge of disloyalty; written 392 B.C.

On the Refusal of a Pension to the Invalid – A funny character sketch.

Against Pancleon, Showing That He Was Not a Plataean

❧ SIGNIFICANT EXCERPTS ❧

Against Pancleon

2-11 – Picturesque glimpses of Athenian town life.

Against Agoratus

1-48 – An account of the conduct of Agoratus as an agent of the Thirty. Describes the Athenian surrender to Sparta when Sparta besieged Athens in 404 B.C. Lysias was present in Athens at the time of the siege.

Against Eratosthenes

1-24 – Lysias tells us the story of what happened to him and his brother during the reign of the Thirty.

Marcus Aurelius
A.D. 121-180
Marcus Aurelius Antoninus

Marcus Aurelius was Emperor of Rome (A.D. 161-180). Some consider him to be the last of the "good" emperors. As a youth, he was given the finest education, although the Greek moral philosophy of the Stoics came to be the most important to him. His writings express the Stoic viewpoint. He wrote his *Meditations* in Greek.

❧ EXTANT WORKS ❧

Meditations – A journal of the thoughts and observations of Marcus Aurelius.

❧ SIGNIFICANT EXCERPTS ❧

Meditations

1.1ff. – Description of the old Roman family education and the importance of family life and training

2.1, 17; 4.23, 41, 48; 5.27; 6.7, 10, 44, 54; 7.18, 28, 49;

8.16, 59; 9.23; 10.10; 11.3-4; 12.26, 32, 36 – Examples of the Stoic writings of Marcus Aurelius.

Martial
A.D. 40-104
Marcus Valerius Martialis

Martial was a Roman who made his living by writing miscellaneous verse (epigrams). Fifteen books of verse on all manner of subjects have come down to us today. He wrote to please the public, and many of his writings (one out of five, estimated) are obscene.

❧ EXTANT WORKS ❧

Epigrams

Menander
342-293 B.C.

Menander was a Greek poet and dramatist of comedy. We possess only fragments of his works.

Nepos
C. 99-24 B.C.
Cornelius Nepos

Nepos was a Roman historian and the earliest biographer. The only work of his that survives is a book of biographies of great men of Greece and Rome.

❧ EXTANT WORKS ❧

On Famous Men – Only about 25 biographies are extant.

❧ SIGNIFICANT EXCERPTS ❧

On Famous Men

Life of Atticus 13 – Atticus was Cicero's banker (and the Atticus of Cicero's letters); describes the life of a rich, cultured and nonviolent Roman.

Life of Hannibal 1-13

Life of Aristides 1-3

Life of Datames 1-11

Life of Eumenes 1-13

Nicolaus of Damascus
FL. FIRST CENTURY A.D.

Nicolaus was a Greek historian and philosopher of Damascus, and a friend of both Augustus and Herod the Great.

❧ EXTANT WORKS ❧

Life of Augustus

Universal History (in fragments)

Autobiography

❧ SIGNIFICANT EXCERPTS ❧

Life of Augustus

19-22 – A possible firsthand account (and perhaps the only one we have) of the murder of Julius Caesar in 44 B.C.

Nicomachus of Gerasa
C. A.D. 60-120

Nicomachus was a Roman mathematician, music theorist, and one of the leading members of the Pythagorean School. His *Introduction to Arithmetic* was the first work which treated arithmetic as a separate subject from geometry, and the first Greek text with a multiplication table. It also used Arabic numerals rather than Greek numerals. Nicomachus gave no abstract proofs for his theorems, as Euclid did, but only stated the theorems and gave examples for each. The work contains some elementary errors and it is believed Nicomachus had no proofs to give. For over 1,000 years this was the standard arithmetic text.

❧ EXTANT WORKS ❧

Introduction to Arithmetic

Manual of Harmonics – Concerns musical notes and the octave, along with tuning a stretched string.

The Theology of Numbers

❧ SIGNIFICANT EXCERPTS ❧

Introduction to Arithmetic

Origen
C. A.D. 185-254
Origenes Adamantius

Origen was born into a Christian home at Alexandria. He was a Biblical translator, theologian, and writer. Origen attempted to synthesize Christianity with Greek philosophy, especially Neoplatonism and Stoicism. Most of his writings have disappeared, although many have been preserved in the writings of Eusebius.

❧ EXTANT WORKS INCLUDE ❧

Against Celsus – An answer to Celsus's book *The True Word* (published about A.D. 178), which was an attack on Christianity. Celsus objects that Christians enter into secret meetings (meaning the love feasts), some of which are illegal; the origins of Judaism were barbarous; Christians practice their doctrines in secret; the morality of Christianity is neither old nor new; miracles of Christianity were done by demons; Christianity is a blind faith; Moses borrowed his ideas from other nations; the followers of Moses gave various names to their god; the Jews practiced witchcraft and worshiped angels; etc.

On First Principles – One of the first systematic theologies.

On Prayer

Letters 1 & 2

❧ SIGNIFICANT EXCERPTS ❧

Against Celsus

Book 1 – Origen lists Celsus's objections to Christianity.

Book 2 – Origen's answers to these charges.

Ovid
43 B.C.-A.D.18
Publius Ovidius Naso

Ovid was a Roman who wrote love poetry and poems about mythology. Much of his work is extremely obscene.

❧ EXTANT WORKS ❧

Amores – Love poems.

Heroides – Letters from mythical heroines to their absent husbands or lovers.

Metamorphoses – Ovid's greatest achievement; a collection of myths; the chief source of popular knowledge of mythology.

On the Care of the Face – The title tells us all.

Art of Love – One of the most immoral poems in existence; caused him to be banished.

Cure of Love – Offers various ways for freeing oneself from the bonds of passion.

Fasti – Calendar of Roman festivals.

Pacuvius
220-130 B.C.
Marcus Pacuvius

Pacuvius was a Roman who wrote tragedies based on the Greek plays. Only thirteen titles plus some fragments remain.

❧ EXTANT WORKS INCLUDE ❧

Antiopa

Armorum Iudicium

Atalanta

Chryses

Dulorestes

Hermiona

Pentheus

Niptra

Iliona

Medus

Periboea

Teucer

Pausanias
C. A.D. 143-176

Pausanias was probably born in Lydia, was a traveler of Greece, Asia Minor, Syria, Palestine, Egypt, Macedonia, and Epirus, and a geographer during the height of Roman rule. His most important work is the *Description of Greece*, which is a valuable text describing ancient ruins. The *Description of Greece* survives (in ten books) in the form of a tour of Greece starting in Attica. The first book seems to have been completed after A.D. 143, but before A.D. 161. No event after A.D. 176 is mentioned in the work. Pausanias begins his description of each city with a summary of its history followed by descriptions of monuments, temples, tombs, shrines, altars, statues, and paintings. He also discusses local daily life, ceremonial rituals, legend, and folklore. He concentrates on artistic work from classical Greece, especially religious art and architecture. His descriptions of buildings have been shown to be accurate. Pausanias used earlier writings as historical and legendary source material. The anthropologist and classical scholar Sir James Frazer said of Pausanias, "Without him, the ruins of Greece would for the most part be a labyrinth without a clue, a riddle without an answer." There is much mythology included in the writings of Pausanias.

❧ EXTANT WORKS ❧

Description of Greece – 10 books

    Book 1 – Attica and Megaris.

    Book 2 – Corinth and Argolis.

    Book 3 – Laconia.

    Book 4 – Messenia.

    Books 5-6 – Elis, including Olympia.

    Book 7 – Achaea.

    Book 8 – Arcadia.

    Book 9 – Boeotia.

Book 10 – Phocis, including Delphi.

❧ SIGNIFICANT EXCERPTS ☙

Description of Greece

1.28.8-11 – Law courts of Athens.

1.35 – The islands near Attica.

2.28.1-2; 37.4-6 – The serpents of Corinth.

5.7-9 – History of the Olympic games.

5.11 – The statue of Zeus.

5.12 – Description of the horns of different animals; the woolen curtain of Olympia.

7.16 – The decisive battle when Rome conquers Greece.

Pericles
c. 490-429 B.C.

Pericles was an Athenian statesman and orator who, from 443 B.C. until his death, assumed the leading position in the State. Pericles did not write anything himself, but his speeches were recorded by others.

❧ SIGNIFICANT EXCERPTS ☙

FROM OTHERS WRITING ABOUT PERICLES OR INCLUDING HIS WRITINGS IN THEIR WORKS

Thucydides – *History of the Peloponnesian War,* 1.139-146 – Pericles advises the Athenians to go to war against Sparta, written 432 B.C.; called "First Speech."

Thucydides – *History of the Peloponnesian War,* 2.13 – Delivered by Pericles before the Assembly at the beginning of the first campaign of the Peloponnesian War; called "Summary of a Speech."

Thucydides – *History of the Peloponnesian War,* 2.34-46 – Given at the funeral of those soldiers who were the first to die in the Peloponnesian War; a valuable statement about Athenian democracy in the fifth century; considered to be one of the finest classical speeches; written 431 B.C.; called "Funeral Speech" or "On Those Who Died in the War."

Thucydides – *History of the Peloponnesian War,* 2.59-65 – Delivered after the second invasion by the Spartans before an assembly in Athens called for the purpose, after violent criticism had been made of his influence in bringing on the Peloponnesian War; written 430 B.C.; called "Third Speech" or "In Defense of Himself."

Plutarch – *The Lives of the Noble Grecians and Romans,* Pericles 3-5, 7-9, 12-13, 29-33.

Aristotle – *The Athenian Constitution,* 27 – The dates of Pericles' enactments as derived from an official document; Aristotle gives his opinion of Pericles.

Philo
c. 20 B.C.-A.D. 45
Philo of Alexandria

Philo was a Jewish philosopher and representative of the Hellenistic Jew. He did much to advance the mixing of the Jewish religion with Greek philosophy. There are about forty extant works of Philo.

❧ EXTANT WORKS INCLUDE ☙

The Therapeutae

Embassy to Gaius

Against Flaccus

Every Good Man Is Free

On the Creation of the World

❧ SIGNIFICANT EXCEPTS ☙

Embassy to Gaius

349-373 – An historical record of an interview which some Jews had with Emperor Gaius in A.D. 40.

On the Creation of the World

1-30

The Therapeutae

  1-4 – Pre-Christian ascetics.

Every Good Man Is Free

  75-87 – On the Essenes.

Pindar
C. 522-441 B.C.

Pindar was a lyric poet born at Thebes whose only surviving works are victory odes for winners at games at Olympia, Delphi, Nemea, and the Isthmus. The poet was connected with the worship of Apollo, and his odes are religious in content.

❧ EXTANT WORKS INCLUDE ❧

Olympian Ode

Plato
427-348 B.C.

Plato was a Greek philosopher, a pupil of Socrates, and the teacher of Aristotle. He was founder of the Academic School, and was known for his dialogues in which his ideas are presented in dramatic form. According to Plutarch, Plato was one of those ancient philosophers who approved of boys taking on male lovers.

❧ EXTANT WORKS ❧

LISTED IN MORE OR LESS CHRONOLOGICAL ORDER IN
WHICH THEY WERE WRITTEN BY PLATO

Hippias Minor

Alcibiades

Apology of Socrates – This work is an account of Socrates'
defense at his trial in 399 B.C. before an Athenian court of law.

The Euthyphro – Plato describes how Socrates characterizes the virtue of piety, or fulfilling one's obligation to god and humanity.

Crito – Socrates' defense of the law and his refusal to escape from prison.

Hippias Major

Charmides

Laches

Lysis

Protagorus

Gorgias – Centered upon the never-ending conflict existing between egoistic self-interest and the demands of moral values.

The Meno – This dialogue between Socrates and Meno concerns virtue.

Phaedo – Plato's picture of the death of his master.

The Symposium – Describes a banquet which takes place in Agathon's house in 416 B.C. to honor his first victory at the dramatic festival in the Theater of Dionysus in Athens; a lewd work.

Phaedrus

Ion – In this dialogue between Socrates and Ion of Ephesus, Socrates refutes Ion's boasts.

Menexenus

Euthydemus

Cratylus

The Republic – These are the political and social views of Plato and are different in spirit and theory from the philosophy of Socrates. Plato's most famous work.

Parmenides

Theatetus

Sophist

Statesman – States some of Plato's political views more precisely than in *The Republic*.

Philebus

Timaeus – Plato's most important scientific work; a sequel to *The Republic*.

Critias

The Laws – Adapts in practical fashion his political
  dreams to human nature.

Epinomis

❧ SIGNIFICANT EXCERPTS ❧

The Republic

  7.514-521 – The allegory of the cave.

  7.525-530 – The quadrivium.

  8.555b-562a – Democracy.

  10.614a-621d – The Vision of Er.

The Laws

  3.676-703 – A survey of history, beginning with
    primitive man (the survivors of the Flood); tracing
    the origin and development of civic communities
    and their laws.

  3.700 – The decline in music and its demoralizing
    effects.

  5.726-750 – The just society.

  Book 7 – Regulations for the education of children
    in the perfect state.

  7.817e-820d – Mathematics.

Apology of Socrates

  17a-42a – Socrates' defense, his counterproposal for
    the penalty; final address to the court.

The Phaedo

  113d-118a – Death of Socrates.

Crito

  50-54 – Socrates tells us why he cannot escape from
    prison.

Gorgias

  515-517 – Plato's view of Periclean democracy.

Symposium

  219e – Describes Socrates as a soldier in 424 B.C.

Protagoras

  342e-343a – Thales.

Plautus
250-184 B.C.
Titus Maccius Plautus

Plautus was a Roman who wrote comedy plays for the
theater. His plays are Latin versions of the Greek comedies, mostly from Menander. These plays had Greek
settings and characters who were called mostly by Greek
names, but he uses Roman customs and institutions. According to Terence, the plays of Plautus were all written
to appeal to a rude and boorish audience who were more
attracted by an exhibition of boxing or walking on the
tightrope than by drama. Today we possess twenty
complete plays plus one play in fragments.

❧ EXTANT WORKS ❧

Amphitryon – Involves Jupiter's seduction of Alemena to
  conceive Hercules.

The Pot of Gold – From Menander's story of an old miser
  who discovers a treasure.

Bacchides – A young man tries to obtain money from his
  father to help him in a love affair.

The Prisoners of War – Master and slave change places to
  win back the hero's son from captivity.

The Casket Comedy – A foundling girl is reunited with
  her parents.

Menaechmi – This is the original of Shakespeare's *Comedy
  of Errors*.

Ghost Story – A young man obtains a mistress and fools
  his father.

Boastful Soldier – The boaster ends up unhappy in love.

Pseudolus – Deals with a dishonest slave merchant.

The Rope – A free-born heroine is rescued from ship-
  wreck by a villainous man.

Three Bob Day – A story of two young men.

Epidicus – The long-lost sister theme.

The Comedy of Asses – A young man asks his father for
  money to buy a beautiful prostitute.

Casina – The most obscene of Plautus's plays.

The Merchant – Similar plot to *Casina*.

Curculio – A slave merchant is about to sell the hero's
  sweetheart to a soldier.

The Girl from Persia – A graphic story of the immoral world of prostitutes.

The Little Carthaginian – A comedy concerning a pimp.

The Churl – A braggart soldier is infatuated with a scheming prostitute.

Stichus – A father tries to persuade his two daughters, whose husbands have been gone for three years, to marry again.

Pliny the Elder
C. A.D. 23-79
Gaius Plinius Secundus

Pliny was a government official during the early empire who died in the eruption of Mount Vesuvius while he was commander of the fleet at Misenum. He was a scholar and wrote numerous works. The only extant work we have is *Natural History* in 37 books, a work not particularly great, but useful for the information it contains. He preserves excerpts from hundreds of ancient writers whose works have otherwise disappeared.

EXTANT WORKS

Natural History (37 books) – Comprises thousands of facts about life, including cosmology and astronomy, physical and historical geography, physiology, zoology, botany, metallurgy, geology, etc.

SIGNIFICANT EXCERPTS

Natural History

2.2 – The shape of the earth.

2.4 – Of the elements and the planets.

2.6 – Of the nature of the stars and the motion of the planets; astrology discarded.

2.7 – Of the eclipses of the moon and the sun.

2.32-36 – The planets.

2.41-43 – The moon.

3.1.3-5 – The three parts of the earth: Europe, Asia, and Africa.

3.5 – Description of Italy and Rome – races, geography, and climate.

7.21-23 – India and Ethiopia abound with marvels.

11.69 – Physiology of the heart.

25.9-11 – Predicting eclipses.

29.112-113 – Remedies for headache.

33.6 – Complains of the Roman luxury of the times; the wearing of rings.

33.13 – The earliest coins.

35.6 f. – Early Italian painting.

36.24 – Description of the first-century A.D. city of Rome, along with some of the buildings.

Pliny the Younger
C. A.D. 62-113
Gaius Plinius Caecilius Secundus

Pliny was a Roman orator and politician, the governor of Bithynia. He was a prolific writer and one of the wealthiest private persons in the empire.

EXTANT WORKS

Letters (10 books)

Books 1-9 – Personal correspondence; 247 letters.

Book 10 – Correspondence with Emperor Trajan; 121 letters to and from Trajan.

Panegyric on Trajan – A speech delivered in the senate flattering the Emperor Trajan; this is the chief source of information concerning the history of the earlier years of Trajan's rule.

SIGNIFICANT EXCERPTS

Letters

1.6 – To Cornelius Tacitus (the historian) about how he (Pliny) likes to write even while hunting.

1.13 – To Sosius Senecio on how the people are lazy about attending the public recitations of poets and how the poets don't receive the respect due them.

2.6 – To Avitus on avoiding self-indulgence and meanness.

4.13 – To Cornelius Tacitus asking him to be on the lookout for good teachers.

6.4 – To Calpurnia his wife asking about her health.

6.16, 20 – To Tacitus describing how his uncle, Pliny the Elder, died in the eruption of Vesuvius in A.D. 79.

9.6 – Pliny complains about how grown men enjoy the chariot races.

9.36 – To Fuscus describing how he (Pliny) spends a typical day.

10.16-17, 33-34, 42-43, 62-63 – Trajan's correspondence with Pliny on various matters of state.

10.96-97 – Letter to Trajan; Pliny asks Trajan how to handle the Christians, and Trajan's answer.

Panegyric on Trajan

1-5, 12-13, 16, 21-24, 44-45, 47, 65-68, 80, 83, 94-95 – Excerpts which give a sense of this speech.

Plutarch
c. A.D. 50-125

Plutarch was a Greek biographer. After a period of study in philosophy in Athens and of travels in Egypt, Asia Minor, and Italy, Plutarch spent the remainder of his life in his native town writing books. The last twenty years of his life he served as the head priest at Delphi. His works fall into two groups, the *Moral Essays* and *The Lives of the Noble Grecians and Romans*. The *Moral Essays* are about eighty essays on various topics relating to everyday life of the Greeks and Romans – these essays are a combination of Biblical-like moralizing and pagan beliefs, along with a smattering of lewd digressions – Plutarch has been called "the first essayist." Plutarch's original plan for his *Lives* was to pair notable Greeks from past history with Romans whose careers were similar. Today only twenty-three pairs of Greeks and Romans and four single life stories remain. Most would consider Plutarch the greatest historian, even though some of his writings are rather inaccurate.

❧ EXTANT WORKS ❧

The Lives of the Noble Grecians and Romans:

Theseus and Romulus

Lycurgus and Numa

Solon and Publicola

Themistocles and Camillus

Pericles and Fabius Maximus

Alcibiades and Coriolanus

Timoleon and Aemilius Paulus

Pelopidas and Marcellus

Aristides and Cato the Elder

Philopoemen and Flamininus

Pyrrhus and Caius Marius

Lysander and Sulla

Cimon and Lucullus

Nicias and Crassus

Sertorius and Eumenes

Agesilaus and Pompey

Alexander and Julius Caesar

Phocion and Cato the Younger

Agis and Cleomenes

Tiberius and Caius Gracchus

Demosthenes and Cicero

Demetrius and Antony

Dion and Brutus

Aratus

Artaxerxes

Galba

Otho

Moral Essays:

The Education of Children

How to Tell a Flatterer from a Friend

How to Profit by One's Enemies

Advice to Bride and Groom

On Abundance of Friends

Against Running in Debt

etc.

❧ SIGNIFICANT EXCERPTS ❧

The Lives of the Noble Grecians and Romans (also called *Lives*)

Demosthenes

5-11 – Demosthenes did not possess natural speaking abilities, but had to work very hard to perfect his art.

16-18 – Demosthenes warns his fellow Greeks against Philip of Macedonia.

Pericles

3-5 – Description of Pericles.

7-9 – He rises in power among the people.

12-13 – Pericles encourages numerous building projects in Athens.

29-33 – Plutarch on the causes of the Peloponnesian War.

Alexander

4-8 – Childhood; the taming of Bucephalas; Aristotle is hired as tutor.

14-15 – Alexander prepares for an expedition against Persia.

20-21 – Alexander defeats Darius and takes the spoils.

38 – Alexander burns the Persian palace.

45 – Alexander adopts the dress of the Persians.

Solon

14 – Solon's political poetry.

24 – Solon's reforms.

29-31 – Solon and Pisistratus.

Aristides

6-8 – His virtues and faults.

22-24 – Aristides vs. Themistocles.

Numa

17 – His reforms.

Lycurgus

1-6 – Early history of Lycurgus.

8-12 – His reforms.

16-20 – The early training of boys in Sparta.

27-31 – More reforms.

Themistocles

6-15 – The Battle of Salamis.

19 – Themistocles deceives the Spartans and rebuilds the wall of Athens.

Cimon

10-11 – His generosity.

Camillus

18, 22, 27-30 – The sack of Rome by the Gauls in 390 B.C.

Marcellus

14-19 – Marcellus and Archimedes at Syracuse in 212 B.C.

Cato the Elder

4 – Cato's manner of life.

20 – Cato educates his son.

21 – How Cato treats his slaves.

23 – Cato dislike Greek learning.

25-26 – The destruction of Carthage.

Crassus

8-11 – Spartacus and the slave revolt in 73 B.C.

Gaius Marius

13 – Marian mules.

32-35 – Marius vs. Sulla.

Sulla

31-33 – Sulla's reign of terror.

Pompey

24-29 – The war against the pirates.

Julius Caesar

15 – Caesar surpasses all men.

57-58 – Caesar is kind to his enemies and makes plans for numerous projects.

59 – The calendar is adjusted.

62-69 – Caesar is murdered.

Aratus

4-9 – How Aratus took Sicyon from the tyrant Nicocles.

Moral Essays:

Against Running in Debt

Polybius
c. 200-123 B.C.

Polybius was a Greek historian who lived during the Roman conquest of Greece. He wrote about the period of Roman history from 264 B.C. (outbreak of the First Punic War) to 144 B.C. (destruction of Carthage and Corinth). Polybius states why he wrote this universal history: "Can anyone be so indifferent or idle as not to care to know by what means, and under what kind of polity, almost the whole inhabited world was conquered and brought under the domination of the single city of Rome, and that too within a period of not quite fifty-three years?" (Book 1, section 1)

Polybius lived his first thirty years in Greece. He held high offices in the government. In 168 B.C. he was taken as hostage to Rome, where he lived for the next 20-25 years. He had total freedom in Rome to study all the many books and documents which the city was acquiring rapidly with all Rome's conquests. He became a tutor and advisor to the head of Rome's armies, so he was able to add to his knowledge an understanding of Rome's military power. He witnessed campaigns and battles and went on numerous rare sea voyages. These travels and studies provided material for his great work, *The Histories*, which consisted of forty books, of which only Books I to V have survived intact, while we have only fragments of the other books.

Here is an interesting passage from Book VI, section 5:

"Now the natural laws which regulate the transformation of one form of government into another are perhaps discussed with greater accuracy by Plato and some other philosophers. But their treatment, from its intricacy and exhaustiveness, is within the capacity of only a few. I will therefore endeavour to give a summary of the subject, just so far as I suppose it to fall within the scope of a serious history and the intelligence of ordinary people. . . ."

Apparently students have always had a hard time understanding Plato!

EXTANT WORKS

The Histories

Book 1 – The earlier history of Rome; Roman interventions with Greek city-states; the first Punic War in 264 B.C.

Book 2 – Rivalry between Romans and Carthaginians in Spain; Carthaginians led by Hamilcar, then Hasdrubal.

Book 3 – Outbreak of Second Punic War; Hannibal's crossing of the Alps into Italy.

Book 4 – Greek affairs.

Book 5 – Treaty by King Philip V of Macedonia with Hannibal, leading to subsequent Roman intervention.

Book 6 – State constitutions.

Book 7 – Begins annalistic style, describing events year by year; each book covers an Olympiad (four-year period).

Books 7-15 – Second Punic War to Scipio the elder's victory at Zama.

Book 16 – Second Macedonian War.

Book 31 – Full portrait of Scipio Africanus the younger.

Final Books – Scipio's conquest of Carthage in the Third Punic War; sack of Corinth, 144 B.C.

❧ SIGNIFICANT EXCERPTS ❧

The Histories

1.1-5 – Polybius tells us he is writing this history to show how great Rome has become; describes the three great empires which came before Rome and how Rome is greater than all three.

1.35 – Why study history.

1.56-58 – Hamilcar.

1.59-63 – The description of the final Roman effort and the terms of peace in 241 B.C.

2.1 – Hamilcar.

2.14-16 – Description of Italy.

2.17 – The Etruscans.

2.37-63 – Aratus of Sicyon and the Achaean League (established in 280 B.C.).

3.6-10, 14-15, 20-22, 27-30 – Causes of the Second Punic War.

3.22 – The first treaty between Rome and Carthage (509 B.C.).

3.33-56 – Hannibal crosses the Alps.

3.91 – Description of Italy.

5.84-86 – How elephants fought in Hellenistic armies.

6.2-19, 21-24, 38-39, 43-57 – Description of the Roman Constitution and the Roman army.

8.5.3-5 – Archimedes.

9.22-26 – The character of Hannibal.

11.19 – The greatness of Hannibal.

18.28-32 – Comparison between the armies of the Romans and the Macedonians.

38.3-6 – The misery of the fall of Greece.

38.7 – Description of Hasdrubal the Carthaginian general during the Roman destruction of Carthage in 146 B.C.

38.9-11 – Outbreak of the Achaean War.

Priscus
FL. FIFTH CENTURY A.D.

Priscus wrote (in Greek) a history in eight books, but only fragments remain.

❧ EXTANT WORKS ❧

History

❧ SIGNIFICANT EXCERPTS ❧

History

Fragment 8 – A visit by Priscus in A.D. 448 to the court of Attila the Hun; gives a picture of the Huns which is different from other sources.

Prudentius
C. A.D. 348-410
Aurelius Clemens Prudentius

Prudentius was the greatest of the Latin Christian poets. He held a high position in the Roman court, but later devoted himself to religious asceticism.

❧ EXTANT WORKS ❧

Against Symmachus – Shows how the Christian writers joined with pagans in regarding Rome as sovereign.

Book of Hymns for Every Day – A collection of lyric poems for the sanctification of the hours of the day or for particular important occasions.

Book of the Martyrs' Crowns – A collection of lyric poems dedicated to the martyrs.

The Divinity of Christ – A teaching poem on the doctrine of the Trinity.

The Origin of Sin – A teaching poem on the doctrine of the origin of sin.

The Spiritual Combat – The battle for the soul of man; an allegorical poem on morals and apologetics.

Scenes from Sacred History – A teaching poem on the events of the Old and New Testaments.

❧ SIGNIFICANT EXCERPTS

Against Symmachus

Pyrrho of Elis
C. 365-275 B.C.

Pyrrho was a Greek philosopher and founder of the Skeptic school.

❧ SIGNIFICANT EXCERPTS ❧

FROM OTHERS WRITING ABOUT PYRRHO OR INCLUDING HIS WRITINGS IN THEIR WORKS

Diogenes Laertius – *Lives of the Philosophers*, Pyrrho

Pythagoras
C. 582-500 B.C.

Pythagoras was a Greek philosopher, mathematician, and founder of a religious order. He taught the transmigration of the soul. He was one of the first to hold that the earth and the universe are spherical in shape. None of his writings have survived.

❧ SIGNIFICANT EXCERPTS ❧

FROM OTHERS WRITING ABOUT PYTHAGORAS OR INCLUDING HIS WRITINGS IN THEIR WORKS

Diogenes Laertius – *Lives of the Philosophers*, Pythagoras.

Strabo – *Ancient Geography*, 10.3.10 – Pythagoras's theory of music.

Diodorus Siculus – *Historical Library*, 10.3-11.

Quintilian
C. A.D. 35-100
Marcus Fabius Quintilianus

Quintilian was a man of great influence under Domitian. He had special skills in oratory, and was trained in rhetoric by his father. He believed that oratory was the highest expression of human thought and human life, and that the education of an orator should begin in his cradle.

❧ EXTANT WORKS ❧

The Education of an Orator (12 books) – The first book is about the elements of elementary education and contains interesting observations on family life; the second book is about the fundamental principles of rhetoric; the next five books deal with oratory under the main headings of invention and disposition; four books concern expression and all that is included in the word "style," with a discussion of memorizing and delivery; and the last book discusses the needed moral qualities and self-discipline of the orator.

❧ SIGNIFICANT EXCERPTS ❧

The Education of an Orator

Preface 24-25 – Quintilian's view of dry textbooks.

Preface 26-27 – Without the help of nature (voice, strong lungs, good health, etc.), precepts and techniques are powerless.

1.1 – The early education of an orator; learning to read and write letters, syllables, and complete words.

1.2 – Should the future orator be taught at home or in school?

1.3 – Advice to teachers on determining abilities in children; against corporal punishment.

1.8 – Reading for boys.

1.10 – What other arts should the orator learn?

2.1 – At what age should a student be sent to the rhetor?

2.7 – The value of memorization.

2.15 – The nature and purpose of rhetoric.

2.19 – Which matters more, nature or teaching?

3.3 – The five divisions of rhetoric.

10.1.105-112 – Cicero's and Demosthenes' merits as orators.

10.3 – How to write.

10.7 – The power of improvisation.

Quintus Curtius
FL. MID-FIRST CENTURY A.D.
Quintus Curtius Rufus

Quintus Curtius was a Roman. He wrote a biography of Alexander the Great which is the only such work in Latin to come down to us. His work originally consisted of ten books – the first two are lost, and the remaining are incomplete. His work is very easy to read.

EXTANT WORKS

History of Alexander

SIGNIFICANT EXCERPTS

History of Alexander

3.11 – A description of the battle between Alexander and Darius.

4.4.1-5 – A huge sea monster appears during Alexander's siege of Tyre.

4.4.10-21 – The fall of Tyre.

4.7 – Alexander's difficult journey through the desert to Egypt to visit the oracle of Jupiter Ammon; the priest says Alexander is the son of Jupiter and Alexander agrees that he is a deity.

4.9 – Alexander crosses the Tigris River in pursuit of Darius.

Alexander on horse

4.10.1-7 – Alexander's soldiers are frightened by an eclipse of the moon, but are persuaded to continue.

5.1.17-35 – Alexander takes Babylon; description of Babylon.

5.7 – Alexander, in a drunken stupor, orders the burning of the palace at Persepolis.

7.4.20-25 – The Hindu Kush.

8.9 – Alexander marches into India; a description of India.

9.9 – Alexander finally reaches the ocean.

10.5 – Alexander dies.

Sallust
86-34 B.C.
Gaius Sallustius Crispus

Sallust was a Roman historian. He served as quaestor and tribune in his early life, and devoted himself to historical writing in his later years. He is considered a primary source because he wrote about the history he helped to make. In his writings, Sallust appears as an opponent of the nobility and a defender of the popular party. He describes the corruption and greed of the senate and he praises the hero Marius. His political bias sometimes causes him to distort the truth, but his work is still of historical value. He imitates the style of Thucydides, and he introduces speeches and letters written by the persons he is writing about.

❧ EXTANT WORKS ❧

The Conspiracy of Catiline – The conspiracy of the year 66 B.C., which was abandoned; the conspiracy of the years 64-63 B.C., which became a serious problem to Rome until it was exposed by Cicero in 63 B.C.

The Jugurthine War – Describes the war waged by Rome against Jugurtha, King of Numidia from 111-105 B.C.

The Histories – Recorded events from 78 to 67 B.C.; only fragments remain.

❧ SIGNIFICANT EXCERPTS ❧

The Conspiracy of Catiline

1 – Opening words of the document.

31 – The terror at Rome when the greatness of the danger from the conspiracy of Catiline became known.

51 – Speech of Caesar to the Senate on the punishment of the conspirators.

The Jugurthine War

10 – The last words of Micipsa to his grandson Jugurtha.

63-65 – Life and character of Marius.

84-86 – Marius, on his election as Consul, addresses the people upon the obstructive policy of the Nobles.

Salvian
C. A.D. 400-492

Salvian was born in Gaul. He became a priest and a monk, and he was a well known preacher and teacher of rhetoric.

❧ EXTANT WORKS ❧

Of God's Government (8 books) – Salvian believed that the troubles of the present times were punishments from God which the Romans had brought upon themselves by their sin and greed. He believed that the Romans, though educated and civilized, were inferior to the barbarians, who were untaught, and that the Germanic invaders were becoming acceptable to many people. It was Salvian's belief that the circus, amphitheatre, and theatre had a corrupting influence on the people.

Against Avarice – Salvian encourages people to be generous in giving money to the Church.

9 Letters

❧ SIGNIFICANT EXCERPTS ❧

Of God's Government

5.4 – The oppression continues after Diocletian.

6.1-18 – The people love the public games and theatre more than going to church.

7.6 – Comparison of Romans and barbarians.

7.16 – An example of the moral condition of the empire.

7.23 – Salvian's view of Socrates.

Letters

4 – Letter to Salvian's in-laws after Salvian and his wife decide to end their marriage and become a monk and a nun.

Sappho
C. 610-570 B.C.

Sappho was a female lyric poet from the island of Lesbos. Her poems are about love and yearning and have a sensual nature about them. Most of her poems have been lost.

Seneca
4 B.C.-A.D.65
Lucius Annaeus Seneca

Seneca was a Roman philosopher, statesman, orator and

author of tragedies. He was tutor to the child Nero, and was later influential in helping Nero to run the empire. He wrote much, and although most of his works are now lost, we still possess nine tragedies (which are mostly imitations of Greek tragedies), moral letters, philosophical treatises (Seneca is the most complete communicator of the Stoic philosophy as it developed at Rome), a satire on the death of Claudius, and a few epigrams. Some say that Seneca was a hypocrite who did not practice what he preached in his Stoic writings. Some tradition says that Seneca exchanged fourteen letters with the Apostle Paul, but there is no proof of this.

❧ EXTANT WORKS ❧

9 Tragedies:

Medea (an imitation of the tragedy of Euripides by the same name)

Hercules Furens

Troades

Phoenissae

Phaedra

Oedipus

Agamemnon

Thyestes

Hercules on Mount Oeta

124 *Moral Letters* (20 books) – Letters (actually sermons) addressed to Lucilius, procurator of Sicily; these are philosophical works.

Studies of Nature (7 books) – On astronomy, physical geography, and meteorology from the Stoic perspective.

Apocolocyntosis – A political satire on the death of Claudius.

12 *Moral Essays* – On Providence; On Firmness; On Anger; On Mercy; On Consolation to Marclam; On the Happy Life; On Leisure; On Tranquility of Mind; On the Shortness of Life; On Consolation to Polybius; On Consolation to Helvia; On Benefits.

❧ SIGNIFICANT EXCERPTS ❧

Moral Letters:

7 – Seneca's opinion of the arena and of crowds.

47 – Slaves are human beings.

84 – What we read should be properly digested.

Essay on Benefits

3.27 – Seneca shows how Augustus became more lenient and kind during the last part of his reign.

4.5-7; 1.2 – God's gifts to man.

Essay on Providence

4 – How a Stoic should react to calamity.

Studies of Nature

Book 3 Preface – A Stoic message.

Essay On Consolation to Helvia

16.1 – Letter to comfort his mother.

Socrates
c. 470-399 B.C.

Socates was a Greek philosopher in Athens. As far as we know, he wrote nothing. We include him here because he is so often written about.

Sir Alexander Grant writes concerning Socrates:

Xenophon omits to mention one peculiarity of Socrates which we learn from Plato – namely, his strange fits of protracted reverie, almost amounting to trance. But he is full of allusions to the Daemon, or divine mentor, under whose guidance Socrates laid claim to act. The whole life of Socrates was represented by himself as being ordered under the direction of internal signs from the gods, which told him what to do and what not to do. He thoroughly believed in the reality of these intimations . . . . But Socrates by habit learnt more and more to recognize and obey. And thus his whole life took the form of a mission, which consisted in improving others, both in intellect and character, by his conversations. . . .

He voluntarily adopted a life of austere simplicity and poverty, entirely devoted to what he considered his spiritual calling. India of the present day throws light on many of the features of ancient Greek society, and in India such lives of renunciation and of contented poverty are not unfrequent. Often in the Indian bazaars may you see Socrates, or something like him, in the person of some stout Brahman, good-humouredly lounging about in loose robes and with bare legs, ready to discuss for hours, with all comers, any topic that may turn up. . . .

Socrates' last hour

Socrates, it appears, made a point of not departing from conformity with the usual religious ceremonies of his country. He also encouraged others in the use of divination, while he himself relied on the intimations of his daemon or familiar spirit. . . ." (Sir Alexander Grant, *Xenophon* [Edinburgh: William Blackwood and Sons, 1871])

Xenophon records the words of Socrates in the following two works:

Memorabilia – As a young Athenian noble, Xenophon became a disciple of Socrates, and preserved his recollections of his teacher in four books. It is a collection of discussions between Socrates and young Athenian men, and is in defense of the philosopher.

The Apology of Socrates

Plato records the words of Socrates in:

Apology of Socrates – This work is an account of Socrates' defense at his trial in 399 B.C. before an Athenian court of law.

The Euthyphro – Plato describes how Socrates characterizes the virtue of piety, or fulfilling one's obligation to god and humanity.

Crito – Socrates' defense of the law and his refusal to escape from prison.

The Meno – This dialogue between Socrates and Meno concerns virtue.

The Phaedo – Plato's picture of the death of his master.

Ion – In this dialogue between Socrates and Ion of Ephesus, Socrates refutes Ion's boasts.

❧ SIGNIFICANT EXCERPTS ☙

FROM OTHERS WRITING ABOUT SOCRATES

Plato, *Apology of Socrates* 17a-42a – Socrates' defense, his counterproposal for the penalty; final address to the court.

Plato, *The Phaedo* 113d-118a – The scene where Socrates dies.

Plato, *Crito* 50-54 – Socrates tells us why he cannot escape from prison.

Plato, *Symposium* 219e – Describes Socrates as a soldier in 424 B.C.

Diogenes Laertius, *Lives of the Philosophers*, Socrates

Socrates Scholasticus
C. A.D. 380-439

Socrates Scholasticus was a Church historian who continued the work of Eusebius for the period A.D. 305-439. His work (written in Greek) is considered to be objective and depends on primary sources (acts of councils, the chronicle of Constantinople, letters of kings and bishops). He also included details of the military history of the time.

❧ EXTANT WORKS ☙

History of the Church

    Book 1 – Constantine (305-337)

    Book 2 – Constantius (337-360)

    Book 3 – Julian and Jovian (360-364)

    Book 4 – Valens (364-378)

    Book 5 – Theodosius the Great (379-395)

    Book 6 – Arcadius (393-408)

    Book 7 – Theodosius the Younger (408-439)

❧ SIGNIFICANT EXCERPTS ☙

History of the Church

    1.2 – How Constantine became a Christian.

    1.5-6 – The beginnings of the Arian controversy.

    1.9 – The Council of Nicea; letters from Constantine.

    1.16 – Constantine founds Constantinople.

    1.17 – Constantine's mother Helena finds the actual cross of Christ in Jerusalem.

    1.18 – Constantine abolishes paganism.

    1.40 – The funeral of Constantine.

    3.1 – The account of the Emperor Julian.

    3.11 – Julian takes money from the Christians.

    3.12 – Julian forbids Christians from entering literary pursuits.

    3.13 – Julian persecutes the Christians; the fake Christians are revealed.

3.16 – Julian forbade Christians to study Greek literature; Socrates' argument for why Christians should study Greek literature.

4.11 – Large hail and earthquakes.

4.12 – Nicene Creed.

5.17 – The symbol of the cross found in the Temple of Serapis, claimed by Christians and pagans alike.

5.22 – The author's views on Easter, baptism, fasting, marriage, the eucharist, etc.

7.10 – Rome taken by Alaric.

7.15 – Murder of Hypatia, the female philosopher.

7.16 – Jews kill a Christian child and are punished.

7.22 – Virtues of Theodosius II.

7.42 – Panegyric of Theodosius II.

Solon
C. 638-558 B.C.

Solon was an Athenian statesman who also wrote poetry. He was known as one of the Seven Wise Men of Greece. His reforms prepared the way for the introduction of democracy in Athens. Few of his poems have survived except in fragments.

❧ SIGNIFICANT EXCERPTS ☙

FROM OTHERS WRITING ABOUT SOLON OR INCLUDING HIS WRITINGS IN THEIR WORKS

Plutarch – *The Lives of the Noble Grecians and Romans*, Solon 14, 24, 29-31

Aristotle – *The Athenian Constitution* 5-12

Demosthenes – *On the Embassy* 255

Diogenes Laertius – *Lives of the Philosophers*, Solon

Herodotus – *The History* 1.29-33

Diodorus Siculus – *Historical Library* 9.1, 3-4, 20, 26-27

Sophocles
C. 495-406 B.C.

Sophocles was one of the trio of great Greek tragic dra-matists (Sophocles, Aeschylus, Euripides). His tragedies centered around the familiar fables and myths of his culture. He was a very sexually perverse and immoral man. Only seven of his original 123 works are extant today. The plots of all of the tragedies of Sophocles, Aeschylus, and Euripides are not original with these men. Rather, they are the retelling of myths which had been around for many centuries, mostly from Homer and Hesiod.

❧ EXTANT WORKS ☙

Ajax – When Achilles is killed, his armor is offered as a prize to the best of the other Greeks, but it is awarded to Odysseus instead of to Ajax. Ajax tries to murder Odysseus and the leaders of the army, Agamemnon and Menelaus. However, Athena (a goddess) drives him mad, so that he attacks the cattle, torturing and killing them and making a fool of himself. Ajax kills himself.

Oedipus the King (*Oedipus Rex*) – Jocasta and Laius, the rulers of Thebes, learn from an oracle that their son will kill his father and marry his mother. When Jocasta gives birth to Oedipus, he is set out in the field to die. He is saved from death, however, and later kills Laius, not knowing he was his father. When Thebes is afflicted by the Sphinx, who kills all who cannot answer her riddle, he solves the riddle, and the Sphinx kills herself. In reward, Oedipus becomes king, and marries his mother, Jocasta. They give birth to four children. Eventually he learns the truth. Jocasta hangs herself, and Oedipus puts out his own eyes. Sigmund Freud appropriated the plot of *Oedipus* in his perverse theories of sexuality.

Antigone – Antigone is one of the four children (Antigone, Ismene, Eteocles, Polynices) of Oedipus, king of Thebes, and Jocasta (mother, then wife, of Oedipus). At the beginning of this play Oedipus is dead, his two sons, Eteocles and Polynices, quarrel over the kingship, and end by killing each other. Creon, Jocasta's brother, becomes king. Creon orders Eteocles to be buried with due rites, and Polynices to be left unburied, as a traitor. Antigone says that Creon has no right to do this, and attempts to bury her brother Polynices. Creon has Antigone shut up in a lonely vault. He later changes his mind and opens the vault, but Antigone has hanged herself. Creon's son, who was to have married Antigone, commits suicide. Creon's wife hangs herself. Considered to be one of the world's greatest plays.

The Women of Trachis – A woman, Deianeira, learns that her husband, the great hero Heracles, loves another woman. She sends him a robe anointed with what she thinks is a love potion. It is poisonous, and causes his death. She kills herself.

Electra – Agamemnon sacrifices his daughter Iphigeneia to the goddess Artemis when she becalms the Greek army at Aulis, so that it cannot sail for Troy. In his long absence, his wife Clytemnestra takes a lover, Aegisthus, and the pair kills Agamemnon on his return. Orestes, Agamemnon's son, grows up in exile and at last comes home and kills Aegisthus and his mother with the help of his sister, Electra.

Philoctetes – Philoctetes is an archer who leads seven ships to Troy. He owns the bow of Heracles, whose arrows were inescapable. But on the way to Troy, he is bitten by a serpent during a sacrifice, and the wound festers. The Greeks therefore leave him on the island of Lemnos. But when the Trojan prophet Helenus is captured by Odysseus and tells them that Philoctetes is needed if Troy was to be taken, Diomedes goes to Lemnos and brings Philoctetes. The hero is healed by Machaon the physician, and then with his bow kills Paris, whose abduction of Helen was the cause of the war.

Oedipus at Colonus – The story of the death of Oedipus.

Sozomen
c. a.d. 400-448
Hermias Salamanes Sozomenus

Sozomen was a Church historian, born in Palestine to Christian parents. His *Ecclesiastical History* continued where Eusebius ended and is similar to the work of Socrates Scholasticus.

❧ EXTANT WORKS ❧

Ecclesiastical History (9 books) – Covers history from Constantine in A.D. 323 down to the death of Honorius in A.D. 423.

Books 1-2 – The reign of Constantine.

Book 3-4 – The reigns of Constantine's sons.

Book 5-6 – The reigns of Julian, Jovan, Valentinian I, and Valens.

Book 7-8 – The reigns of Gratian, Valentinian II, Theodosius I, and Arcadius.

Book 9 – The reign of Theodosius the Younger (incomplete).

❧ SIGNIFICANT EXCERPTS ❧

Ecclesiastical History

1.15 – The Arian heresy.

1.20-21 – Constantine condemns Arius.

2.3 – Constantine begins to transform Byzantium into the new Christian capital of the Roman Empire in A.D. 324.

Constantine

2.32 – Constantine prohibits people from holding church in any place but the Catholic Church.

5.1, 3-5, 16 – Julian's measures against the Christians and his favors towards the pagans.

5.18 – Julian forbids the children of Christians to be instructed in the writings of the Greek poets and authors and to go to the public schools.

Strabo
c. 66 b.c.-a.d. 24

Strabo was a Greek historian and geographer writing in the early days of the Roman Empire under the first two Roman emperors, Augustus and Tiberius. (His history has been lost.) Much of his geographical information is from his personal observation from his many travels. In a passage from his second book he says: "Our descriptions shall consist of what we ourselves have observed in our travels by land and sea, and of what we conceive to be credible in the statements and writings of others; for in a westerly direction we have traveled from Armenia to that part of Tyrrhenia which is over against Sardinia; and southward, from the Euxine to the frontiers of Ethiopia. Of all the writers on geography, not one can be mentioned who has traveled over a wider extent of the countries described than we have. Some may have gone farther to the west, but then they have never been so far east as we have; again, others may have been farther east, but not so far west; and the same with respect to north and south. However, in the main, both we and they have availed ourselves of the reports of others, from which to describe the form, size, and other peculiarities of the country." The seventeen volumes of his *Ancient Geography* provide information on the geography of the ancient world from the Atlantic Ocean in the west to the Indus River in the east.

EXTANT WORKS

Ancient Geography

Books 1-2 – Preliminaries and theory; definition of geography; critique of predecessors.

Book 3 – Spain.

Book 4 – Gaul, Britain, Alps.

Book 5 – Northern Italy.

Book 6 – Southern Italy and Sicily.

Book 7 – Northern and Central Europe; epitome of Thrace and Macedon.

Book 8 – Macedon and Greece.

Book 9 – Attica, Boeotia, Thessaly.

Book 10 – Aetolia, Crete.

Book 11 – Asia Minor.

Book 12 – Asia Minor.

Book 13 – Asia Minor.

Book 14 – Asia Minor.

Book 15 – India and Parthia.

Book 16 – Assyria, Babylonia, Syria, Arabia.

Book 17 – Egypt, Ethiopia, Libya.

SIGNIFICANT EXCERPTS

Ancient Geography

1.1.20-21 – The condition of science at this time.

1.4.1-9 – Critique of Eratosthenes.

1.4.9 – Character of Alexander.

2.5.1-4 – Description of Strabo's principles.

3.5.11 – The Cassiterides Islands.

4.1.4,5 – Massalia.

5.3 – The founding and grandeur of Rome.

5.4.8 – Mt. Vesuvius pre-eruption – it erupted August 24, A.D. 79.

6.3.1 – Colossus of Zeus.

7.6.2 – Byzantium.

8.1.2 – The tribes of Greece and their Greek dialects.

9.1.16-17 – On Attica.

10.3.10 – Pythagoras's theory of music.

11.14.2 – The Tigris and Euphrates Rivers.

16.1.5 – Description of the walls and hanging gardens of Babylon.

16.1.7 – Bats used for food.

16.1.9-13 – The canals of Babylon.

16.1.14-15 – The products of Babylon.

16.2.22-24 – Physical description of Sidon and Tyre.

16.2.26 – A strange occurrence of the sea.

16.2.34-46 – Judea; Strabo's version of the Moses story.

17.1.4 – Description of the Nile River.

17.1.6-10 – The city of Alexandria.

17.1.52-54; 17. 2.4-5 – A description of Egypt under the principate.

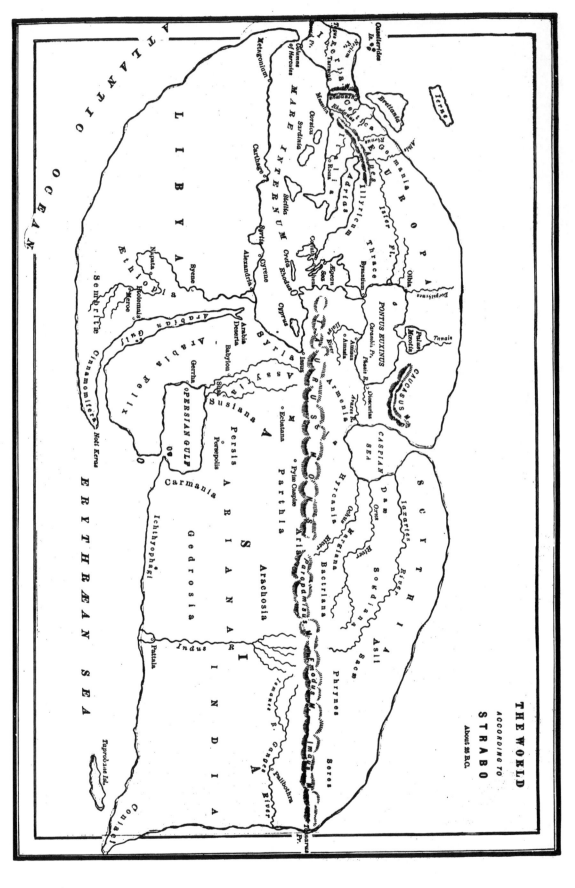

Map of the world according to Strabo

Suetonius

C. A.D. 75-150

Gaius Suetonius Tranquillus

Suetonius was Latin secretary to the Emperor Hadrian, and had access to important archives. This made it possible for him to write a careful biography of the twelve Caesars based on primary sources which are now lost. He was not a great writer, but he was a diligent and impartial compiler of interesting information. Suetonius had a flair for the sensational, and recorded many of the scandalous stories and gossip concerning the emperors. Portions of his work are not suitable to read.

❧ EXTANT WORKS ❧

Lives of the Twelve Caesars (8 books) – Julius Caesar, Augustus, Tiberius, Caligula, Claudius, Nero, Galba, Otho, Vitellius, Vespasian, Titus, and Domitian; published in A.D. 121.

On Illustrious Men – A series of biographies of Latin poets, orators, historians, philosophers, grammarians, and rhetoricians. Much is lost.

❧ SIGNIFICANT EXCERPTS ❧

Lives of the Twelve Caesars

Julius Caesar 1-2, 10, 14, 20, 25, 31-36, 55-56, 82.

Nero

Nero 6-10, 20, 30-31, 38, 49, 57.

Nero 16.2 – Nero persecutes the Christians in A.D. 64.

Claudius 4 – A letter written by Augustus in A.D. 10 and preserved by Suetonius; describes the character of the young Claudius; 25.4 – The expulsion of the Jews from Rome (cf. Acts 18.2); 30 – A physical description of Claudius.

Augustus 5, 8, 28, 31, 35, 47-49, 76-77, 81

Tiberius 36 – He suppresses Jewish rites.

Caligula 8.1, 9, 11, 13, 19, 22; 8.23.2; 8.26.2-5; 8.30.1; 8.50; 8.54; 8.55.3; 8.57.1-2; 8.58

Vitellius 13 – The gluttony of Vitellius in A.D. 69.

Vespasian 1, 4-5, 7-9, 16, 18, 25

Domitian 4 – Domitian amuses the Roman people by providing games and arena massacres.

Tacitus coin

Tacitus

A.D. 55-120

Publius Cornelius Tacitus

Tacitus was a Roman public speaker, government official, and historian. After he retired, he devoted his time to writing. He purposed to leave a record of the evils of tyranny under the emperors from Tiberius to Domitian.

❧ EXTANT WORKS ❧

Dialogue on Orators – An inquiry into the causes of the decay of oratory; published in 79-81.

Germania – This is the earliest extant connected account of Germany and the inhabitants of northern Europe.

Agricola – A biography of Gnaeus Julius Agricola, Tacitus's father-in-law; published in A.D. 98.

Histories (4 books and a fragment are extant) – A history of Tacitus's own times; most is lost, but the year A.D. 69-70 is left to us.

Annals (16 books) – A history of events before the time of Tacitus (from the death of Augustus to the death of Nero); much of this is lost, but the extant portions cover the reign of Tiberius, the last seven years of Claudius, and the first twelve years of Nero's reign.

❧ SIGNIFICANT EXCERPTS ❧

Histories

1.1-50 – Galba.

3.32 – Sack of Cremona by the troops of Vespasian.

Annals

1.1-15 – Brief description of Roman political history before Augustus; purpose of Tacitus in writing the Annals; Augustus had undermined republican liberty; Tiberius and the early events of his reign.

1.16-30 – The mutiny of the Pannonian Legions in A.D. 14 after the accession of Tiberius.

2.47, 86-87 – Administration of Tiberius.

4.1-2, 57-58, 64 – Tiberius is unpopular.

6.16-17 – A business dilemma in Rome in A.D. 33 which reveals business conditions at the time; the currency; laws concerning interest.

6.51 – Tiberius is unpopular.

11.13, 23-25 – Reforms of Claudius.

11.14 – Short history of the alphabet – Claudius adds three letters which are later abandoned.

12.23-24 – Reforms of Claudius.

13.15-17 – Nero murders Britannicus – an example of the sort of crimes Nero perpetrated.

13.31-32 – The trial of Pomponia Graecina in A.D. 57 (reference to Christianity, a foreign superstition).

13.50-51 – Nero.

15.38-44 – The great fire at Rome in A.D. 64; how Nero blamed the Christians.

Agricola

2 – Tacitus gives his reasons for having written nothing during the reign of Domitian; his view of the imperial government in the first century.

10-12, 29-30 – Britian.

19-21, 39-40 – Domitian.

46 – Agricola's name shall live forever.

Dialogue on Orators

28-29, 34-35 – On the education of children – the old way and the new.

Germania

4-23, 45-46 – Customs of the Germans in A.D. 100.

Terence
195-159 B.C.
Publius Terentius Afer

Originally a slave, Terence wrote comedy plays (in Latin) imitating the Greek classics of Menander and Apollodorus. Most of his plays involve an immoral love intrigue. Six of his plays are extant.

❧ EXTANT WORKS ❧

Girl From Andros

Mother-in-Law

Self-Punisher

Eunuch

Phormio

Adelphi

Tertullian
C. A.D. 160-230
Quintus Septimius Florens Tertullianus

Tertullian was born in North Africa and was brought up as a pagan, but was converted to Christianity as an adult. Tertullian was a prominent defender of the Christian faith and rejected Greek or Roman philosophy. He is known as the first of the Latin Church Fathers for his great achievement of developing a vocabulary adequate to express in Latin the Biblical theology which was already expressed in Greek. His writing is easy to understand and is filled with witty and amusing statements. There are only thirty-one extant treatises left to us of Tertullian's works.

❧ EXTANT WORKS ❧

Prescriptions against Heretics – How to debate with the heretics; how not to use the Bible when arguing with pagans.

Against Hermogenes – Hermogenes promoted ideas about the material universe.

Against the Jews – Compares Judaism with Christianity.

To Scapula – A letter to the Proconsul, telling him it will be dangerous to persecute the Christians because it may hurt the province.

Against Marcion – An argument against Marcion's Bible which omits the Old Testament.

Against Praxeas – Tertullian invents the word "Trinity."

Against the Valentinians

Apology – It is the pagans who should be spoken against, not the Christians.

On the Testimony of the Soul – An appendix to the *Apology.*

To the Nations – Similar to the *Apology.*

On the Soul

On Baptism – Discusses baptism.

On the Flesh of Christ – How Christians should conduct themselves in the world.

To the Martyrs – Encouragement to the persecuted.

To My Wife – Advice to his wife if he should die.

On the Garland – More on persecution.

On Female Fashion

On an Exhortation to Chastity – Discusses the matter of remarriage for the widowers and widows.

On Running Away from Persecution

On the Resurrection of the Flesh

Antidote to the Gnostics – Tertullian's answer to the heretics who say that it is alright to swear to pagan gods to avoid persecution.

On Monogamy – Remarriage is sin.

On Prayer – The Lord's Prayer.

On Repentance – Church discipline.

On the Philosopher's Cloak – Christianity is the only true philosophy.

On Patience

On Modesty – The church is made up of the body of Christ, not of a group of bishops.

On Idolatry – How to live in the world without being corrupted by it.

On Fasting, Against the Carnal Believers – Can Christians serve Christ and still live like pagans.

On the Games – Christians shouldn't be going to the games.

On Head-Coverings for Unmarried Girls

❧ SIGNIFICANT EXCERPTS ❧

Apology

2 – Tertullian on persecution.

5 – Bad emperors are the only persecutors; Marcus Aurelius was a good emperor.

29-32 – Christian loyalty to the emperor.

39 – How the Church helps the poor and those in jail.

Against the Jews

4 – The observance of the Sabbath.

7 – Christianity has spread to all the world.

Prescriptions against Heretics

7 – The place of ancient philosophy in Christianity.

Against Marcion

4.5 – The condition of the canon of the Bible.

On Idolatry

10 – It is difficult to be a schoolmaster and a Christian.

11 – Certain trades should be avoided.

12 – Answers the question, "Then, how am I to live?" regarding which trade to take; not participating in idolatry.

18 – Dress and idolatry.

To the Nations

2-3 – Philosophers did not succeed in discovering God.

Against Praxeas

2 – The term Trinity is first used.

Thales
C. 624-546 B.C.

Thales is the first known Greek philosopher, scientist, and mathematician. He apparently left no writings, but we can learn about him in the writings of others.

❧ SIGNIFICANT EXCERPTS ❧

FROM OTHERS WRITING ABOUT THALES OR INCLUDING
HIS WRITINGS IN THEIR WORKS

Diogenes Laertius – *Lives of the Philosophers*, Thales.

Aristotle

Metaphysics, 983b 20-28.

On the Soul, 405a 20-22; 411a 7-8.

On the Heavens, 294a 28-66.

Politics 1259a 6-23.

Herodotus – *The History*, 1.74-75.

Josephus – *Against Apion*, 1.2.

Plato – *Protagoras*, 342e-343a.

Theocritus
FL. C. 270 B.C.

Theocritus was a Greek poet and writer of short epics. His themes were the typical subjects of Greek interest: love and romance.

Theodoret
C. A.D. 386-457

Theodoret was born in Antioch and raised in a well-to-do Christian home. He spent much of his early life in voluntary poverty in a monastery, received a thorough education, and became an overseer of Cyrus in A.D. 423. He was a well known preacher and writer, and many of his writings are extant.

❧ EXTANT WORKS ❧

Ecclesiastical History (5 books) – From the time of Constantine in A.D. 324 until A.D. 429; intended to be supplementary to the ecclesiastical histories of Socrates and Sozomen and a continuation of the ecclesiastical history of Eusebius. This work is easy to read.

48 *Letters*

Commentaries on numerous books of the Bible

Philotheus – A record of the lives of about thirty anchorites.

Eranistes, or Polymorphus – Dialogues promoting the doctrine that Jesus Christ is both man and God.

On Heresies – A detailed account of the errors held by various sects.

A Series of Ten Discourses on Providence – Discourses on natural theology.

Remedy for the Diseases of the Greeks

Discourse on Charity

Sermon upon St. John

Confutation of St. Cyril's Twelve Chapters

❧ SIGNIFICANT EXCERPTS ❧

Ecclesiastical History

3.1-28 – Julian the Apostate rules.

5.17-18 – How Ambrose humiliated Theodosius the Great (the last ruler of the undivided empire).

Theodosius II
A.D. 408-450

Theodosius was a Christian and the Roman emperor of the East from A.D. 408-450. The *Theodosian Code*, published in A.D. 438 during the reign of Theodosius II, was a collection of the laws of the Roman Empire issued by Constantine and the succeeding emperors. Some of the laws showed favor to the Christians.

Thucydides
C. 460-399 B.C.

Thucydides was a Greek historian who wrote *The History of the Peloponnesian War* (the Greek civil war). He takes up history where Herodotus leaves off. Thucydides is considered to be the first writer of contemporaneous history (writing about events as they occurred in his own lifetime).

Here is the first paragraph of his *History*: "Thucydides, an Athenian, wrote the history of the war in which the Peloponnesians and the Athenians fought against one another. He began to write when they first took up arms, believing that it would be great and memorable above any previous war."

This is a military history, a chronicle of the events of the very long war between Athens and Sparta. Most historians would consider Thucydides' *History* to be accurate and impartial, and Thucydides assures us that he went to great effort to find the truth from people who actually witnessed the events when he was not there himself to witness them.

❧ EXTANT WORKS ❧

The History of the Peloponnesian War

Book 1 – A summary account of Greece from Minoan times to the Persian Wars; the origins of the Peloponnesian War; Pericles' speech persuading his fellow citizens to go to war; preparations for war.

Book 2 – Initial military operations; Pericles' funeral speech for the dead; description of the plague in Athens in 430 B.C. (of which he himself fell ill); first, second, and third years of the war.

Book 3 – Fourth, fifth, and sixth years of the war; revolt of Mytilene from Athens.

Book 4 – Seventh, eighth, and ninth years of the war; Athenian success at Pylos; capture of Nisea; fall of Amphipolis.

Book 5 – Tenth through sixteenth years of the war; Deaths of Cleon and Brasidas; treaty between Athens and Sparta; breaking up of the League.

Books 6 and 7 – Seventeenth through nineteenth years of the war; Athenian expedition against Syracuse in Sicily; retreat and annihilation of the Athenian army.

Book 8 – Nineteenth through twenty-first years of the war; Ionian rebellions against Athenian rule; Persian intervention; the book ends in 411 B.C., before the war is over.

❧ SIGNIFICANT EXCERPTS ❧

The History of the Peloponnesian War

1.2-11 – History of very early Greece.

1.12-23 – The beginnings of the Peloponnesian War.

1.31-44 – The Corcyraean Alliance, which was one of the turning points of the war.

1.66-71 – The Corinthians contrast the Athenian and Spartan temperaments.

1.89-99 – History of the time period between Persian Wars and Peloponnesian War.

1.103-113 – The Athenian empire at its height.

1.139-146 – The Spartan ultimatum and Pericles' reply.

2.2-9 – How the Peloponnesian War began at Plataea.

2.13 – Speech of Pericles.

2.34-46 – The Funeral Oration of Pericles (431 B.C.).

2.47-54 – The Plague in Athens in 430 B.C.

2.59-65 – Speech of Pericles.

2.65 – The historian's estimate of Pericles.

3.20-24 – The Siege of Plataea

3.36-50 – The Mytilenian Debate.

3.82-84 – Civil War in Corcyra (427 B.C.).

4.3-14 – The affair of Pylos.

5.17-19 – Terms of the peace of Nicias.

5.77-79 – The treaty between Lacedaemon and Argos in 418 B.C.

5.84-116 – The Melian Dialogue.

6.1-5 – History of Sicily.

6.24-32 – The Sicilian Expedition.

7.70-71 – The last fight in the harbor of Syracuse.

7.72-87 – Destruction of the Athenian Expedition (413 B.C.).

8.1-2 – The consequence of the Sicilian disaster and Athens' response to the defeat of 413 B.C.

8.48 – General Phrynichus's view of oligarchy, democracy, and empire.

Tyrtaeus
FL. SEVENTH CENTURY B.C.

Tyrtaeus was a Greek poet and soldier who lived in Sparta. About twelve fragments of his work survive today, including three complete poems. They were written in praise of the Spartan constitution and of King Theopompus, and to stimulate the Spartan soldiers to deeds of heroism in the field.

❧ EXTANT WORKS INCLUDE ❧

Apollo Proclaims the Rhetra

Marching Song

To the Soldiers After a Defeat

Spartan Soldier (also called *Elegies 6-7*, or *How Can Man Die Better*)

Code of the Citizen Soldier

❧ SIGNIFICANT EXCERPTS ❧

Marching Song

To the Soldiers After a Defeat

Spartan Soldier

Spartan Soldier

Code of the Citizen Soldier

Varro
116-27 B.C.
Marcus Terentius Varro

Varro was a Roman poet, satirist, historian, jurist, geographer, meteorologist, scientist, and philosopher. He was considered the greatest scholar of Rome in his day. He wrote much, but most has been lost.

❧ EXTANT WORKS ❧

On Agriculture (3 books extant) – A systematic treatment of agriculture, of stock-raising, and of poultry, game, and fish; written in 40 B.C.

On the Latin Language (6 books extant of the 25) – A technical treatise on the derivation of words.

❧ SIGNIFICANT EXCERPTS ❧

On Agriculture

1.17.4 – Treatment of slaves should be more humane.

Vegetius
FL. A.D. 400
Publius Flavius Vegetius Renatus

Vegetius was a Christian and a Roman military expert who wrote an important manual of Roman military practices. He wanted to return to the traditional organization of the Roman legion. His book was widely used during the Middle Ages and the Renaissance.

Digest of the Art of Caring for the Diseases of Mules – A veterinary work on the diseases of horses and cattle.

Military Institutions of the Romans (4 books)

Book 1 – Discusses camp construction and the training of recruits.

Book 2 – Discusses the organization of the legion, the relationship between the legions and the auxiliaries, causes of legion decay, duties of cohorts, legion officers, tribunes of the soldiers, legionary horse, and order of battle.

Book 3 – Discusses operations, logistics, tactics and strategy.

Book 4 – Discusses naval tactics and siege fortifications.

🙢 SIGNIFICANT EXCERPTS 🙠

Military Institutions of the Romans

Prologue 3

Roman Soldiers

1.3-4, 6-12, 14-20, 26 – Training men for war.

Velleius
C. 19 B.C.-A.D. 31
Marcus Velleius Paterculus

Velleius was a Roman historian. He wrote a compendium of Roman history from the dispersion of the Greeks after the siege of Troy down to the death of Livia in A.D. 29. The time period from the death of Julius Caesar to the death of Augustus is given the most detail.

🙢 EXTANT WORKS 🙠

History of Rome (2 books)

🙢 SIGNIFICANT EXCERPTS 🙠

History of Rome

1.14 – Describes Roman colonization and the extension of citizenship to its colonies.

2.104.3-4 – Describes Tiberius as a great general.

2.126.1-4 – Tiberius as a great emperor.

Virgil
70-19 B.C.
Publius Vergilius Maro

Virgil was a Roman poet. He grew up on a farm, but was well educated. He was influenced by Epicurean philosophy and was a close friend of the Emperor Augustus, whom he deifies in his poetry. Throughout the Middle Ages, Virgil was the most popular Roman poet.

🙢 EXTANT WORKS 🙠

Georgics (4 books) – A didactic (teaching) poem on farming which concentrates on Italian products and Italian methods. Some mythology. Considered to be the most perfect of Virgil's works. It is an imitation of Hesiod's *Works and Days*.

Aeneid (12 books) – An epic poem very similar to *The Iliad* and *The Odyssey* and other Greek tragedies. Written at the request of Augustus. Tells of the mythical origin of the Roman race and of the greatness and glory of Rome which reached its height under the leadership of the Julian family, which claimed direct descent from Aeneas. Considered to be the greatest poem of Roman times. The first six books tell of the adventures of Aeneas on his voyage from Troy to Italy. The last six books tell of the struggles of Aeneas and his followers against the warriors who opposed their settlement in Italy.

Eclogues – Ten poems depicting the country life of herdsmen and their lovers. Mythology. Much of it is simply translations of the Greek poet Theocritus.

SIGNIFICANT EXCERPTS

Georgics

1.176-203 – Rules of husbandry.

1.351-392 – Signs of bad weather.

1.461-483 – Signs of the weather given by the sun.

2.109-135 – Soil and trees.

2.136-225 – Praise for the land of Italy and her products.

2.458-460 – The blessings of the farmer's life.

3.9-18 – The poet's love for his native Mantua and his homage to Augustus.

4.67-85 – The battle of the bees.

4.149-280 – Description of the life of the bee hive.

Vitruvius

FL. LATE FIRST CENTURY B.C. & EARLY FIRST CENTURY A.D.
Marcus Vitruvius Pollio

Vitruvius was a Roman writer, engineer, and architect for the Emperor Augustus. He also served as a military engineer during the civil wars and Caesar's African wars, and was well educated and well traveled. His *On Architecture* is a handbook of the classical principles of architecture. His is the only ancient work on architecture which has survived.

EXTANT WORKS

On Architecture (10 books) – Covers the history of architecture; city planning and civil engineering; construction methods and materials for buildings of all kinds; Ionian, Corinthian, Doric, and Tuscan capitals; floor paving and ornamental plaster work; water supply and aqueducts; military engines.

SIGNIFICANT EXCERPTS

On Architecture

1.2.1-7 – Of what things architecture consists.

1.4.1-7 – Choosing a site.

1.4.9-12 – On inspecting the livers of animals for testing the quality of the air.

1.5.1-4 – On the foundations of walls and the establishment of towns.

5.8.1-2 – On acoustics.

7.7.1-5 – On natural colors.

7.11.1-2 – On blue and yellow.

7.13.1-3 – On purple.

8.1.1-7 – On finding water.

8.4.1-2 – On testing water.

10.9.1-7 – On measuring a journey.

Xenophon

C. 430-350 B.C.

Xenophon was a Greek historian and a pupil of the philosopher Socrates. His writing style is much more lively and interesting than Thucydides', and he interjects interesting personal descriptions which keep the reader's interest to the end. On the other hand, Xenophon is not as historically accurate as Thucydides. According to Plutarch in his essay "On Education," Xenophon was one of the ancient writers (along with Socrates, Plato, and Euripides) who approved of allowing boys to have male lovers.

EXTANT WORKS

His work may be divided into three main categories: Historical, Socratic (Xenophon records his conversations with his teacher Socrates), and Minor Works (essays on various topics of ancient Greece).

Historical

Anabasis – This is Xenophon's most successful work. *Anabasis* is a narrative of the war in 401 B.C. between Cyrus the Younger and his brother Artaxerxes II, King of Persia, and of the retreat of the ten thousand

Greek mercenaries in the service of Cyrus. Xenophon himself served on the expedition, and he is prominent from Book 3 onwards. He was elected their general after the death of Cyrus. This work is regarded as historically accurate and would be considered a primary source.

Hellenica (Hellenic History) – Xenophon's attempt at carrying on the work of Thucydides; a history of Greece from 411-362 B.C. It is the story of Sparta's triumph over Athens and of her overthrow by Thebes. *Hellenica* would be considered a fairly strong primary source for the history of Greece for the half-century which it covers, although Xenophon's bias towards Sparta shows through. *Hellenica* is composed of seven books in three parts.

Part I. (Book 1.1.1 - Book 2.3.10) – Brings the story of the Peloponnesian War to a conclusion (411-404).

Part II. (Book 2.3.11 - Book 5.1.36) – From the close of the Peloponnesian War to the Peace of Antalcidas (386 B.C.).

Part III. (Book 5.2.1 - the end) – From the Peace of Antalcidas to the battle of Mantinea (362 B.C.).

Cyropaedia or the Education of Cyrus the Great – This is a biography of Cyrus the Great of Persia (553-529 B.C.). The first part of this book covers the youth of Cyrus, in which the author writes about the value of education; the second tells of his conquests; the third shows him as the monarch of Asia. Part of this work is actual history, part is legend, and part is romance, and it is thought by some "to be a precursor of the later novel." We would probably call it historical fiction. Definitely worth reading, though it must be kept in mind that this is not a primary source.

Agesilaus – This is a biography of King Agesilaus of Sparta (c. 444-360 B.C.). It is one of the first true biographies in Greek literature.

Socratic

Memorabilia – As a young Athenian noble, Xenophon became a disciple of Socrates, and preserved his recollections of his teacher in four books. It is a collection of discussions between Socrates and young Athenian men, and is in defense of the philosopher.

The Apology of Socrates

Economics – A Treatise on the Science of the Household in the form of a Dialogue – This is a series of dialogues divided into two parts. In the first, Socrates discusses with Critobolus the principles of private economy, in which he defines economics as the art of administering one's house well. In the second part, Xenophon writes of a conversation with a friend and describes his view of the education of women.

Hiero, or The Tyrant: A Discourse of Despotic Rule

Symposium, or the Banquet – A description of the conduct and discussion at a banquet at Athens; a lewd work.

Minor Works

Treatise on Horsemanship – On choosing, keeping, and sitting on the horse.

Constitution of the Lacedaemonians – The Spartan educational system.

Agesilaus – Xenophon's admired patron, the King of Sparta.

Polity of the Athenians – A political tract.

Revenues, or Ways and Means – Some of Xenophon's ideas on finance and political economy.

Cavalry Officer's Manual – Suggestions by an experienced officer for the improvement of the cavalry arm of the Athenian service.

On Hunting

SIGNIFICANT EXCERPTS

Anabasis

1.8.14-29 – Cyrus is killed.

1.9 – The character of Cyrus.

1.10 – The head and right hand of Cyrus are cut off.

2.1 – The Greeks are surprised to hear of the death of Cyrus.

2.2 – The Greeks form an alliance with Ariaeus.

2.3 – The king proposes a truce.

2.4 – The Greeks march apart from the Persians.

2.5 – Clearchus tries to put an end to the distrust between the Persians and the Greeks.

2.6 – The characters of the five generals who were put to death.

3.1.4-47 – How Xenophon was led to join in Cyrus's expedition.

4.4 – The Greeks arrive at the Teleboas.

4.5 – Retreat of the ten thousand through the snows of Armenia.

4.7 – The first glimpse of the sea.

Hellenica

1.6.24-38 – The Battle of Arginusae.

2.1 – The Battle of Aegospotami – the final disaster for Athens.

2.4 – The fall of the thirty.

5.3-4 – The violence of Sparta.

6.4 – Thebes defeats Sparta.

7.5 – The Battle of Mantinea.

Cyropaedia

1.2 – Persian education.

1.3 – Cyrus and his grandfather.

1.4 – The youth of Cyrus.

8.7 – The death of Cyrus.

Constitution of the Lacedaemonians

2-5, 7-8, 10 – The Spartan educational system

Zeno of Citium
C. 336-264 B.C.

Zeno was a Greek philosopher and founder of the Stoic school in Athens. We possess only fragments of his works.

❧ SIGNIFICANT EXCERPTS ❧

FROM OTHERS WRITING ABOUT ZENO OR INCLUDING HIS WRITINGS IN THEIR WORKS

Diogenes Laertius – *Lives of the Philosophers*, Zeno.

Return of the Ten Thousand

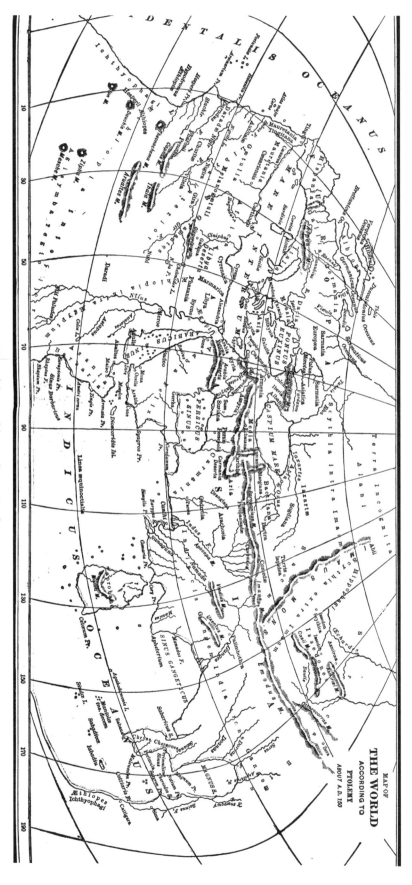

Map of the world according to Ptolemy

Appendices

Four Approaches to the Study of Ancient Literature

The purpose of this article is to help Christians to develop their own Biblical approach to evaluating literature. We cannot describe every possible approach, but we will briefly describe three common approaches to the study of classical literature, then we will explain our own distinct approach.

Nobody has appointed us judge over what others think or do, but we do have to judge what we ourselves think and do, and others may be able to use our opinions to help them explore the issues themselves.

❧ 1. A SECULAR-INTELLECTUAL ❧ APPROACH

Secular literally means *of the generation or age*, and refers to temporal and worldly matters to the exclusion of spiritual matters. The idea, or thesis, of a Secular-Intellectual Approach is that everyone should be intimately familiar with the standard collection of classical literature in the Western tradition – a collection often called *the Western canon. Canon* is a Greek word meaning a measuring line, a standard for measurement, a rule, a basis for judgment.

This *Western canon* – or standard literature in Western culture – includes such works as those of Homer, Herodotus, Plato, Aristotle, Dante, Shakespeare, Gibbon, and so forth. The *Harvard Classics* or the *Great Books* philosophy represents this approach.

Robert M. Hutchins describes this approach in terms of engaging in "the great conversation:"

> The tradition of the West is embodied in the Great Conversation that began in the dawn of history and that continues to the present day. . . . No dialogue in any other civilization can compare with that of the West in the number of great works of the mind that have contributed to this dialogue. The goal toward which Western society moves is the Civilization of the Dialogue. . . . The exchange of ideas is held to be the path to the realization of the potentialities of the race. (Robert M. Hutchins, "The Tradition of the West," published in *The Great Conversation: Substance of a Liberal Education, Vol. 1, The Great Books of the Western World* [Chicago: Encyclopaedia Britannica, Inc., 1952], 1-6)

The idea of "the great conversation" is that Western man is perfecting himself toward an understanding of intellectual truth, moral virtue, and aesthetic beauty, by means of an historical dialogue with his cultural past. Mortimer Adler describes it this way:

> People who scorn the study of the past and its works usually assume that . . . we can learn nothing worthwhile from the past. . . . But, although social and economic arrangements vary with time and place, man remains man. We and the ancients share a common human nature and hence certain common human experiences and problems. . . . The ancient poets speak across the centuries to us, sometimes more directly and vividly than our contemporary writers. And the ancient prophets and philosophers, in dealing with the basic problems of men living together in society, still have something to say to us. . . . Exclusive preference for either the past or the present is a foolish and wasteful form of snobbishness and provinciality [sic]. We must seek what is most worthy in the works of both the past and the present. When we do that, we find that ancient poets, prophets, and philosophers are as much our contemporaries in the world of the mind as the most discerning of present-day writers. Some of the ancient writings speak more directly to our experience and condition than the latest best sellers. (Dr. Mortimer J. Adler, *Great Ideas from the Great Books* [New York: Washington Square Press, 1961], 127)

This approach highly esteems the traditions of Western civilization. It is humanist in principle because it implicitly measures all things by human standards. We are reminded of Paul's expression in II Corinthians 10: 12, "they measuring themselves by themselves, and comparing themselves among themselves, are not wise." Humanism implicitly rejects all absolute standards, and replaces them with man's ever-changing and progressively evolving standards. Man's supposed progress leads us ever upward to as close to a god as man can get.

2. A RELIGIOUS-DEVOTIONAL APPROACH

This approach is the opposite, or antithesis, of the Secular-Intellectual Approach. The Religious-Devotional Approach holds to a smaller, more denominational canon consisting of religious and devotional literature, which may include confessions and catechisms, theologies and commentaries, devotional and practical works. The religious tradition or denomination will determine what particular literature is included. Many of those who follow this approach will discourage reading outside of the canon of their own denomination. They tend to withdraw from the secular world into their own private circle. They particularly fear the defilement which can come from reading much worldly literature, particularly the Western canon of classical literature.

William Penn serves as an example of this approach.

> Have but few books, but let them be well chosen and well read, whether of religious or civil subjects. . . . Shun fantastic opinions; measure both religion and learning by practice; reduce all to that, for that brings a real benefit to you; the rest is a thief and a snare. And indeed, reading many books is but a taking off the mind too much from meditation. . . . Reading yourselves and nature, in the dealings and conduct of men, is the truest human wisdom. The spirit of a man knows the things of man, and more true knowledge comes by meditation and just reflection than by reading; for much reading is an oppression of the mind, and extinguishes the natural candle, which is the reason of so many senseless scholars in the world. (William Penn, *Advice to His Children* [1699])

It would be unfair and uncharitable to brand this approach with the uncomplimentary label of "anti-intellectual," for many of these men are great thinkers. Nevertheless, the contrast is between the first approach, which has a secular outlook and focuses on the abstract, academic, and intellectual, and the second approach, which has a religious outlook and focuses on the devotional and practical.

3. A RELIGIOUS-INTELLECTUAL APPROACH

This approach uses the identical Western canon of classical literature of the Secular-Intellectual Approach, to which it adds some religious literature, although the religious literature is much broader in perspective than the denominational canons of the Religious-Devotional Approach.

Os Guinness explains his perspective:

> We can be assured that the classics have an intrinsic human, cultural, and spiritual worth. . . . Their value far transcends such commonly claimed benefits as adult education or personal self-improvement – let alone such false motivations as "culture snobbery." . . . The classic works are a "great conversation," the Western contribution to the ongoing discussion of the primary themes of life and death, right and wrong, triumph and tragedy, which we all confront in being human. . . . [I]t is time and past time for a new championing of the great literary classics of our Western civilization. . . . [W]ith endless controversies swirling around the Western masterworks, individual followers of Christ and the church of Christ as a whole have a unique responsibility to guard, enjoy, and pass them on. (Louise Cowan and Os Guinness, editors, *Invitation to the Classics* [Grand Rapids, Mich.: Baker Books, 1998], 14)

If the Secular-Intellectual and the Religious-Devotional Approaches were opposites to each other (the thesis and the antithesis), then the Religious-Intellectual Approach is the compromise between them (the dialectical synthesis). By blending the two more extreme approaches, more territory is covered and a broader balance is thus achieved – or so it seems.

However, the Religious-Intellectual Approach uses the same Western canon as the Secular-Intellectual Approach, which places Humanism in the driver's seat, and improperly exposes the young to graphic descriptions and clever justifications of the degeneracies of men. We believe the authority of the Word of God must be brought forward as the absolute standard by which to measure all literature. So we propose yet a fourth way.

4. A DISTINCTIVELY CHRISTIAN APPROACH

What we need is a distinctively Christian approach. By distinctively Christian, we mean *identifiably and unmistak-*

ably built upon Christian principles and absolutes.

A Secular-Intellectual Approach obviously is not Christian. A Religious-Devotional Approach is too narrow and truncated and withdrawn. A Religious-Intellectual Approach compromises distinctive Christian principles in order to gain the broader perspective. Christians should step outside of this *dialectical* atmosphere of extremes and compromises, and into the world of real principles, and of moral absolutes, and of ultimate accountability to God. We should begin with the principle of the absolute authority of the Word of God, and we should stand upon this principle alone, reason carefully from it, apply it everywhere, defend it always, and never back down from it. The authority of God's Word will never change. The Word of our God is a Rock. Whatever falls upon it will be broken, and whatever it falls upon will be crushed (Matt. 21:44).

Christians should focus neither upon the academic and the intellectual, nor upon the religious and the practical, nor upon a compromise – a synthesis – between the two, but upon the God of both intellect and of practice. A mature Christian intellectual is someone who is thoroughly familiar with the Scriptures and who knows how to apply practically the truths of Scripture to every facet of human culture. So Christians should hold to Scripture alone as their canon – their rule of measure – and they should use this canon to judge *all other literature:* the Western canon of the Secular-Intellectual, the private canon of the Religious-Devotional, the hybrid canon of the Religious-Intellectual, and any other literature.

Everything which we need to know is found – at least in seed form – in the Scriptures. As John Wycliffe put it, "There is no subtlety, in grammar, neither in logic, nor in any other science that can be named, but that it is found in a more excellent degree in the Scriptures." The Bible alone is the best foundation for culture, and the only foundation upon which to build a civilization. Again, John Wycliffe said, "The Bible is for government of the people, by the people, for the people."

Christians should not necessarily shun nor should they necessarily embrace other literature until they first determine from where it comes, and to where it leads. Whatever will not measure up to the standard of Scripture we must either transform for use in service to God, or else we must confine to the catalogue of historical relics. We recognize that Western civilization has been influenced by a Biblical culture, but we also recognize many other influences upon Western civilization, not the least of which is the pagan humanism which received its thrust forward with Homer and the Greeks.

As Michael Kelley writes:

[Should] the older traditionalists who believe in the goodness of Western culture . . . be heeded who suggest that the ideals of classical man need to be recovered in order to revive the lost vision of culture that made the West what it is . . .? Should we accept the argument of those who wish to restore . . . the medieval synthesis of Christianity and Humanism? . . . From a Christian perspective, each and every cultural endeavor of man . . . must be subjected to a careful scrutiny based upon what . . . does not derive from man in any sense. . . . [T]he Christian perspective on all human life and endeavor must ultimately rest upon . . . the Divine point of view, in other words, on revelation! (Michael W. Kelley, *The Impulse for Power: Formative Ideals of Western Civilization* [Minneapolis, Minn.: Contra Mundum Books, 1998])

We should not blindly accept any work of literature. Each family is accountable to God for what they choose to use. So, in submission to the Word of God, each family should determine for itself whether something meets the standards which they have established for their family under God.

If we are mature in our faith, then we will neither blindly accept, nor blindly reject, but we will test and prove all things, and we will hold fast to that which is good (I Thess. 5:21), proving what is acceptable to the Lord (Eph. 5:10). There is often more than one way to apply Biblical principles, especially in different situations. What one family cannot use, another family may have the skill and the resources to be able to transform and use. But to press some classical standard beyond a family's ability to handle it is to cause that family to stumble, which is not Christian at all (Matt. 18:7; Rom. 14:13,20,21; Rev. 2:14). We must each apply the principles of Scripture in proper balance to our own situation, recognizing that exceptional situations may call for exceptional applications. It is nevertheless perfectly appropriate for each of us to establish such rules within our own home with our own children.

The proper balance between Christian principles and any literature – classical, religious, or whatever – is that Scripture always wins, and literature always submits. We can call ourselves both classical and Christian as long as we understand that the *classical* must always submit to the *Christian*.

In summary, the Secular-Intellectual Approach ends up making man the master; the Religious-Devotional Approach ends up throwing out works of man which may be made to serve the true Master; the Religious-Intellectual Approach ends up attempting to serve two masters. We think a more mature approach would put everything in its proper place: God's Word is master, and man's works must either be made to serve the true and living God or else be set aside – lest they serve the gods of humanism.

Some persons may find much use in certain classical authors. We find most of the ancient histories useful. But though these writings may supply us with some practical information, we nevertheless know that we cannot properly evaluate them apart from the Scriptures. We must maintain a proper balance between Christian principles and our appetites.

However, it may be quite inappropriate to impose upon others our passions for certain things. If someone can consume a quart of strawberry cheesecake almond fudge ice cream a day and maintain a healthy nutritional balance, that's fine. But most people may have difficulty in maintaining that same balance, and we would be causing them to stumble if we should urge them to try it. We are not judges of other men's uses. They must answer for their own uses. There may be things which they can use but which we cannot, and vice versa, simply because of the differences in our constitutions, abilities, and experiences.

The presupposition with which we approach the subject of literature is that we should employ cautious reserve and prudent discretion.

> But strong meat belongeth to them that are of full age, even those who by reason of use have their senses exercised to discern both good and evil. (Hebrews 5:14 K.J.V.)

There is such a thing as age appropriateness, and there are also some things which are not ordinarily appropriate for any age and therefore must be approached with the highest discretion.

Nothing is Neutral

The Lord did not create the world neutral. He created it for Himself.

> Thou art worthy, O Lord, to receive glory and honour and power: for thou hast created all things, and for thy pleasure they are and were created. (Revelation 4:11 K.J.V.)

We, as Christians, should not approach anything as if it is neutral, but as if it is the Lord's.

> For of him, and through him, and to him, are all things: to whom be glory for ever. Amen. (Romans 11:36 K.J.V.)

We are to do everything from Him and through Him and to Him, and He is to receive the glory in all things. This is not limited to curricula or education, but it encompasses all of life.

Knowledge Level: We must acknowledge every fundamental fact as God's gift. He is the source of all of the particulars of which we have knowledge.

Understanding Level: We must acknowledge God as the One Who establishes the proper order and connection between things. Only through God can we understand how everything should fit together.

Wisdom Level: We must acknowledge God as the One Who gives direction and goals to everything which we do. All lesser goals must be harnessed to ultimately serve God, doing all things to Him, according to His direction, and for His glory.

To fail to acknowledge God in everything amounts to practical agnosticism or atheism.

> The wicked, through the pride of his countenance, will not seek after God: God is not in all his thoughts. (Psalm 10:4 K.J.V.)

Nothing in this world is neutral. All things belong to Christ and to those in Him.

> For all things are yours. . . . And ye are Christ's; and Christ is God's. (I Corinthians 3:21,23 K.J.V.)

As soon as we place something into the category of neutral, we make it available to those who will not acknowledge God's sovereign ownership over all things. When the devil proposes a compromise, he says: "What's mine is mine, and what's yours is negotiable." Whatever we surrender to the neutral category becomes negotiable. Once it is placed in negotiable territory, it is slowly lost by a war of attrition. What we used to consider our territory slowly erodes into neutral territory, then negotiable territory, and finally enemy territory. Why? Because, in principle, we surrendered what is in fact ours when we placed it in the neutral category to begin with. Our compromises are the devil's victories.

❧ EDUCATION IS NOT NEUTRAL ❧

No true education can take place without reference to God. Education is for a purpose. If the purpose does not have God in view, then it is godless education, and it will eventually produce godless results. The objective of education is not service to self, the community, business, church, or state, but service to God. Education which does not serve God is an empty education, and that emptiness will be filled by other gods to serve. To develop capacities for service, but to omit the One Who is to be served, is to manufacture a monster.

Modern government education does what ancient pagan education did – namely, teach without reference to God, which is ultimately to promote ignorance.

> Behold, the fear of the Lord, that is wisdom; and to depart from evil is understanding. (Job 28:28 K.J.V.)

> Come, ye children, hearken unto me: I will teach you the

fear of the LORD. (Psalm 34:11 K.J.V.)

The fear of the LORD is the beginning [/principal part] of wisdom: a good understanding have all they that do his commandments: his praise endureth for ever. (Psalm 111:10 K.J.V.)

The fear of the LORD is the beginning [/principal part] of knowledge: but fools despise wisdom and instruction. (Proverbs 1:7 K.J.V.)

For that they hated knowledge, and did not choose the fear of the LORD. (Proverbs 1:29 K.J.V.)

Then shalt thou understand the fear of the LORD, and find the knowledge of God. (Proverbs 2:5 K.J.V.)

The fear of the LORD is the beginning [/principal part] of wisdom: and the knowledge of the holy is understanding. (Proverbs 9:10 K.J.V.)

The fear of the LORD is the instruction of wisdom; and before honour is humility. (Proverbs 15:33 K.J.V.)

And the spirit of the LORD shall rest upon him, the spirit of wisdom and understanding, the spirit of counsel and might, the spirit of knowledge and of the fear of the LORD; And shall make him of quick understanding in the fear of the LORD: and he shall not judge after the sight of his eyes, neither reprove after the hearing of his ears. (Isaiah 11:2,3 K.J.V.)

And wisdom and knowledge shall be the stability of thy times, and strength of salvation: the fear of the LORD is his treasure. (Isaiah 33:6 K.J.V.)

❧ REFINEMENT OF IGNORANCE ☙

Generally speaking, the more experience we have, the more refined our knowledge and understanding becomes. But refinement is not necessarily a good thing. One can progress in righteousness, or he can progress in wickedness – and, outwardly, it is sometimes difficult to tell the difference. The man who gets better and better at blaspheming or burglarizing or swindling can be easily identified as progressing in wickedness. But the man who gets better and better at lying or cheating or hypocrisy – the more he progresses in his wickedness, the harder he is to detect. The same is true of cultures. The culture which degenerates into open idolatry and debauchery is identifiably declining. The culture

which refines its monetary deceit and intellectual fraud is likewise declining, but the decline is identifiable only to those who have absolute cultural standards by which to measure.

From where do such absolute cultural standards come? Humanism declares that man is the measure of all things. But Scripture declares that the Lord, man's Maker, reveals the standards for measuring man and his culture. There is no truly passive, objective, or neutral ground:

He that is not with me is against me; and he that gathereth not with me scattereth abroad. (Matthew 12:30 K.J.V.)

Nor is there any shared middle ground:

No servant can serve two masters. . . . (Luke 16:13 K.J.V.)

The notion that there is common ground between believers and unbelievers is a lie. In the Lord's providence, the unbelievers share many good things with believers.

For he maketh his sun to rise on the evil and on the good, and sendeth rain on the just and on the unjust. (Matthew 5:45 K.J.V.; cf. Luke 6:35; Psalm 145:9)

Who in times past suffered all nations to walk in their own ways. Nevertheless he left not himself without witness, in that he did good, and gave us rain from heaven, and fruitful seasons, filling our hearts with food and gladness. (Acts 14:16,17 K.J.V.)

But the unbeliever takes the gifts which the Lord provides to him, and he uses them from the framework of his false philosophy – his erroneous worldview – which leaves the true and living God out of the picture. His facts are not the same as the believer's facts. The facts may appear the same on the surface, but they have an entirely different meaning, because they are interpreted from an entirely different framework.

❧ THE TAIL WAGGING THE DOG ☙

It is the framework which gives every word, or fact, or message, its meaning, and therefore its ultimate truth value. The fact that dogs wag their tails actually becomes a lie in any other framework of interpretation than the Christian framework. The Christian framework says that the true and living God created the heavens and the earth, and on the sixth day he created dogs to wag their tails, which ultimately brings glory and delight to God (among other things). The naturalist framework says that an impersonal big bang billions of years ago set in motion the shape and form of things which eventually evolved by chance into a chemically determined activity of a dog whereby he wags his tail for no ultimate purpose.

When an unbeliever says a dog wags its tail, we regularly interpret that statement from our own framework, so we are prone to agree to the outward and formal truth of that statement. But we must look behind that statement and recognize that *it arose from his framework*. It makes no difference whether he is self-conscious of his framework, his meaning is nevertheless derived from that framework. What looks like truth *to us – from our perspective* – does not at all have the same meaning to the unbeliever. He sees the world apart from God. He believes a lie. His dog's wagging tail is necessarily incorporated into his own interpretive framework – his false mythology – which imports an entirely different meaning to what we might like to call "the outward objective fact" of the wagging tail. There is no evolved dog wagging its tail by chemical determination. *Evolutionary* dogs cannot wag their tails because *evolutionary* dogs do not exist. There is only a dog created by God to wag its tail.

Everything which is not understood in its proper relation to God is ultimately understood in a false relation which, ultimately, will break down. Teaching anything – no matter how innocuous it may seem – while leaving out its relation to God, amounts to a lie – ultimately, a disintegrating lie. We must be very careful about agreeing with the unbelieving world, lest we be entrapped by a very subtle but genuine equivocation arising from our different interpretive frameworks. If we aren't careful, we may end up with the proverbial "tail wagging the dog" (pun fully intended). Instead, we need to entrap unbelievers in our interpretive framework. We must take tail-wagging dogs and remove them from the darkness of evolutionary mythology, and we must place them under the light of Biblical revelation. And we must take the statements of pagans and remove them from the darkness of humanist mythology, and we must place them under the light of Biblical revelation.

Worldliness may be reduced to the failure to make this simple distinction between interpretive frameworks. Worldliness creates a so-called neutral zone of shared providences and "uninterpreted" facts. The equivocation is precisely there, for the facts are indeed interpreted – as being neutral! The lie here is that there is no difference between a "fact" in the Christian worldview and a "fact" in any other worldview – as if *all* worldviews are relative and biased but "facts" are absolute and neutral, which is precisely the naturalist worldview. No. Whatever form of knowledge which the unbeliever has regarding God,

he suppresses it (Rom. 1:18,19). There is an absolute perspective, a Biblically-correct worldview, and God communicates this worldview to us by His Word, and we should spend our lives interpreting what we observe as "facts" in the world according to the absolute perspective of His Word. The moment we give credence to a neutral point of view, we in principle deny God His place of authority in the universe, and we submit ourselves to the ongoing competition between various humanist worldviews.

No matter what superficial similarities may appear to exist between them, at the base and core, the unbeliever's philosophy drives him in any direction except towards the one true and living God. He does not love God with all his heart, soul, mind, and strength. His fleshly mind *is* enmity against God (Rom. 8:7) which causes all of his faculties to be set *at* enmity against God, so that not only is he not truly subject to the Law of God, it is not possible in the nature of things that he ever would be. As he continues to interpret his experience by wrong – unbelieving, skeptical, humanistic – presuppositions, he actually becomes more and more ignorant – that is, he builds up more and more false interpretations of the reality over which he blindly stumbles. He progresses in building a false culture. But those who evaluate their experiences by true presuppositions – presuppositions drawn from the Bible – revise their understanding more and more into conformity to the truth revealed to them. They progress in building a true culture.

THE BABY AND THE BATHWATER

Then, have we no lawful use for the works of unbelievers? We certainly do.

> All things are lawful for me, notwithstanding, all things do not necessarily benefit. All things are lawful for me, notwithstanding I-myself will not be brought under the inordinate control of anything. . . . All things are lawful for me, notwithstanding, all things do not necessarily benefit. All things are lawful for me, notwithstanding, all things do not necessarily edify. (I Corinthians 6:12; 10:23 V.L.T.)

All things are lawful for us as Christians, but only so long as we use them lawfully – according to their proper use.

> But we know that the law is good, if a man use it lawfully. (I Timothy 1:8 K.J.V.)

> Meats for the belly, and the belly for meats: but God shall destroy both it and them. Now the body is not for

fornication, but for the Lord; and the Lord for the body. (I Corinthians 6:13 K.J.V.)

We must not abuse things in a way which contradicts God's law.

Paul narrows the field of uses down to those things which do benefit. The word translated "benefit" literally means to bring things together so as to make a helpful contribution. What we use must bring things together for us in a helpful and profitable way. Pythagoras and Euclid may have developed useful geometry, but their philosophy is foolishness. A study of their philosophy would be useful only as a study in the carnal speculative mind – a study which has much more limited use than geometry. All things must be made to serve the Lord Jesus, or else they serve no good purpose. Lest you think we are advocating some extremely narrow and strict philosophy of use, well, we aren't – Jesus is.

"All things are lawful" does not mean all things are beneficial. "All things are lawful" only means that there is a lawful use for each and every thing. It does not mean that every way something has been used, or conceivably might be used, is necessarily lawful. All things have lawful uses, but not all uses are lawful. An idol is in itself nothing (I Cor. 8:4), but idolatry is not a lawful use for anything (I Cor. 10:14).

Unbelievers have put together many things – even many intellectual things – which are useful. But that which is common and unclean must first be tested and purged with fire and purified with water of separation (Numbers 31:23; Psalm 66:12) before it can be set apart for lawful use. It must first be washed and reshaped for the Master's use before it can be used "in house," that is, among Christians, or before it can be used "outside the house," that is, in apologetic evangelism, calling out the Lord's people from among the world.

❧ "NEUTRAL" CURRICULA OPTIONS ❧

How does this all apply to curricula and to higher education?

Some of the materials and curricula which are available are explicitly Christian. Maybe some of this isn't as consistently Christian as we might like, but at least it makes no claims to being neutral. Some of the materials and curricula which are available are explicitly hostile to Christianity. Many more are hostile, but not so openly. But the vast majority of curricula in the world will implicitly or explicitly claim to be neutral. From their point of view, what they mean is that they grant no favors to religious points of view. They are inclusive. They may even give the religious point of view a little space, and they may not even try to make it seem stupid.

What's wrong with this picture? God is not just one among many options. Of Him and through Him and to Him are all things. That's not optional. All options which exclude that option are necessarily false.

So what do we do with this "neutral" curricula or material? The same thing we do with the professedly Christian and the professedly non-Christian material: we either redeem it or we look for something else. It has to be transformed or trashed. Transformation means:

1. We must remove it from its dark surroundings of a false worldview and expose it to the light of God's truth in the Biblical worldview.
2. We must separate the precious from the vile, drawing distinct lines between good and evil, truth and error, holy and unholy, just and unjust.
3. We must set it at liberty by putting it into lawful service within the correct order of things under God.

For example, if we have a history program which relates everything from man's point of view, then we should critique the humanist perspective and show God's providential hand and moral judgment in everything. If we have some science text which relates everything from a naturalistic perspective, then we need to critique the naturalism and show God's eternal power and Godhead in everything. Whatever the program, text, or curriculum, it must be brought under the light of God's Word, the proper distinctions must be drawn, and it must be put into its lawful place in the order of things.

❧ RESPONSE TO THE COUNTER ❧ ARGUMENT

Someone might try to counter the "nothing is neutral" philosophy by quoting, "he that is not against us is for us" (Luke 9:50 K.J.V.) understanding this as if someone who is neutral – at least not openly opposed to the Lord – is as good as on our side because at least he's not opposing the Lord.

That is not at all what Jesus is saying.

Then there arose a reasoning among them, which of them should be greatest. And Jesus, perceiving the thought of their heart, took a child, and set him by him, And said unto them, Whosoever shall receive this child in my name receiveth me: and whosoever shall receive me receiveth him that sent me: for he that is least among you all, the same shall be great. And John answered and said, Master, we saw one casting out devils in thy name; and we forbad him, because he followeth not with us. And Jesus said unto him, Forbid him not: for he that is not against us is for us. (Luke 9:46-50 K.J.V.)

Jesus' point is that there are only two classes – those against Him and those for Him. If someone is casting out devils in the name (by the authority) of Jesus – that is, they did this in the same way which the Apostles themselves had done – then he's not in the class of those who are against the Lord. That leaves only one other possibility: he is for the Lord. He may not be directly commissioned by the Lord, but he who truly receives a gift in the name of (by the authority) the Lord receives it from the Lord.

Mark 9:33-50 encompasses a larger context, where the Lord concludes:

> For every one shall be salted with fire, and every sacrifice shall be salted with salt. Salt is good: but if the salt have lost his saltness, wherewith will ye season it? Have salt in yourselves, and have peace one with another. (Mark 9:49,50 K.J.V.)

Either we have salt, or we don't. The words "if the salt have lost his saltness," is literally, "if the salt has become no salt." There is no neutral ground. We may have more or less salt, but the salient point is whether or not we have any salt at all.

Some might accuse this of being a *false dilemma*. A false dilemma is a fallacy where someone limits the possible options – usually to two options – when in fact there may be several options. We are forced to choose between either this or that. "Either you marry me or I'll just die." Well, maybe there are some other possibilities. In this case, "Either you are for the Lord or you're against Him." Are there any other legitimate options? Is neutrality a legitimate option?

APPLYING THE TRIVIUM

When we evaluate what someone is saying, we should apply the Trivium.

Knowledge Level: When we wish to learn something, we must begin at the Grammar Level by gaining an accurate knowledge of the facts – what someone actually says, and what they really mean by what they say. Primary source evidence is considered more reliable than hearsay evidence because it has not passed through a filter of personal perspective and bias. If we hear about a broken window in our house from our son who is angry at the neighbor boys because they won't let him play baseball with them, the facts may come across in a distorted way which makes it look as if the neighbor boys

hit the baseball through the window. But if we consult the neighbors, we may find that the boys weren't in a position to hit a baseball through our window.

Understanding Level: If we begin to draw conclusions before we have an accurate knowledge of the facts, then our conclusions are necessarily built upon a wrong foundation. But we must also be careful to reason accurately with the facts we know. There is a difference between what something could possibly mean and what it necessarily means. A small ball in the middle of our living room floor, with glass trailing back to a broken window – these things might possibly mean the neighbors have been playing baseball. Likely – yes. Necessarily – no. The lawn mower could have flung a rock through the window – a rock which we have not discovered. The baseball could be our own, which fell off the mantle when the rock hit it.

Wisdom Level: If we begin to apply our conclusions before we have accurately ascertained the facts and carefully reasoned with them, then we may take actions which are unwarranted and may, in the end, prove damaging or embarrassing. We may send the neighbor kids their baseball along with a bill for window repair. We may slander our neighbors for not raising their children to take responsibility for their actions. Then we may discover it was our own lawnmowing which caused the problem. So, in the end, it is ourselves who appear to have acted irresponsibly.

Here are a few Scripture texts which speak to the subject.

> Go not forth hastily to strive, lest thou know not what to do in the end thereof, when thy neighbour hath put thee to shame. (Proverbs 25:8 K.J.V.)

> He that answereth a matter before he heareth it, it is folly and shame unto him. . . . He that is first in his own cause seemeth just; but his neighbour cometh and searcheth him. (Proverbs 18:13, 17 K.J.V.)

> Doth our law judge any man, before it hear him, and know what he doeth? (John 7:51 K.J.V.)

Now to get back to the question.

EITHER FOR OR AGAINST

"He that is not with me is against me." (Matthew 12:30 K.J.V.)

"He that is not against us is for us." (Luke 9:50 K.J.V.)

We're either for Christ or against Him. We're either against Christ or for Him. Jesus doesn't leave any other options. On the temperature scale, there are an infinite number of points between freezing and boiling. In a book, there is a margin between the edge of the paper and the print. With a balancing scale, there is a knife's edge where things could stay level or teeter one way or totter the other way. But with a light switch, there is only an on and an off, and with reference to Christ, there is only a *for Him* or an *against Him*. This is not a false dilemma: this is a true dilemma. Here are some other examples of true dilemmas, some either-or realities:

Light or Darkness

To open their eyes, and to turn them from darkness to light, and from the power of Satan unto God. (Acts 26: 18 k.j.v.)

Grace or Works

And if by grace, then is it no more of works: otherwise grace is no more grace. But if it be of works, then is it no more grace: otherwise work is no more work. (Romans 11:6 k.j.v.)

Self-Possessiveness or Discipleship

So likewise, whosoever he be of you that forsaketh not all that he hath, he cannot be my disciple. (Luke 14:33 k.j.v.)

EXPERIENCE VERSUS REALITY

But our experience seems to say otherwise. There are people who are openly hostile to Christ, but there are also people who are not openly hostile to Christ. We think they are neutral because we do not detect their bias. We frame our thoughts in terms of openly hostile or not openly hostile to Christ. What we don't see is that to be supposedly "neutral" to Christ is in fact to be hostile to Christ, because "neutral" means negotiable, when it isn't negotiable at all. Satan proposed that pure obedience to God's word was negotiable when he said, "Yea, hath God said, Ye shall not eat of every tree of the garden. . . . Ye shall not surely die: For God doth know that in the day ye eat thereof, then your eyes shall be opened, and ye shall be as gods, knowing good and evil" (Gen. 3:1,4,5).

We imagine that since there are different degrees of direction between true north and true south, that there must be different degrees of direction between good and evil. But as far as God and Christ are concerned, true north is the only direction which counts. Every other direction does not head toward God. The wider our angle away from true north, then the more quickly we depart from God's way. True south would be the fastest departure. However, the closer we are to true north – without actually being on compass north – then the more deceptive we become, because someone would need to follow our course out much farther into the future in order to see how it departs from God's way.

ONLY TWO RELIGIONS

There are really only two religions: Biblical Christianity and all the others.

When it comes to sorting this all out on a practical level, things may appear blurry and indistinct to us. That's because our sight needs correcting, and more light needs to be shed on the subject.

The reason people have trouble seeing beyond the myth of neutrality is because neutrality is the prevailing philosophy of our day. "We shouldn't judge. There is no right or wrong. Right or wrong is determined by the way we choose to think about it. If someone else chooses a different set of values, we must be tolerant." If there is no God, then there can be no logical standard by which we can judge anything. Everything is neutral until someone has clarified the situation from his own perspective and decided to place his own personal value upon it.

NOT!

This is God's world, whether or not we choose to acknowledge it.

SO!

Nowadays, this "no-neutrality" philosophy can be a very frustrating philosophy. By refusing to acknowledge God, and ignoring all reference to God, our culture declares, in every nook and cranny, the foolish philosophy of "No God" (Psalm 14:1; 53:1). It educates in the deliberate absence of the knowledge of God, which is to educate – in a proactive and aggressive way – in ignorance. It matters not that they profess themselves wise; they have nevertheless become fools, and exchanged the glory of the incorruptible God into naturalistic philosophy (Rom. 1:22,23).

The appearance of neutrality comes from considering things without reference to God. Unbelievers see many things, but the one thing which they are blind to is the glory of God in everything (II Cor. 4:4), and they want us to see the world the way it appears to them – neutral, which is, in fact, biased against reality.

Appearances mean everything to the one who wants us to let our guard down so that he can then gain the advantage over us. All he wants is for us who stand on principle to compromise that principle – even in the slightest way. Once we surrender the principle, then how far we will fall from the principle is only a matter of taste, imagination, perception, and circumstances. We have moved off of the solid rock and onto the slippery slope. Yes, *slippery slope* is the name of a fallacy. But as with the either-or fallacy or the false dilemma, so with the slippery slope: there are fallacious applications, and there are genuine applications, and we must learn the difference, or we fall prey to the *Fallacy of Appearances*.

Was Paul a Classical Greek Scholar?

It is one thing to deal with classical Greek myths, and quite another to deal with myths about classical Greek. One such myth, which has had rather wide circulation, is the notion that Paul was a scholar of classical Greek literature and philosophy.

It is alleged that the Apostle Paul quoted several classical Greek authors, and this is presented as conclusive and irrefutable evidence of his classical scholarship. We will first examine the three quotations – real or alleged – which are presented as the primary examples for Paul's scholarship.

> Whence did he get the saying, 'The Cretans are always liars, evil beasts, slow-bellies,' but from a perusal of The Oracles of Epimenides, the Cretan Initiator? Or how would he have known this 'For we are also his offspring,' had he not been acquainted with The Phenomena of Aratus the astronomer? Again this sentence, 'Evil communications corrupt good manners,' is a sufficient proof that he was conversant with the tragedies of Euripedes. (Socrates Scholasticus, *History of the Church*, 3.16)

❧ ACTS 17:28 ❧

In Acts 17, Paul is addressing a tribunal gathered to hear his answer to the charge of introducing strange gods. Among the many words which he speaks in his defense, he says,

ἐν αὐτῷ γὰρ ζῶμεν καὶ κινούμεθα καί ἐσμεν·

For in Him we live and we move and we exist,

ὡς καί τινες τῶν καθ᾽ ὑμᾶς ποιητῶν εἰρήκασι,

as also some of the poets – according to you – have said,

τοῦ γὰρ καὶ γένος ἐσμέν.

'For we are also from among His offspring.' (Acts 17:28 V.L.T.)

The First Alleged Quotation of Acts 17:28

Some assert that the expression "For in Him we live and we move and we exist" is a poetic quotation from Epimenides. There is no surviving manuscript of any Greek poet saying this; and the statement does not follow a Greek poetic form; and the connection to Epimenides is very conjectural. Paul did not exactly overwhelm the Greeks with his knowledge of their philosophy, but he did know enough to address them with what they needed to hear in the way which they needed to hear it. Paul may even have been alluding to what his interrogators had already told him, for when he says, "as also some of the poets – according to you – have said," that may refer to his previous words as well as to his following words. Perhaps Paul had heard a similar expression in his discussions in the Athenian marketplace, or in remarks previously made by others at this hearing in the Areopagus. Perhaps these words are from a Greek poet. Perhaps Paul reformulated them here in order to serve his purposes. Perhaps.

A sentiment similar to this first alleged quotation may be found in Plautus:

> O Jupiter, who dost cherish and nourish the race of man;
> by whom we live, and with whom is the hope of the life of all men.

But why do we not look further, for the same sentiment is expressed in much older Hebrew Scripture?

> In whose hand is the soul [/life] of every living thing, and the breath of all mankind [/flesh of man]. (Job 12:

10 v.l.t.)

Thou dost search out my path and my lying down, and thou art acquainted with all my ways. (Psalm 139:3 v.l.t.)

The Second Alleged Quotation of Acts 17:28

The last phrase, "for we are also from among his offspring," is more likely to be some kind of a quotation. This phrase matches, word-for-word, the first half of the fifth line of a half-hexameter *Hymn to Zeus* (Jupiter), a famous poem, dealing mainly with astronomy, found in Τα` Φαινόμενα *The Phaenomena* (5), an astronomical poem written about 270 B.C. by Aratus (c. 324-240 B.C.), a native of Solis, a city of Cilicia, not far from Tarsus, where Paul was born. A similar expression (ἐκ σοῦ γα`ρ γένος ἐσμέν) is attributed to a *Hymn to Jove* (Jupiter) (5), written by Cleanthes of Assos (300-220 B.C.) who taught at Athens, and who was the successor of Zeno, founder of the Stoics. A similar sentiment is also found in the poet Homer and several other places, such as:

> Spiritus intus alit, totamque infusa per artus mens agitat molem.

> The Spirit doth nourish within, and the Mind, being dispersed throughout all the limbs, doth set in motion the whole mass. (Virgil, *Aeneid* 6.724-727)

Now, contrary to what Aratus and others asserted, we are emphatically *not* Jupiter's offspring. Paul conceded no authority to the quotation itself, but reframed it – placed it within the framework of a different worldview – in order to serve his own purpose. This is precisely what we Christians must do with everything which we use from the world – we must reframe it into the Christian worldview in order to serve our purposes. Paul's purpose was to point to the sentiment – which existed even among the heathen – that we are all related to deity by creation. In this incident, it served Paul's purpose to quote out of context! But the sentiment is not a heathen concept at all, for it is found throughout Scirpture.

> Then the LORD God formed the man [Adam] out of dust from the ground, and breathed into his nostrils the breath of life; and the man [Adam] became a living soul. (Genesis 2:7 v.l.t.)

> Adam, who was the son of God. (Luke 3:38 v.l.t.)

> The spirit shall return to God who gave it. (Ecclesiastes 12:7 v.l.t.)

> Thus says God the LORD, He Who created the heavens, and stretched them out; He Who spread forth the earth, and what comes out of it [its offspring]; He Who gives breath to the people upon it, and spirit to those who walk in it. (Isaiah 42:5 v.l.t.)

> But now, O LORD, Thou art our Father; we are the clay, and Thou art our potter [Former]; and all we are the work of Thy hand. (Isaiah 64:8 v.l.t.)

> The God in whose hand is thy breath of life [/spirit], and to whom belongs all thy ways. (Daniel 5:23 v.l.t.)

> Is there not one father for us all? Has not one God created us? (Malachi 2:10 v.l.t.)

Paul himself also eloquently expressed elsewhere the sentiment of both statements in Acts 17:28.

> One God and Father of all, Who is above all, and through all, and in you all. (Ephesians 4:6 v.l.t.)

So Paul here may have used an ad hominem argument (not adversative) with the pagans, even as he later used an ad hominem argument with the Pharisees against the Sadducees (Acts 23:6-9).

In quoting a very common Greek expression, what is there to indicate that Paul was a scholar of Greek literature and philosophy? Nothing.

❧ I CORINTHIANS 15:33 ☙

In I Corinthians, we find another passage where many believe Paul quotes a Greek poet.

> Φθείρουσιν ἤθη χρηστα΄ ὁμιλίαι κακαί

> Evil associations corrupt excellent characters. (I Corinthians 15:33 v.l.t.)

This appears to quote a senary iambic verse from the lost dramatic comedy *Thais*, by Menander (c. 342-293 B.C.), the comic poet of Athens who himself probably lifted his expression from a lost tragedy of Euripides (Socrates Scholasticus, *History of the Church*, 3.16).

The quotation was a very common proverb in Paul's time. Furthermore, the same sentiment is found frequently in Scripture.

> Forsake the foolish [/simple ones], and live; and walk in the way of understanding. (Proverbs 9:6 v.l.t.)

> He who walks with the wise shall become wise: but the companion of fools will suffer harm. (Proverbs 13:20 v.l.t.)

A little leaven leavens the whole lump. (I Corinthians 5: 6 v.l.t.)

But be standing aloof from the profane empty chatterings, for they will force their way toward further irreverence, and their discourse will have an expansion like gangrene . . . who did swerve around the truth. (II Timothy 2: 16,17,18 v.l.t.)

Lest any root of bitterness, springing up, should cause trouble, and through this root, many may become defiled. (Hebrews 12:15 v.l.t.)

And many shall follow their destructive ways through to conclusion, on account of whom the way of truth shall be blasphemed. (II Peter 2:2 v.l.t.)

For in uttering haughty words of emptiness, they continually allure – by the desires of the flesh, by sensualities – those who are actually just escaping from those who walk in error. While promising to them liberty, they themselves are all that time constituted bondservants of corruption: for by whom anyone has been decisively defeated, to the same he is irrevocably held in bondservitude. (II Peter 2:18,19 v.l.t.)

It is not unlikely that this very common expression was actually carved on public monuments throughout the Greek speaking world. What do we find here to indicate that Paul was a scholar of Greek literature and philosophy? Nothing.

❧ TITUS 1:12 ❧

There is only one passage, Titus 1:12, where Paul expressly states that he is quoting an author, although Paul does not identify that author.

εἶπέν τις ἐξ αὐτῶν ἴδιος αὐτῶν προφη´της,

A certain one of themselves, a prophet of their own, said,

Κρῆτες ἀει` ψεῦσται, κακα` θηρία, γαστέρες ἀργαί.

Cretans are always liars, evil wild-beasts, lazy gluttons. (Titus 1:12)

Why does Paul call this person a *prophet*? The ancient Greeks used the word *prophet* [προφη´της] to refer to one who explained or interpreted the obscure expressions of the oracles of the gods. They included poets and wise men among the *prophets*, whom they considered "sons of the gods" (Plato, *Politics*). So Paul is not using the term prophet in the sense it is commonly used in Scripture, but in the common pagan sense.

Indeed, Paul apparently quoted here a poem entitled, Περι` Χρησμῶν, *Concerning Oracles*, written around 600 B.C. by the pagan prophet and wandering fortune-teller Epimenides, a Cretan by birth, of the city of Cnossus. It is a hexameter line, quoted by Callimachus in a *Hymn to Zeus* (5.8), and is quoted by others elsewhere. It resembles a line from Hesiod's *Theogony*, written in the eighth century B.C., from which Epimenides may have copied. The sentiment is found frequently in ancient literature.

(Epimenides himself took on mythical proportions, supposedly living for 289 years, including 57 years in which he slept in a cave without waking.)

The Syllogistic Puzzle

The reputation of Cretans throughout the ancient world was that of liars. To *Cretanize* [κρητίζειν] meant simply to tell a lie. Eubulides, the Megarian philosopher of Miletus (c. 350 B.C.), is said to have discussed a syllogistic puzzle, called Ψευδόμενον *The Liars* (a.k.a. *Epimenides' Paradox*), which was very common in the ancient world.

Epimenides said that the Cretans were liars.
But Epimenides was a Cretan.
Therefore Epimenides was a liar.
Therefore the Cretans were not liars.
Therefore Epimenedes was not a liar.
(Diogenes Laertius, *Lives of the Philosophers* 2.108)

If we *do* believe what Epimenides says about Cretans being liars, then, since Epimenides is himself a Cretan, we *must not* believe what Epimenides says about Cretans being liars, for Epimenides must be a liar. But if we *do not* believe what Epimenides says about Cretans being liars, then Epimenides is a liar, so we *must* believe what Epimenides says about Cretans being liars, for Epimenides is a Cretan.

Chrysippus, a Stoic logician (c. 297-206 B.C.), wrote numerous books and treatises on "The Liar" (Diogenes Laertius, *Lives of the Philosophers* 7:196-198). In medieval times, this puzzle was known as an "Insoluble." We have our own modern versions of this puzzle, such as, "I am now lying," or "This statement is not true."

Paul solved the puzzle in the only way possible, by declaring, not that Epimenides was truthful, but only that "this testimony is true," stepping outside of the endlessly repeating cycle and shifting the focus to the saying apart from the messenger.

This is what Christians must always do with all information emitted by non-Christian worldviews. False worldviews are self-contradictory by their very nature. They "borrow" the form of truth from reality, then they position this formal ornament of truth within their own false interpretive framework – their worldview, which then transforms the truth into a lie (cf. Rom. 1:18,25). In other words, they have what might be characterized as a multitude of little fragments of truth, but they weave them as embroidery into a garment which is a fabrication – a lie. These fragments appear true to us because we interpret them according to our Biblical worldview. But it is the connection of these fragments of truth within the interpretive framework of the false worldview which transforms these fragments of truth into servants of a lie, regardless of how they appear to us. We can convert them back into truth by putting them back into their proper place within the Biblical worldview, which is reality. [See Appendix 2: "Nothing is Neutral."]

From a Christian worldview, when Epimenides, a Cretan, said Cretans are always liars, he pointed to the inherent contradiction within any non-Christian worldview. Nevertheless, when reinterpreted from a Christian worldview, both Epimenides and Cretans are characteristically liars, and indeed, all men in their fallen condition are always liars walking about in darkness.

> The wicked ones go astray from the womb: they err from their birth, speaking lies. (Psalm 58:3 V.L.T.)

> Surely the sons of Adam are emptiness, the sons of men are a lie: they go up in the scale balances, together they are lighter than emptiness. (Psalm 62:9 V.L.T.)

Knowing the general reputation of Cretans as liars, the popularity of Epimenides' expression for describing the Cretans as liars, and the popularity of the syllogistic puzzle *The Liars*, do we find anything here to indicate that Paul was a scholar of Greek literature and philosophy? Not at all.

❧ OTHER PASSAGES ❧

We have now covered the three passages most often cited as evidence for Paul's Greek scholarship. There are a few other passages from Paul's writings which may receive honorable mention as alleged quotations or allusions to some author outside of Scripture.

More of Paul's Alleged Allusions to the Writings of Greek Authors

1. The expression "necessity is laid upon me" in I Corinthians 9:16 is compared to the same expression found in Socrates' *Apology*:

> What can the god mean? and what is the interpretation of this riddle? for I know that I have no wisdom, small or great. What can he mean when he says that I am the wisest of men? . . . but **necessity was laid upon me** – the word of God, I thought, ought to be considered first. And I said to myself, Go I must to all who appear to know, and find out the meaning of the oracle. (Plato, *Apology* 21)

The same expression appears again in *Hellenica,* recorded by Xenophon:

> "Men of Miletus, **necessity is laid upon me** to obey the rulers at home; but for yourselves, whose neighborhood to the barbarians has exposed you to many evils at their hands, I only ask you to let your zeal in the war bear some proportion to your former sufferings. (Callicratidas, addressing the men of Miletus, quoted in Xenophon, *Hellenica* 1.6.8)

2. The discussion in I Corinthians 12:12-31 about the importance of every member of the body is compared to the ancient fable of *The Belly and the Limbs.*

> The Belly and the Limbs. Back in the days when the various parts of the body did not necessarily all agree with each other, as they do now, but each had its own ideas and its own voice, some of the parts began to think that it was unfair that they should have to worry and toil to provide everything for the belly, while the belly just sat there in their midst with nothing to do but to enjoy the bounty they brought to it. They therefore conspired together, and agreed that the hands would no longer carry food to the mouth, the mouth would no longer open for food, and the jaws and teeth would no longer grind up what they received. The belly growled and tossed about in protest; but the limbs remained steadfast in their angry resolve to starve the belly into submission. Soon though, they began to feel weak. Their fatigue grew worse and worse, until they, the belly, and the entire body nearly perished from starvation. Thus, it had become clear that even the seemingly idle belly had its own task to perform, and returned as much as it received; by digesting the food brought to it and returning nourishment to the limbs via the blood. (Menenius Agrippa c. 503 B.C., quoted in Livy, *The Early History of Rome* 2:32)

3. The statement in I Timothy 6:10 about the relationship between money and evil is compared to expressions

found in Bion, and variously ascribed to Democritus, or Diogenes the Cynic of Sinope, etc.

The sinews of affairs are cut. (Demosthenes [Greek orator and statesman 382-322 B.C.], quoted in Aeschines, *Against Ctesiphon* 53)

Riches are the sinews of business [/of the state] (Bion of Smyrna [Greek poet and philosopher, c. 325-255 B.C.], quoted in Diogenes Laertius, *Lives of the Philosophers* 4.7.3)

He who first called money the sinews of the state seems to have said this with special reference to war. (Cleomenes, quoted in Plutarch, *The Lives of the Noble Grecians and Romans*, Life of Cleomenes 27)

[Money is expressly called] the sinews of war. (Libanius, *Orat.* 46; Pindar, *Olymp.* 1.4; Photius, *Lex.* 5)

Boundless riches are the sinews of war. (Cicero [Roman philosopher, statesman, and orator, 106-43 B.C.], *Philippics* 5.2)

He has not acquired a fortune; the fortune has acquired him. [Said of a wealthy man who was known to be miserly.] (Bion of Borysthenes, quoted in Diogenes Laertius, *Lives of the Philosophers* 4.7.3)

The love of money is the center [metropolis] of all evil. (Theon of Alexandria, *Progymnasmata: Chreia* 125-126)

Paul's Alleged Allusions to the Jewish Greek Apocrypha

1. Romans 9:21 is compared to the *Wisdom of Solomon* 15.7. (Compare Isa. 64:8; Jer. 18:1-6; II Tim. 2:20.)

For the potter, tempering soft earth, laboriously molds each vessel for our service. Nay, from the same clay he fashions both the vessels which serve clean uses, and those which serve contrary uses, making all in like manner. But the craftsman himself is the judge of what is the use of each. (Apocrypha, *Wisdom of Solomon* 15.7)

2. I Corinthians 6:2 is compared to the *Wisdom of Solomon* 3.8. (Compare Psalm 149:9; Dan. 7:18,22; Matt. 19:28; Luke 22:30; Jude 14,15; Rev. 2:26,27; 3:21; 20:4.)

They shall judge nations, and have dominion over peoples, and the Lord shall reign over them for evermore. (Apocrypha, *Wisdom of Solomon* 3.8)

3. Ephesians 6:10-17 is compared to the *Wisdom of Solomon* 5.17-23. (Compare Deut. 20:3,4; Isa. 11:15; 49:2; 52:7; 59:17; Rom. 10:15; 13:12; II Cor. 6:7; 10:4; I Thess. 5:8; Heb. 4:12.)

He shall take His zeal for His whole armor, and He shall arm all creation to repel His enemies; He shall put on righteousness for a breastplate, and He shall wear impartial judgment for a helmet; He shall take holiness for an invincible shield, and He shall sharpen His stern wrath for a sword, and the world shall fight with Him against the unwise. Bolts of lightning shall fly with true aim, and they shall leap to the target as from a well-drawn bow of clouds, and hailstones full of wrath shall be hurled as from a catapult; the water of the sea shall rage against them, and rivers shall cruelly drown them; a mighty wind shall rise up against them, and like a storm it shall blow them away. Thus lawlessness shall lay waste the whole land, and evil-practice shall overturn the thrones of the mighty. (Apocrypha, *Wisdom of Solomon* 5.17-23)

❧ OBSERVATIONS ❧

We have gone far out of our way to try to find every shred of evidence we could in order to support the theory that Paul was a scholar of Greek literature and philosophy. Our purpose has not been to dispute the possibility that any or all of these words of Paul were expressions which Paul deliberately borrowed from authors – particularly pagan authors – outside of Scripture. For the sake of argument, we will grant them all without another word. So, assuming that these all are indeed quotations from pagan authors, we must ask ourselves this question, "Does the apostle Paul quote these pagan authors to display his classical learning?" Not at all.

If we assume that Paul has indeed intentionally quoted or alluded to pagan Greek authors, then how should we understand Paul's use of these quotations? Paul expected that all, or at least most, of his listeners and readers would readily recognize and understand these expressions. But very few, if any, of his listeners and readers were scholars of classical literature and philosophy, so how could they recognize them, unless they were expressions not confined to the scholarly classics? Paul simply did what we all do from time to time – he borrowed common expressions which he had learned from living in the Greek and Roman culture, removed them from their context, and transformed them for his own use. All of these expressions were among the most common and customary, passed around like coins of the realm, often quoted in literature before and during Paul's earthly lifespan, and possibly inscribed on ancient monuments. Paul only quotes the most obvious material, and never the more obscure.

If this kind of evidence proves that Paul "was thoroughly trained in classical languages, literature, and philosophy," then we would be forced to conclude, on this same kind of evidence, that the apostle Peter was a scholar of Greek philosophy because in II Peter 2:22 he appears to quote Heraclitus (and other sources); "A sow, having washed, to her wallowing in the mire."And, by the same criteria, Jesus was also a scholar of Greek tragedies, because in Acts 9:5 and 26:14, Jesus used the expression "it is hard for thee to kick against the goads," which also appears in *Bacchae*, 794, by Euripides (c. 480-406 B.C.), and in Aeschylus' (c. 525-455 B.C.) play *Agamemnon*, 1624. But in fact, these lines were familiar proverbs of the ancient world.

We can explain the matter with a simple illustration. If we used the words "government of the people, by the people, for the people," would that mean that we had thoroughly studied the literature of the War Between the States, the life and writings of Abraham Lincoln, and that we were thoroughly familiar with the philosophical trends of the mid-nineteenth century? Or would it simply mean that this selection from the Gettysburg Address is a common expression in our day? For that matter, did Lincoln craft this expression himself, or did he overhear it from some unknown source, or did he borrow it from John Wycliffe, who happened to have used this identical expression five hundred years earlier? Paul's quotations and allusions are as ordinary as our ability to quote the proverb, "A penny saved is a penny earned" which is attributed to Benjamin Franklin, but who knows who really coined it.

Paul was not trying to impress his audience with his own pagan learning, nor with the authority of the pagan authors whom he cited. He simply borrowed a common expression from a pagan context, and he put it to his own use. Indeed, the Greek vocabulary of the New Testament could be said to be appropriated from the pagans for Christian use. (Some have also argued that Paul borrowed his vocabulary from Greek philosophers.) We also appropriate the English vocabulary for our own Christian use – even as we are doing at this very moment.

In Paul's writings, he can scarcely write a half dozen sentences without quoting or alluding to the Hebrew Scriptures. If Paul was an erudite scholar of Greek literature, then what truly needs to be explained is why, in all of his writings (2,033 verses, plus many more were we to add up all of his dialogue in Acts, and still more if we include Hebrews), Paul may have quoted at most only a half-dozen very common pagan Greek expressions which everyone obviously recognized and understood. If Paul knew as much as some claim for him, yet he showed so little of this branch of his learning in his writings, then there can be no other explanation than that Paul studiously avoided quoting anything except Scripture. Paul was a very articulate man, and he demonstrates a common knowledge of Greek culture, but he displays no special Greek learning.

> I did not come according to a personal superiority of discursive speech or of philosophical wisdom. (I Corinthians 2:1 V.L.T.)

Paul does display some fondness for some very common classic Greek rhetorical figures of speech (alliteration, anakoluthon, antithesis, asyndeton, chiasmus, climax, euphemism, hyperbaton, litotes, oxymoron, paradox, paraleipsis, paronomasia, zeugma, etc.). It has been suggested that he may have picked up some elementary "classic rhetoric" during his childhood in Tarsus, before he moved to Jerusalem to study under the rabbis. But this seems most unlikely, if for no other reason than that they did not teach such rhetoric to children. However, other writers of both the Hebrew and Greek Scriptures use many of these same figures, and we cannot discern whether Paul was any more educated than others in these figures and therefore would have employed these figures more self-consciously than others. (Compare E. W. Bullinger, *Figures of Speech Used in the Bible*, London: Messrs. Eyre and Spottiswoode, 1898; reprinted Grand Rapids: Baker Book House, 1968, xlvii+1,104 pages.)

Paul also adopted matters of heathen life for the illustration of Christian truth.

Greek Theater

> For I think that God has exhibited us the apostles last, as it were appointed to death: for we are made a spectacle [/theater] to the world, and to angels, and to men. (I Corinthians 4:9 V.L.T.)

Paul here describes himself and the other apostles as if standing in a Greek amphitheater, surrounded by thousands of spectators – the world, angels, and men. Those who were exhibited "last" – who were brought out at the conclusion of the games in order to fight – were doomed to death with no allowance made for escape.

> And those who are using this present world should be as those who are not making full use of it, for the scene of this present world is passing away [off stage]. (I Corinthians 7:31 V.L.T.)

Paul here compares the world to a Greek drama where the scenes change and the imposing and splendid pageantry is shifted around and passed off and away out of sight. So this world is unreal, continues but a short time, and soon changes scenes.

> Indeed this for one example, being exposed as a spectacle both to reproaches and to afflictions; and this for another example, having become companions with those passing through [the theater] in this manner. (Hebrews 10:33 v.l.t.)

This describes a common scene, where Greeks and Roman magistrates customarily led criminals through the theater before they were put to death, exposing them to public scorn, ridicule, insult, and reproach.

Greek Athletics

> Know ye not that those who run in a race [/stadium] run all, but only one receives the prize? So run, that ye may grasp the prize. Now everyone who strives for the prize is temperate in all things. However, they do so in order that they may receive a corruptible crown; but we do so in order that we may receive an incorruptible crown. Therefore, I so run, not as uncertainly; I so prize-fight, not as one who beats the air: But I bruise my body with blows, and I enslave it: lest perchance, after I have proclaimed to others, I myself should prove to be a rejected combatant. (I Corinthians 9:24-27 v.l.t.)

The Corinthians would know well the Isthmian athletic games which were celebrated every fourth year, on the isthmus which joined the Peloponnesus to the mainland, north of Corinth. (There were also the Pythian or Delphic games in Phocis, at the foot of Mount Parnassus, the Nemean games at Nemaea, a town of Argolis, and the Olympic games in Olympia, on the western part of the Peloponnesus.) At these games, athletes competed for the glory of an earthly garland and a crowd's acclaim, both of which soon passed away. They prepared themselves for these contests by a long course of discipline, exercise, and self-denial.

> That I did not run in vain, nor did I toil [/work out] in vain. Not that I have already taken hold of, or that I have already been brought to the goal, but I am still pursuing it, if I may even take hold of this goal for which purpose I have also been fully taken hold of by Christ Jesus. Brethren, I myself do not account my own self to have fully taken hold of this goal, but one thing I have taken hold of: Indeed, forgetting those things out of view behind me, yet stretching myself forward upon these things in view before me, I am pursuing toward the visible goal for the prize of the high calling from God in Christ Jesus. (Philippians 2:16; 3:12-14 v.l.t.)

In running a race, one does not look behind, but strains forward, with his eyes fixed on the mark or goalpost before him. To arrive at the goalpost first was to win the prize. The winner would take hold of the pole which marked the goal, thereby securing one's claim to victory in the race.

> Crown of joyful boasting. (I Thessalonians 2:19 v.l.t.)

The goal of the games was a garland crown over which the victor joyfully boasted.

> Be constantly contending in the noble contest of the faith, be laying hold on the life eternal, to which goal thou wast also called, and thou didst confess the noble confession in the presence of many witnesses. (I Timothy 6:12 v.l.t.)

If one wanted to take hold of the goal and receive the crown before the witnesses of the games, he must faithfully pursue the contest.

> Now also if anyone should be competing in athletic games, he is not to be crowned as winner, unless he shall have competed according to the rules. . . . I have contended in the noble contest to the end, I have finally finished the race course, I have safely guarded the faith from injury. There remains reserved for me the victor's crown of justice which the Lord – the Just Judge of the games – shall award to me at that day, yet He shall not award this crown to me alone, rather, He shall also award this crown to all those who have always devotedly loved His glorious appearing. (II Timothy 2:5; 4:7,8 v.l.t.)

One is not crowned unless he has followed the rules of the game. Paul has followed the rules and finished the race, so he expects the just judge of the games to give him the crown.

Roman Military Triumph

> Having Himself stripped the principalities and the authorities of their power, He made an open exhibit of them in public, having led a triumph over them by this cross. (Colossians 2:15 v.l.t.)

> Now thanks be to God, Who always leads us everywhere to triumph in Christ, and Who, by us, makes manifest the fragrance of His knowledge in every place. For we are to God a sweet fragrance of Christ, among those who are being saved, and among those who are perishing: To the latter one we are the fragrance of death to death; and to the former one we are the fragrance of life to life.

And who is sufficient for these things? (II Corinthians 2:14-16 V.L.T.)

Paul here refers to a triumphal procession, when a victorious general returns from a decisive victory, makes a magnificent entrance into the capital, rides in a magnificent chariot, usually drawn by two white horses, and he is accompanied by his captains, by the spoils of war, and by the nobles, generals, and peoples whom he has subdued. Flowers are scattered in the way, diffusing a grateful smell, and incense is burned on the altars of the gods while sacrifices are offered. The incense is a fragrance of life to the victor, but of death to the vanquished, who are put to death near the end of the procession. So the gospel is a fragrance of life to those who march with Christ, and of death to those who do not.

CONCLUSION

Where, in all of these alleged quotations and examples, is the evidence that Paul was formally schooled in Greek or Roman literature, history, or philosophy? Paul simply used to his advantage whatever he had learned from living in the Greek and Roman culture. Paul actually displays a paucity of Greek learning. In the words of F. W. Farrar:

> The notion that he [Paul] was a finished classical scholar is, indeed, as we have shown already, a mere delusion; and the absence from his Epistles of every historical reference proves that, like the vast mass of his countrymen, he was indifferent to the history of the heathen, though profoundly versed in the history of Israel. (F. W. Farrar, *The Life and Work of St. Paul* [London: Cassell and Company, 1891], 296)

Paul was a Pharisee of Pharisees, who studied at the feet of the great Jewish Rabbi, Gamaliel.

> I-myself [Paul] am a Pharisee, the son of a Pharisee. (Acts 23:6 V.L.T.)

> In accordance with the most exact sect of our ceremonial religion, I [Paul] lived a Pharisee. (Acts 26:5 V.L.T.)

> I-myself [Paul], indeed, am an adult male, a Jew, having been born in Tarsus of Cilicia, but having been brought up in this city [Jerusalem] at the feet of Gamaliel, having been instructed according to the exactitude of the ancestral law, being in my personal constitution zealous for God. (Acts 22:3 V.L.T.)

What is the likelihood that the very strictest Pharisee, raised from childhood in Jerusalem, placed directly and continuously under one of the seven greatest Jewish rabbis of all time, taught the law in the fullest and strictest manner known, and personally zealous for it all, was also an erudite scholar of Greek philosophy and literature? Somewhere between zero and none!

It is said of the eleven other apostles

> Now observing the boldness of Peter and John, and having perceived that they were formally uneducated [/unlettered] and professionally untrained men, they were captivated with astonishment, and they were one after another recognizing who they were – that they had been with Jesus. (Acts 4:13 V.L.T.)

There is no real evidence that any New Testament writer was well read in Greek literature and philosophy. If any were, then they were not at all burdened to display it. Their burden was different.

> For I decided not to know anything among you, except Jesus Christ, and Him once-and-for-all-time crucified. (I Corinthians 2:2 V.L.T.)

> Let no one continue to be deceiving himself. Assuming someone among you supposes himself to be wise in regard to things of this present age, let him become foolish to this age, in order that he may become wise. For the wisdom of this present world is foolishness with God. For it stands written, He it is Who entraps the wise in their shrewd craftiness. And again, The Lord knows the reasonings of the wise, that they are empty [/without content]. (I Corinthians 3:18-20 V.L.T.)

The Bible Chronology Puzzle

*C*hronology comes from χρόνος *a segment or division of time*, and λογία *a collection or study of something.* Biblical chronology is the study of segments of time recorded in the Bible, with the primary goal of compiling one continuous and interlocking sequence of time from creation down to as late a date as possible, and the secondary goal of lining up this chronology with secular dates in order to arrange a continuous sequence of dates down to present time.

Biblical chronologists differ with one another on many seemingly minor things, and a few major things. We make no claim to being experts in Biblical chronology. Our "Timeline of Ancient Literature" is based largely upon our study of several well known chronologists. At the end of this article is a comparative chart of several different systems of chronology. From this chart you should at least learn that honest and learned men may honestly and learnedly differ among themselves.

❧ WHY IS CHRONOLOGY ❧ IMPORTANT?

The Scriptures contain records of dates and measurements of time periods. If the Scriptures are inerrant, then these records of time are also inerrant. The Scriptures themselves identify precise calculations of certain important periods of time.

> In the six hundredth year of Noah's life, in the second month, the seventeenth day of the month, the same day were all the fountains of the great deep broken up, and the windows of heaven were opened. (Genesis 7:11 K.J.V.)

> And it came to pass in the fortieth year, in the eleventh month, on the first day of the month, that Moses spake unto the children of Israel, according unto all that the

> LORD had given him in commandment unto them. (Deuteronomy 1:3 K.J.V.)

> And it came to pass in the four hundred and eightieth year after the children of Israel were come out of the land of Egypt, in the fourth year of Solomon's reign over Israel, in the month Zif, which is the second month, that he began to build the house of the LORD. (I Kings 6:1 K.J.V.)

We are commanded in the Scriptures to study the Scriptures, and chronology is one area of study which other men in the Scriptures have pursued.

> In the first year of his [Darius] reign I Daniel understood by books the number of the years, whereof the word of the LORD came to Jeremiah the prophet, that he would accomplish seventy years in the desolations of Jerusalem. (Daniel 9:2 K.J.V.)

The theory of Biblical chronology is that these dates and periods can be assembled into an uninterrupted sequence, then aligned with an absolute and universally accepted baseline date in order to give exact dates for Biblical events. This theory sounds simple enough to test. All one would need to do is to assemble the chronological data in Scripture and to align this all into one continuous string of events. In practice, however, this is not such a simple thing to do. There are three major problem areas in Biblical chronology: (1) problems of text, (2) problems of interpretation, and (3) problems of finding an absolute baseline date from which to count.

1. Textual Problems

Our modern printed editions and translations of the Bible are based upon ancient handwritten copies of the Hebrew Old Testament Scriptures. Men do not copy thousands of words without making mistakes. Because there are many handwritten copies of these ancient Hebrew Scriptures which survive, there are (as you can well imagine) many minor differences in these copies. Among the many differences are differences in the dates recorded in the genealogies of Scripture. So it might be nice to have something to compare these dates with in order to verify these dates. So what do we have to compare with? With the Hebrew Scriptures, there are four main sources to compare:

1. The *Masoretic* text, which is considered the most accurate tradition of the Hebrew Scriptures.
2. The *Samaritan Pentateuch*, which is an ancient Aramaic translation of the five books of Moses.
3. The *Septuagint*, which is an ancient Greek translation of the Old Testament.
4. The *Antiquities of the Jews*, written by Josephus, who was a Hebrew priest who wrote in Greek, and who wrote accounts in the first century which parallel the genealogies and other records of Scripture.

What happens when we compare these dates? As we can observe in the chart below, there are some *major* differences in dates. For example, for the age when an individual fathered the next son in the genealogies of Genesis 5 and 11, the Greek *Septuagint* translation often adds 100 years to the ages we find in the Hebrew *Masoretic* text. Furthermore, in the Aramaic *Samaritan Pentateuch* translation, the genealogy from Arphaxad to Serug often agrees with the Greek Septuagint in adding 100 years to the Hebrew ages. To add to the confusion, in the Greek *Antiquities of the Jews* we find that Josephus generally agrees with the Greek Septuagint, though not always.

A Comparison of Dates in Different Texts

In the following chart, we demonstrate a few of the differences among the four major sources for dates.

1. Items in brackets [ ] are textual variants.
2. Items in parentheses ( ) are ages calculated from the text.
3. Items in braces { } are for comparison, but are not included in the other calculations.

Age of each patriarch when the next patriarch was born.		
	(Hebrew) *Masoretic* text & (Aramaic) *Samaritan Pentateuch* (The Samaritan Pentateuch is mentioned separately only where it does not agree with the Hebrew.)	(Greek) *Septuagint* & (Greek) *Antiquities of the Jews* (Josephus' *Antiquities of the Jews* is mentioned separately only where it does not agree with the Septuagint.)
Adam	130	230 — [/Josephus 330]
Seth	105	205 — [/Josephus 105]
Enos	90	190
Cainan	70	170
Mahalaleel	65	165
Jared	162 — *Samaritan 62*	162
Enoch	65	165 — [/Josephus 65 /187]
Methuselah	187 — *Samaritan 67*	187 [/167] — [Josephus 171]
Lamech	182 — *Samaritan 53*	188 — *Josephus 182* [/82]
{Noah}	{(502)} {already calculated into the Flood and interval below}	{(502)}
Noah at the Flood	600	600
Totals to the Flood	(1656) (*Samaritan 1307*)	(2262) (*Josephus 2256*)
{Shem}	{100} {already calculated into the Flood above and the interval below}	{100}
Interval after the Flood	2 (until Arphaxad is born to Shem)	2 — *Josephus 12*
Arphaxad	35 — *Samaritan 135*	135
[Cainan II]	—	[130 — *Septuagint adds this person*]
Salah	30 — *Samaritan 130*	130
Eber	34 — *Samaritan 134*	134
Peleg	30 — *Samaritan 130*	130
Reu	32 — *Samaritan 132*	132 — *Josephus 130*
Serug	30 — *Samaritan 130*	130 — *Josephus 132*
Nahor	29 — *Samaritan 79*	79 [/179] — *Josephus 120* [/109]
Terah	{(130)} {already calculated into the interval below when Abraham leaves Haran}	(130) [/Josephus 130]
Abraham leaves Haran	{75} {already calculated into the interval below when Terah dies and Abraham leaves Haran}	{75}
Terah dies; God reveals His promises to Abraham	205	205
From the Flood to Abraham's call from Haran	(427) (*Samaritan 1077*)	(1207) — *Josephus* (1128)

From Creation to Abraham's call from Haran	(2083) (Samaritan 2384)	(3469) — Josephus (3384)

As anyone can see, if we chose not to follow the Hebrew *Masoretic* text, but we chose instead to follow the *Samaritan Pentateuch*, the *Septuagint*, or the *Antiquities of the Jews*, then we would end up with radically different totals. Most Biblical chronologists believe the *Masoretic* text is the most reliable, and are content to rely upon it for their dates. However, one does wonder how the dates in the other texts and translations came about.

2. Problems of Interpretation

Once we've settled on what are the actual numbers recorded in the text, then we need to settle on how these numbers are to be added together. That might seem simple at first – until we realize that the Biblical writers adopted many standards for dating events. Sometimes they reckoned from the time of the Exodus.

> On the first day of the second month, in the second year after they were come out of the land of Egypt . . . (Numbers 1:1 K.J.V.)

> And Aaron the priest went up into Mount Hor at the commandment of the LORD, and died there, in the fortieth year after the children of Israel were come out of the land of Egypt, in the first day of the fifth month. (Numbers 33:38 K.J.V.)

> And it came to pass in the four hundred and eightieth year after the children of Israel were come out of the land of Egypt, in the fourth year of Solomon's reign over Israel, in the month Zif, which is the second month, that he began to build the house of the LORD. (I Kings 6:1 K.J.V.)

Sometimes they reckoned from the accession of a king.

> Now in the eighteenth year of king Jeroboam the son of Nebat reigned Abijam over Judah. And in the twentieth year of Jeroboam king of Israel reigned Asa over Judah. And Nadab the son of Jeroboam began to reign over Israel in the second year of Asa king of Judah, and reigned over Israel two years. In the third year of Asa king of Judah began Baasha the son of Ahijah to reign over all Israel in Tirzah, twenty and four years. (I Kings 15:1,9,25,33 K.J.V.)

Sometimes they reckoned from the return from the Exile.

> Now in the second year of their coming unto the house of God at Jerusalem, in the second month, began . . . to set forward the work of the house of the LORD. (Ezra 3: 8 K.J.V.)

In attempting to create a consistent system of Biblical dates relative to each other, the challenge is to determine how these different dating systems line up and overlap with each other. We might compare this to putting together a jigsaw puzzle without benefit of the picture on the cover of the box. If we're not quite sure what it's supposed to look like when we're done, then we have to do much more matching of puzzle parts.

If we adopt the Masoretic Hebrew text as our standard, then there are several segments of time which are generally not arguable.

Dates in the chart below are A.M. – Anno Mundi – in the year of the world.

0	Creation
1656	1,656 years to the Flood (Genesis 5:3-32; see chart above)
1878	222 years to the birth of Terah (Genesis 11:10-25, see chart above)
2008	130 years to the birth of Abraham (Genesis 11:26,32; 12:4; Acts 7:4,5; see explanation below)
2083	75 years to the call of Abraham out of Haran (Genesis 12:4)
2107	24 years to the covenant of circumcision (Genesis 17:1,10,24)
2108	1 year to the birth of Isaac (Genesis 17:17,21; 21:1-5)
	2113 — 5 years (estimated) to the weaning of Isaac (Genesis 17:19-21; 21:8,10,12 — when Isaac was designated the heir of the promise, and Ishmael was cast out)
2168	60 years to the birth of Jacob (Genesis 25:26)
2298	130 years to Jacob's entry into Egypt (Genesis 47:9)
2513	215 years to the Exodus from Egypt (Exodus 12:40,41 — exactly 430 years from Abraham's call out of Haran; see explanation below)
2553	40 years to the entrance into Canaan (Exodus 16:35; Numbers 14:33,34; 32:13; Deuteronomy 2:7; 8:2,4; 29:5; Joshua 5:6; Psalm 95:10; Amos 2:10; Acts 7:36,42; 13:18; Hebrews 3:9,17)
2992	440 years to the beginning of the temple in the fourth year of Solomon's reign (I Kings 6:1,37 — 480 years from the Exodus; see explanation below)
3000	7 ½ years to the completion of the first temple (I Kings 6:38)

We include that last date, A.M. 3000, just to round things off nicely to an even millennium. Within this 3,000-year period, there are three main problems which Biblical chronologists have worked to resolve. There are some apparent contradictions regarding: 1) Terah's age at Abraham's birth, 2) the length of Israel's sojourning, and 3) the length of the period of the judges in relation to the period from the Exodus to the building of Solomon's temple. We must find what puzzle part matches up with the other puzzle parts, and where it matches up; and this can become rather complicated, as you are about to discover.

A. THE PROBLEM OF TERAH'S AGE AT ABRAHAM'S BIRTH
— GENESIS 11:26,32; 12:4; ACTS 7:4,5

Genesis 11:26 appears to suggest that Terah was seventy years old at the birth of Abraham.

And Terah lived seventy years, and begat Abram, Nahor, and Haran. (Genesis 11:26 K.J.V.)

But a comparison of Genesis 11:32, Acts 7:4,5, and Genesis 12:4 indicates that Abraham was seventy-five years old when Terah died at the age of two hundred and five years, making Terah one hundred and thirty years old at Abraham's birth.

And the days of Terah were two hundred and five years: and Terah died in Haran. (Genesis 11:32 K.J.V.)

So Abram departed, as the LORD had spoken unto him; and Lot went with him: and Abram was seventy and five years old when he departed out of Haran. (Genesis 12: 4 K.J.V.)

Then came he out of the land of the Chaldeans, and dwelt in Charran: and from thence, when his father was dead, he removed him into this land, wherein ye now dwell. (Acts 7:4,5 K.J.V.)

If Terah was two hundred and five years old when he died (Gen. 11:32), and if Abram was seventy-five years of age when he went out of Haran to Canaan (Gen. 12: 4), and if Abram did so as soon as his father Haran died there (Acts 7:4), then 205 - 75 = 130, so Abram was not born until the one hundred and thirtieth year of his father's life.

How do we reconcile this computation with the statement in Genesis 11:26? All that Genesis 11:26 actually affirms is that Terah was seventy years old before he begat three sons, and that the names of those three sons were Abram, Nahor, and Haran. It does not affirm that they were triplets, nor that Abram was the oldest son of the three. We may compare the three sons of Noah:

And Noah was five hundred years old: and Noah begat Shem, Ham, and Japheth. (Genesis 5:32 K.J.V.)

And Noah begat three sons, Shem, Ham, and Japheth. (Genesis 6:10 K.J.V.)

In the selfsame day entered Noah, and Shem, and Ham, and Japheth, the sons of Noah . . . (Genesis 7:13 K.J.V.)

And the sons of Noah, that went forth of the ark, were Shem, and Ham, and Japheth . . . (Genesis 9:18 K.J.V.)

Now these *are* the generations of the sons of Noah, Shem, Ham, and Japheth . . . (Genesis 10:1 K.J.V.)

Though Shem is always mentioned first, and the text says that "Shem, Ham, and Japheth" were born after Noah was five hundred years old, we know that Shem was not born in Noah's five hundredth year, because Scripture tells us that Japheth was the oldest.

Unto Shem also, the father of all the children of Eber, the brother of Japheth the elder, even to him were children born. (Genesis 10:21 K.J.V.)

Likewise, the younger Isaac is mentioned before the older Ishmael (Gen. 25:9; I Chron. 1:28), the younger Jacob is mentioned before the older Esau (Gen. 28:5; Josh. 24: 4; Heb. 11:20), and the younger Moses is mentioned before the older Aaron (Exod. 4:28 and about 80 other places).

As Shem became the most distinguished of the three sons and is mentioned first, so Abram, as the father of the Jewish people, likewise became the most distinguished of the three sons and is mentioned first. It cannot be proven from Scripture that Abram was the eldest, and the other facts will not allow him to be the eldest, so Abram must have been born sixty years after Terah begat his eldest son, who most likely was Haran, because Haran died before they migrated.

This may explain how Abraham could marry Sarah.

And Abram and Nahor took them wives: the name of Abram's wife was Sarai; and the name of Nahor's wife, Milcah, the daughter of Haran, the father of Milcah, and the father of Iscah [Sarah's name before marriage]. (Genesis 11:29 K.J.V.)

Abraham was only ten years older than Sarah (Gen. 17: 17). The Scripture commonly uses terms like *brother* and *sister* for *close kin* and *son* and *daughter* for *grandson* or *granddaughter.* Apparently, Haran was Abraham's half-brother, and Sarah was apparently Abraham's half-niece, the daughter of Abraham's much older half-brother Haran.

And yet indeed [Sarah] she is my sister [/close female kin]; she is the [grand-] daughter of my father, but not the [grand-] daughter of my mother; and she became my wife. (Genesis 20:12 K.J.V.)

B. THE PROBLEM OF THE LENGTH OF ISRAEL'S SOJOURN
— GENESIS 15:13; EXODUS 12:40,41; GALATIANS 3:17; ACTS 7:6

The book of Exodus mentions 430 years for the sojourning of the children of Israel until the Exodus.

Now the sojourning of the children of Israel, who dwelt in Egypt, was four hundred and thirty years. And it came to pass at the end of the four hundred and thirty years, even the selfsame day it came to pass, that all the hosts of the LORD went out from the land of Egypt. (Exodus 12:40,41 K.J.V.)

This appears to be calculated exactly to the very day. But the question is, "From *what* day does this text begin its calculation?" At first glance, someone might understand the 430 years to be calculated from the moment Israel's children began their sojourning in Egypt. But chronologically speaking, it is certain that Israel did not sojourn in Egypt 430 years, but rather, about half that amount of time – 215 years or less. So let us begin our own journey of interpretation.

A New Testament passage suggests a different beginning for the 430-year period.

And this I say, that the covenant, that was confirmed before of God in Christ, the law, which was four hundred and thirty years after, cannot disannul, that it should make the promise of none effect. (Galatians 3:17 K.J.V.)

If we assume that both Exodus 12:40,41 and Galatians 3:17 refer to the same period of 430 years, then Galatians 3:17 appears to begin the period of Israel's sojourning with the establishment of a covenant which God made with Abraham.

However, the Biblical record of the fleshly covenant of circumcision with Abraham (Gen. 15:1-21) mentions a different time frame.

Thy seed shall be a stranger in a land that is not theirs, and shall serve them; and they shall afflict them four hundred years. (Genesis 15:13 K.J.V.)

And God spake on this wise, That his seed should sojourn in a strange land; and that they should bring them into bondage, and entreat them evil four hundred years. (Acts 7:6 K.J.V.)

At first glance, all of this seems quite confusing. However, a more careful examination may allow a harmony of these texts.

To begin with, Exodus 12:40,41 does not say that Israel had been in Egypt 430 years. It only says that "the sojourning of the children of Israel" continued 430 years. The phrase "who dwelt in Egypt" may be understood as a parenthetic remark describing where Israel dwelt at that moment. It was inserted here in anticipation of its mentioning in the next verse their Exodus from Egypt. This is a figure of speech called *epitrechon* or *running along*, where an explanatory statement is parenthetically

thrown in. (For other examples of epitrechon, compare I Kings 8:39-42; Matt. 9:6; Acts 1:15; Rom. 3:7,8.)

The Greek *Septuagint* version agrees with this interpretation.

And the sojourning of the children of Israel, which they [(some copies add:) **and their fathers**] sojourned in the land of Egypt **and in the land of Canaan**, was four hundred and thirty years. (Exodus 12:40, Greek Septuagint)

Likewise, the Aramaic *Samaritan Pentateuch* agrees.

The sojourning of the children of Israel, **and of their fathers, in the land of Canaan**, and in the land of Egypt was four hundred and thirty years. (Exodus 12: 40, Samaritan Pentateuch)

Similarly, the two Jewish Talmuds read, respectively, "and the sojourning of the children of Israel, who dwelt in Egypt, *and in all the lands*, were four hundred and thirty years" and "and the sojourning of the children of Israel who dwelt in Egypt *and in the rest of the lands*, were four hundred years." The gloss in the Talmud explains, "from the time that the decree of the captivity was made between them to the birth of Isaac, were thirty years; and from the birth of Isaac, until the Israelites went out of Egypt, were four hundred years; take out of them the sixty of Isaac, and the one hundred and thirty that Jacob had lived when he went down into Egypt, and there remain two hundred and ten; and so is the decree, that 'thy seed shall be a stranger in a land not theirs.'"

So we must not confine the 430 years to the sojourning of Israel in Egypt. Instead, the text extends to the full time when they sojourned "in a land that is not theirs." Abraham, Isaac, and Jacob, dwelt "in a land that is not theirs" before the children of Israel ever went down into Egypt; and from then until they left Egypt, Abraham's children were strangers. All of this time of sojourning may properly be considered one continuous period of promise, which is appropriately contrasted with the Exodus, when the children of Israel actually moved to take possession of the promised land.

Abraham was seventy-five years old when he left Haran (Gen. 12:4). The covenant of circumcision was instituted when Abraham was 99 years old, and Isaac was born when Abraham was 100 years old.

And when Abram was ninety years old and nine, the LORD appeared to Abram, and said . . . This is my covenant, which ye shall keep, between me and you and thy seed after thee; Every man child among you shall be circumcised. . . . But my covenant will I establish with Isaac, which Sarah shall bear unto thee at this set time in the next year. . . . And Abraham was ninety years old and nine, when he was circumcised in the flesh of his foreskin. . . . For Sarah conceived, and bare Abraham a son in his old age, at the set time of which God had spoken to him. . . . And Abraham was an hundred years old, when his son Isaac was born unto him. (Genesis 17: 1,10,21,24; 21:2,5 K.J.V.)

So there would have been about 25 years from Abraham's coming out of Haran until the birth of Isaac. From the birth of Isaac to the birth of Jacob was 60 years (Gen. 25:26), and from the birth of Jacob until he went down to Egypt was 130 years (Gen. 47:9), and from then until Israel came out of Egypt is generally computed as 210 or 215 years. 25 + 60 + 130 + 215 = 430, which is the exact sum. The 400 years must then be computed from 5 years after the birth of Isaac, which many identify as the estimated time of the weaning of Isaac (Gen. 21: 8,10,12) at which time Isaac was designated the heir of the promise, and Ishmael was cast out. (See next page for illustrations.)

An alternative method for calculating this period is to begin when Abraham left Ur. If Abraham stayed at Haran five years before he left, which is probable, then he would have been about 70 years old when he left Ur. So there would have been about 30 years from Abraham's coming out of Ur until the covenant of circumcision or the birth of Isaac. From the birth of Isaac to the birth of Jacob was 60 years (Gen. 25:26), and from the birth of Jacob until he went down to Egypt was 130 years (Gen. 47:9), and from then until Israel came out of Egypt is generally computed as 210 or 215 years. 30 + 60 + 130 + 210 = 430, which again is the exact sum. So, the 400 years must then be computed either from the covenant of circumcision or from Isaac's birth.

Therefore, both periods (430 years and 400 years) end at the same point – the Exodus from Egypt – but they are calculated from two different beginning points. The 430 years (Exod. 12:40,41; Gal. 3:17) refers to the whole dura-tion of the sojourning, beginning either (first method) when Abraham left Haran and God made a covenant with him (Gen. 12:1-4), or else (second method) when Abraham came to Haran. The 400 years (Gen. 15:13; Acts 7:6) dates either (first method) from the weaning of Isaac, an estimated 5 years after his birth, at which time Isaac was designated the heir of the promise, and Ishmael was cast out (Gen. 17:19-21; 21:8,10,12; Rom. 9:7,8), or else (second method) from the covenant of circumcision and the birth of Isaac.

There remains one technical difficulty which needs to be resolved. The text does say ". . . the sojourning *of the children of Israel . . . was* four hundred and thirty years"

(Exod. 12:40). But the 430 years extends back to before Jacob himself was even born. How may we understand "the children of Israel" (Jacobs's descendants) to be *so-journers* before Jacob himself was even born? Well, Levi is said to pay tithes in Abraham because he was in the loins of Abraham when Abraham paid tithes.

And as I may so say, Levi also, who receiveth tithes, payed tithes in Abraham. For he was yet in the loins of his father, when Melchisedec met him. (Hebrews 7:9,10 K.J.V.)

So the children of Israel may be said to have sojourned in the loins of their parents when their parents sojourned.

When parents are mentioned, their children are often included or intended. For example, God said to Abraham, "I will give it [the land] unto thee [Abraham]" (Gen. 13:17), which means that Abraham's descendants would receive the land. Also, God said to Jacob, "I will also surely bring thee [Jacob] up *again* [out of Egypt]" (Gen. 46:4), which means that Jacob's descendants would leave Egypt. Again, David is often named in place of his descendants (I Kings 12:16 Ezek. 34:23 37:24,25). In the same way but reversed, when only the children are mentioned, sometimes their parents are also understood. For example, the deliverance from Egypt is attributed to certain persons when only their ancestors experienced these things.

And the LORD said unto the children of Israel, Did not I deliver you from the Egyptians, and from the Amorites, from the children of Ammon, and from the Philistines? The Zidonians also, and the Amalekites, and the Maonites, did oppress you; and ye cried to me, and I delivered you out of their hand. (Judges 10:11-12 K.J.V.)

The Lord did not deliver those persons during the pe-riod of Judges, but only their ancestors. This may solve another part of the chronology puzzle.

C. THE PROBLEM OF THE PERIOD FROM THE EXODUS TO THE TEMPLE — I KINGS 6:1; ACTS 13:20

I Kings tells us there were 480 years from the Exodus to the beginning of Solomon's temple.

And it came to pass in the four hundred and eightieth year after the children of Israel were come out of the land of Egypt, in the fourth year of Solomon's reign over Israel, in the month Zif, which is the second month, that he began to build the house of the LORD. (I Kings 6:1 K.J.V.)

There is one text which appears to contradict this.

The God of this people of Israel chose our fathers, and exalted the people when they dwelt as strangers in the land of Egypt, and with an high arm brought he them out

First Method for Calculating
the 400 and 430 Years

(Adapted from Martin Anstey)

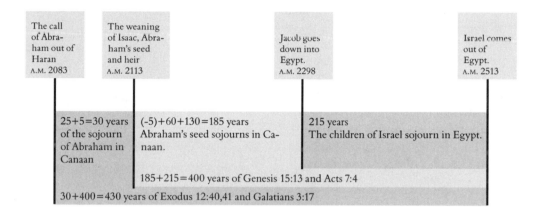

The call of Abraham out of Haran A.M. 2083

The weaning of Isaac, Abraham's seed and heir A.M. 2113

Jacob goes down into Egypt. A.M. 2298

Israel comes out of Egypt. A.M. 2513

25+5=30 years of the sojourn of Abraham in Canaan

(-5)+60+130=185 years Abraham's seed sojourns in Canaan.

215 years The children of Israel sojourn in Egypt.

185+215=400 years of Genesis 15:13 and Acts 7:4

30+400=430 years of Exodus 12:40,41 and Galatians 3:17

Second Method for Calculating
the 400 and 430 Years

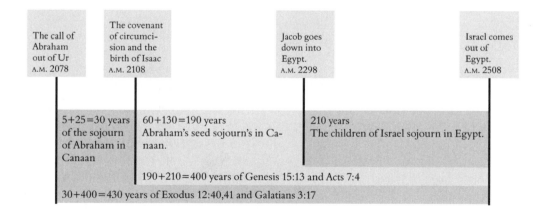

The call of Abraham out of Ur A.M. 2078

The covenant of circumcision and the birth of Isaac A.M. 2108

Jacob goes down into Egypt. A.M. 2298

Israel comes out of Egypt. A.M. 2508

5+25=30 years of the sojourn of Abraham in Canaan

60+130=190 years Abraham's seed sojourn's in Canaan.

210 years The children of Israel sojourn in Egypt.

190+210=400 years of Genesis 15:13 and Acts 7:4

30+400=430 years of Exodus 12:40,41 and Galatians 3:17

of it. And about the time of forty years suffered he their manners in the wilderness. And when he had destroyed seven nations in the land of Chanaan, he divided their land to them by lot. And after that he gave unto them judges about the space of four hundred and fifty years, until Samuel the prophet. (Acts 13:17-20 K.J.V.)

This text seems to assign 450 years to the period of the judges. If there are 480 years from the Exodus out of Egypt until the beginning of the temple (I Kings 6:1), and there are 450 years for the judges (Acts 13:20), that only leaves 30 years for several other events. Let's do the math. If we deduct from 480 years:

40 years of Israel's wandering in the wilderness
7 years in subduing the land before the allotment of the land
10 more years while Israel was under Joshua
40 years of Samuel's judging Israel (or 20 years, or 0 years; see below)
40 years for the reign of Saul
40 years for the reign of David
3 years for the reign of Solomon until his fourth year in which the temple is begun

we are then reduced to 300 years left for the period of the judges down until Samuel the last judge.

40	7	10	300		40	40	40	3
57 years			480 - 57 - 123 = 300 years for the judges		123 years			
57 + 300 + 123 = 480 years from the Exodus to the beginning of the temple								

Some believe Acts 13:20 meant to include the ten years of Joshua, which would bring the period of judges up to 310 years. Some argue that Samuel judged independently for only twenty years before Saul was chosen king (I Sam. 7:2) then judged more years while Saul was king, which would bring the period of judges before Samuel up to 330 years. Some argue that Acts 13:20 means to extend the period of judges through Samuel the judge, which would bring the period of judges up to 350 years.

40	7	350		40	40	3
47 years		480 - 47 - 83 = 350 years for the judges		83 years		
47 + 350 + 83 = 480 years from the Exodus to the beginning of the temple						

We still fall 100 years short of the 450 years given in Acts 13:20.

To add to the confusion, several chronologists have devised schemes which allow the years of the judges actually to add up to 450 years. Below are two examples of how this is done.

Martin Anstey and Philip Mauro	E.W. Bullinger
	20 years entry into the land
1st servitude – 8 years under Cushan (Judges 3:8,11)	1st servitude – 8 years under Mesopotamia
40 years of Othniel (3:11,14)	40 years for Othniel
2nd servitude – 18 years under Eglon (3:14,30)	2nd servitude – 18 years under Moab
80 years for Ehud (3:30)	80 years for Ehud
3rd servitude – 20 years under Jabin (4:3) (includes Shamgar 3:31)	3rd servitude – 20 years under Canaan
40 years for Barak (5:31)	40 years for Barak
4th servitude 7 years under Midian (6:1; 8:28)	4th servitude 7 years under Midian
40 years for Gideon (8:28)	40 years for Gideon
5th usurpation – 3 years for Abimelech (9:22;10:2)	Omit (concurrent with Tola's first three years)
23 years for Tola (10:2,3)	23 years for Tola
22 years for Jair (10:3,8)	4 years for Jair (22-18=4)
6th oppression – 18 years for Ammon (10:8)	Omit (concurrent with Tola's last 18 years)
	This totals to the 300 years mentioned by Jephthah (Judges 11:26)
6 years for Jephthah (12:7)	6 years for Jephthah
7 years for Ibzan (12:8,11)	7 years for Ibzan
10 years for Elon (12:11,14)	10 years for Elon
8 years for Abdon (12:14)	8 years for Abdon
7th servitude – 40 years for Philistia (13:1) (includes 20 years of Samson, 16:31)	5th servitude – 40 years for Philistia
40 years for Eli (I Samuel 4:18)	40 years for Eli
20 years for Samuel (I Samuel 7:2)	40 years for Samuel
Totals 450 years [including 114 years servitude/ oppression]	Totals 451 years [including 93 years servitude]

There have been several inventive solutions proposed to this difficulty. Possibly the most inventive solution is that the 480 years of I Kings 6:1 are reckoned in a way which omits periods when Israel was in servitude. (See the several servitudes noted in the chart above.) Once these periods of servitude are deducted, the numbers seem to add up better. The first problem with this solution is that nothing in the text (or any other text) is advanced to suggest such a novel method for reckoning. It is purely speculative. The second problem is that those who choose this solution cannot agree on the number and length of the periods of omission, or on when to begin or to end the 450 years – they seem to juggle these things arbitrarily in order to come up with the number they happen to be looking for.

Perhaps the most common solution to this whole

problem is found in a more careful examination of the text. If we follow the order of phrases in the Greek text of Acts 13:20, and we allow to be parenthetical the phrase about the number of years, then we may read the text, "And after these things (approximately four hundred and fifty years), He gave judges until Samuel the prophet." This is a perfectly legitimate division of the text. Rather than the 450 years referring to the period of judges, it refers instead to the period from the choosing of the fathers (Acts 13:17) until Israel divided the land by lot (Acts 13:19) which began the period of the judges. The Vulgate Latin version agrees with this division of the text.

> He divided their land unto them, about the space of four hundred and fifty years, and after that he gave unto them judges. (Acts 13:20, Vulgate Latin)

Likewise, the Ethiopic version agrees.

> And after four hundred and fifty years, he set over them governors. (Acts 13:20, Ethiopic version)

Indeed, by all reckoning, this is approximately four hundred fifty years:

1 year from the covenant of circumcision until the birth of Isaac

60 years from the birth of Isaac until the birth of Jacob

130 years until Jacob goes down into Egypt

210 to 215 years until the Israelites come out of Egypt

40 years until the Israelites enter the land of Canaan

7 years until the division of the land

= 448 to 453 years, which is "approximately 450 years" – exactly as the text says.

Since the only absolute measure in Scripture which spans over the period of the judges is the statement in I Kings 6:1, then the period of judges must fit within those 480 years, along with several other historical events. So how do we compress all of the periods of the judges into the 300 to 350 years allowed by I Kings 6:1? Well, it appears that there were at least three judgeships and oppressions which overlapped:

1. Jabin and Shamgar
2. Tola, Jair, Ammonite oppression on the east, and Philistine tyranny on the west
3. Philistine servitude and Samson.

This may signal to us that there were more overlappings of the judgeships, creating more compressions of time which we cannot necessarily discern in a way which would provide a precise chronology. There are other considerations in the Hebrew grammar of Judges – too complicated for us to describe here – which suggest other compressions.

Beyond these three problems (Terah's age at Abraham's birth, the length of Israel's sojourn, the period from the Exodus to the temple), there is the problem of calculating the reigns of the kings of Judah, a period of about 500 years, which is more involved than we have space to address here.

3. Problems of Establishing a Baseline

After we have determined with some certainty a system of Biblical dates relative to each other, then we need to line this whole system up with secular dates established by mere human reckoning.

Some persons want to make the Bible prove their peculiar scheme of predictive prophecy. Some persons want to make the Bible fit secular timelines in order to prove the Bible is true by man's standards. Some persons even want to prove the Bible is contradictory and therefore false or unreliable. These are the kinds of things referred to by Peter when he warned of "they that are unlearned and unstable [who] wrest . . . [the] scriptures, unto their own destruction" (II Pet. 3:16). When someone approaches the Scripture with an agenda, he is tempted to manipulate the words of Scripture to make them say what he wants them to say, instead of allowing Scripture to speak the truth.

Here are some of the suggested baselines from which we can count backwards (and forwards):

1. Ahab died in the sixth year of Shalmaneser III, in 853 B.C., and King Jehu paid tribute to Shalmaneser III twelve years later. Secular sources calculate this to be 841 B.C. This is the anchor date for Edwin Thiele.

2. Secular sources calculate the beginning of the Assyrian captivity of the northern kingdom of Israel to be 722 B.C. (plus or minus two years).

3. The sacking of Thebes by Assurbanipal of Assyria in 664 B.C. is the earliest secular date to which virtually everyone agrees, and it stands almost exactly in the middle between the Assyrian captivity and the destruction of Jerusalem. This, together with the destruction of Jerusalem in 586 B.C., is the anchor date for David Rohl.

4. The following Scripture links the inspired chronology of Hebrew kings with the chronology of secular kings.

> . . . in the fourth year of Jehoiakim the son of Josiah king

of Judah, that was the first year of Nebuchadnezzar king of Babylon. (Jeremiah 25:1 K.J.V.)

This was 607 B.C. according to James Ussher and January 21, 604 B.C. according to Jamieson, Fausset and Brown.

5. The destruction of Jerusalem in 586 B.C. (plus or minus two years) is an established secular baseline.

6. The death of Nebuchadnezzar in 562 B.C. This is the anchor date for James Ussher.

A Comparison of Various Systems of Biblical Chronology

The following chart compares the chronology systems of several Biblical chronologists. In our "Timeline of Ancient Literature," we have chosen to use Edwin Thiele's anchor dates for our own anchor dates. This is not to say that we reject the dating systems of Ussher or the other Biblical chronologists. They all have strong arguments supporting their systems. Thiele's date for the division of the kingdom is 930 B.C. We accept the consensus of A.M dates before that date.

See Appendix 5, "Sources Consulted," for more information on these chronologists.	James Ussher	Martin Anstey; Philip Mauro	Edward Reese	Edwin Thiele	Floyd Nolen Jones	David Rice	David Rohl
Creation	0 [4004]	— [4046]	0 [3976]	—	0 [4004]	0 [3958]	— [c.5500]
To the Flood	1656 [2349]	1656 [2390]	— [2319]	—	1656 [2348]	1656 [2302]	— [c.3113]
To the birth of Abraham	2008 [1996]	2008 [2038]	— [1967]	—	2008 [1996]	2008 [1950]	—
To the covenant with Abraham	2083 [1921]	2083 [1963]	— [1892]	—	2083 [1921]	2083 [1875]	— [1775]
To the weaning of Isaac	2113 [1891]	2113 [1933]	— [1864]	—	2113 [1891]	2113 [1845]	—
To Jacob's sojourn in Egypt	2298 [1706]	2298 [1748]	— [1677]	—	2298 [1706]	2298 [1660]	— [1662]
To the Exodus from Egypt	2513 [1491]	2513 [1533]	— [1462]	—	2513 [1491]	2513 [1445]	— [1447]
To the entrance into Canaan	2553 [1451]	2553 [1493]	— [1422]	—	2553 [1451]	2553 [1405]	—
To the division of the land	2560 [1444]	2559 [1487]	— [1416]	—	2560 [1444]	2559 [1399]	—
To King Saul	2909 [1095]	3023 [1023]	— [1065]	—	2909 [1095]	2908 [1050]	—
To King David	2949 [1055]	3063 [983]	— [1025]	—	2949 [1055]	2948 [1010]	— [1010]
To King Solomon	2990 [1015]	3103 [943]	— [985]	—	2989 [1015]	2988 [970]	— [970]
To the beginning of the 1ˢᵗ temple	2992 [1012]	3106 [940]	— [982]	—	2992 [1012]	2992 [966]	— [966]
To the division of the kingdom	3029 [975]	3143 [903]	— [945]	[930]	3029 [975]	3028 [930]	— [931]
To the Assyrian captivity	3283 [721]	3406 [—]	— [721]	[723]	3283 [721]	3235 [723]	— [724]
To the destruction of the 1ˢᵗ temple	3416 [588]	3539 [—]	— [586]	[586]	3418 [586]	3371 [587]	— [587]
To the decree of Cyrus	3467 [538]	3589 [—]	— [539]	—	3468 [536]	3420 [538]	—
To the completion of the 2ⁿᵈ temple	3489 [515]	3609 [—]	— [517]	—	3488 [516]	3443 [515]	—
To the birth of Jesus	4000 [4]	4038 [—]	— [5]	—	4000 [4]	3956 [2]	—
To the resurrection of Jesus	4036 [A.D. 33]	4071 [—]	— [A.D. 29]	—	— [A.D. 30]	3990 [A.D. 33]	—
To the destruction of the 2ⁿᵈ temple	4074 [A.D. 70]	—	— [A.D. 70]	—	—	4027 [A.D. 70]	—

Dates are A.M. – Anno Mundi – in the year of the world. Dates in brackets are B.C. – Before Christ, unless marked A.D. – Anno Domini – in the year of our Lord

Sources Consulted

PRIMARY SOURCES: ENGLISH TRANSLATIONS OF ANCIENT LITERATURE

Ambrose. *Saint Ambrose.* Translated by Sister Mary Melchior Beyenka. *The Fathers of the Church,* edited by Roy Joseph Deferrari. New York: Fathers of the Church, Inc., 1954.

Arnold, Eberhard, ed. *The Early Christians After the Death of the Apostles: Selected and Edited from all the Sources of the First Centuries.* Rifton, N.Y.: Plough Publishing House, 1972.

Atchity, Kenneth J. *The Classical Roman Reader: New Encounters with Ancient Rome.* New York: Henry Holt and Company, 1997. Excerpts from primary sources.

Auden, W. H., ed. *The Portable Greek Reader.* New York: The Viking Press, 1948.

Augustine. *The City of God Against the Pagans.* Translated by Henry Bettenson. Baltimore, Md.: Penguin Books, 1972.

Augustine. *Confessions and Enchiridion.* Translated by Albert C. Outler. Philadelphia: The Westminster Press, 1955.

Ayer, Joseph Cullen. *A Source Book for Ancient Church History: From the Apostolic Age to the Close of the Conciliar Period.* New York: Charles Scribner's Sons, 1922.

Bailkey, Nels M., ed. *Readings in Ancient History: From Gilgamesh to Diocletian.* Lexington, Mass.: D. C. Heath and Company, 1976. Excerpts from primary sources.

Bettenson, Henry, ed. *Documents of the Christian Church.* London: Oxford University Press, 1963. Excerpts from primary sources.

Botsford, George Willis, and Lillie Shaw Botsford, eds. *A Source-Book of Ancient History.* New York: The Macmillan Company, 1922. Excerpts from primary sources.

Bryan, William Jennings, ed. *The World's Famous Orations. Volume I: Greece. Volume II: Rome.* New York: Funk and Wagnalls Company, 1906.

Cherry, David. *The Roman World: A Sourcebook.* Malden, Mass.: Blackwell Publishers, 2001. Excerpts from primary sources.

Cubberley, Ellwood P., ed. *Readings in the History of Education: A Collection of Sources and Readings to Illustrate the Development of Educational Practice, Theory, and Organization.* Boston: Houghton Mifflin Company, 1920. Excerpts from primary sources.

Davis, William Stearns, ed. *Readings in Ancient History: Illustrative Extracts from the Sources. Volume I: Greece and the East. Volume II: Rome and the West.* Boston: Allyn and Bacon, 1912-1913. Excerpts from primary sources.

Duff, J. Wight. *A Literary History of Rome: From the Origins to the Close of the Golden Age.* London: T. Fisher Unwin, 1910.

Eusebius. *The History of the Church from Christ to Constantine.* Translated by G.A. Williamson. N.p.: Penguin Books, 1965.

Finley, M. I., ed. *The Greek Historians: The Essence of Herodotus, Thucydides, Xenophon, Polybius.* New York: The Viking Press, 1959.

Guinagh, Kevin, and Alfred P. Dorjahn. *Latin Literature in Translation*. New York: Longmans, Green and Company, 1947.

Gwatkin, Henry Melvill, ed. *Selections from Early Writers Illustrative of Church History to the Time of Constantine*. London: Macmillan and Company, 1909.

Hallo, William W., and K. L. Younger, eds. *The Context of Scripture. Volume I: Canonical Compositions from the Biblical World. Volume II: Monumental Inscriptions from the Biblical World*. Leiden: Brill, 1997-2000.

Hardy, Edward Rochie, and Cyril C. Richardson, eds. *The Library of Christian Classics. Volume 3: Christology of the Later Fathers. Volume 7: Augustine*. Philadelphia: The Westminster Press, 1954.

Herodotus. *The History*. Translated by David Grene. Chicago: The University of Chicago Press, 1987.

Hutchins, Robert M., and Mortimer J. Adler, eds. *Gateway to the Great Books. Volume 10: Philosophical Essays*. Chicago: Encyclopaedia Britannica, Inc., 1963. Essays by Epicurus, Epictetus, Plutarch, and Cicero.

Josephus. *Complete Works*. Translated by William Whiston. Grand Rapids, Mich.: Kregel Publications, 1973.

Kaegi, Walter Emil, and Peter White, eds. *University of Chicago Readings in Western Civilization: Volume 2: Rome – Late Republic and Principate*. Chicago: The University of Chicago Press, 1986.

Kagan, Donald. *Problems in Ancient History. Volume I: The Ancient Near East and Greece. Volume II: The Roman World*. New York: The Macmillan Company, 1966.

Knoles, George H., and Rixford K. Snyder, eds. *Readings in Western Civilization*. Chicago: J. B. Lippincott Company, 1954.

Laing, Gordon Jennings, ed. *Masterpieces of Latin Literature with Biographical Sketches and Notes*. Boston: Houghton Mifflin Company, 1903.

Lewis, Naphtali, and Meyer Reinhold, eds. *Roman Civilization Sourcebook II: The Empire*. New York: Harper and Row, 1955.

Lightfoot, J. B., and J. R. Harmer, eds. *The Apostolic Fathers: Revised Greek Texts with Introductions and English Translations*. Grand Rapids, Mich.: Baker Book House, 1987.

Loeb, James, founder. *The Loeb Classical Library*.

Lucretius. *On the Nature of Things*. Trans. Charles E. Bennett. New York: Walter J. Black, 1946.

Mack, Maynard, ed. *World Masterpieces: Volume I: Literature of Western Culture Through the Renaissance*. New York: W. W. Norton and Company, 1956.

Marcus Aurelius and His Times: The Transition from Paganism to Christianity – Comprising Marcus Aurelius, Meditations; Lucian, Hermotimus and Icaromenippus; Justin Martyr, Dialogue with Trypho and First Apology; Marius the Epicurian. New York: Walter J. Black, 1945.

McDermott, William C., and Wallace E. Caldwell. *Readings in the History of the Ancient World*. New York: Holt, Rinehart and Winston, 1967.

McFarlane, Patricia Anne, ed. *Literature of Beginnings*. New York: American Heritage, 1995.

McKeon, Richard, ed. *Introduction to Aristotle*. New York: Random House, Inc., 1947.

Morrison, Karl F., ed. *Readings in Western Civilization: Volume 3: The Church in the Roman Empire*. Chicago: The University of Chicago Press, 1986.

William Penn. *Advice to His Children*. N.p.: n.p., 1699.

Plato. *Great Dialogues of Plato*. Translated by W. H. D. Rouse. New York: The New American Library of World Literature, Inc., 1956.

Plato. *The Last Days of Socrates*. Translated by Hugh Tredennick. New York: Penguin Books, 1979.

Quasten, Johannes, and Joseph C. Plumpe, eds. *Ancient Christian Writers: The Works of the Fathers in Translation. Volume 25: St. Cyprian*. Translated by Maurice Bevenot. New York: Newman Press, 1956.

Richardson, Cyril C., ed. and trans. *Early Christian Fathers*. New York: Macmillan Publishing Co., Inc., 1976.

Roberts, Alexander, and James Donaldson, eds. *The Ante-Nicene Fathers. Volume 4: Tertullian, Commodian, Origen*. Buffalo: The Christian Literature Publishing Company, 1885.

Robinson, James Harvey. *Readings in European History: A Collection of Extracts from the Sources Chosen with the Purpose of Illustrating the Progress of Culture in Western Europe Since the German Invasions*. Boston: Ginn and Company, 1906.

Rose, H. J. *A Handbook of Latin Literature from the Earliest Times to the Death of St. Augustine*. London: Methuen and Company Ltd., 1936.

Sayce, A. H., ed. *Records of the Past: Being English Translations of the Ancient Monuments of Egypt and Western Asia.* London: Samuel Bagster and Sons, Limited, 1888.

Schaff, Philip, and Henry Wace, eds. *Nicene and Post-Nicene Fathers of the Christian Church. Volume 2: Socrates, Sozomenus.* New York: The Christian Literature Company, 1890.

Schuster, M. Lincoln. *The World's Great Letters From Ancient Days to Our Own Time, Containing the Characteristic and Crucial Communications, and Intimate Exchanges and Cycles of Correspondence, of Many of the Outstanding Figures of World History. . . .* New York: Simon and Schuster, 1940.

Thatcher, Oliver J., ed. *The Ideas That Have Influenced Civilization, In the Original Documents. Volume 1: The Ancient World. Volume 2: The Greek World. Volume 3: The Roman World.* Boston: The Roberts-Manchester Publishing Company, 1901.

Theodoret. *History of the Church: From A.D. 322 to the Death of Theodore of Mopsuestia, A.D. 427.* London: Henry G. Bohn, 1854.

Thomas, D. Winton, ed. *Documents From Old Testament Times.* New York: Thomas Nelson and Sons Ltd., 1958.

Thucydides. *History of the Peloponnesian War.* Translated by Rex Warner. N.p.: Penguin Books, 1954.

Workman, B. K., ed. *They Saw It Happen in Classical Times: An Anthology of Eye-witnesses' Accounts of Events in the Histories of Greece and Rome.* New York: Barnes and Noble, Inc., 1964. Excerpts from primary sources.

Xenophon. *The Anabasis or the Expedition of Cyrus.* Translated by J. S. Watson. New York: The Translation Publishing Company, 1920.

❧ BIBLES ❧

Clarke, Adam. *The Holy Bible, Containing the Old and New Testaments: The Text Carefully Printed from the Most Correct Copies of the Present Authorized Translation, Including the Marginal Readings and Parallel Texts, With a Commentary and Critical Notes Designed as a Help to a Better Understanding of the Sacred Writings.* Nashville: Abingdon, first published early 1800s. Follows Ussher's chronology.

The Life and Times Historical Reference Bible: New King James Version. Nashville: Thomas Nelson Publishers, 1997.

The Nelson Study Bible: New King James Version. Nashville: Thomas Nelson Publishers, 1997.

Reese, Edward. *The Reese Chronological Bible.* Minneapolis, Minn.: Bethany House Publishers, 1977.

❧ SECONDARY SOURCES ❧

Adler, Mortimer. *Great Ideas from the Great Books.* New York: Washington Square Press, 1969.

Ball, W. W. Rouse. *A Short Account of the History of Mathematics.* London: Macmillan and Company, 1912. Biographical information on the early philosophers and mathematicians.

Barnes, Timothy David. *Tertullian: A Historical and Literary Study.* Oxford: Clarendon Press, 1971.

Bender, Hermann. *A Brief History of Roman Literature.* Translated by E. P. Crowell and H. B. Richardson. Boston: Ginn and Company, 1901.

Bone, Robert G. *Visual Outline of Ancient History.* Philadelphia: David McKay Company, 1939. A simple, compact outline of ancient history.

Bowen, James. *A History of Western Education: Volume 1: The Ancient World.* London: Methuen and Co., Ltd.

Breasted, James Henry. *Ancient Times: A History of the Early World – An Introduction to the Study of Ancient History and the Career of Early Man.* Boston: Ginn and Company, 1914.

Bullinger, E. W. *Figures of Speech Used in the Bible.* 1898. Reprint, Grand Rapids: Baker Book House, 1968.

Cary, M., et al, eds. *The Oxford Classical Dictionary.* Oxford: Clarendon Press, 1949.

Cowan, Louise, and Os Guinness, eds. *Invitation to the Classics.* Grand Rapids, Mich.: Baker Books, 1998.

Craig, Albert M., et al. *The Heritage of World Civilizations.* New York: Macmillan College Publishing Company, 1994.

Dang, Katherine, ed. *Universal History: Volume 1: Ancient History, Law Without Liberty.* Oakland, Calif.: Katherine Dang, 2000. This large beautiful volume is a compilation of excerpts from 18th, 19th, and early 20th century history texts. Included are numerous timelines, maps, and charts. The Principle Approach appled to ancient history.

Downs, Robert B. *Famous Books, Ancient and Medieval.* New York: Barnes and Noble, Inc., 1964. Outlines of 108 great works that have shaped modern civilization, including biographical information and summaries.

Farrar, F. W. *The Life and Work of St. Paul.* London: Cassell and Company, 1891.

Fowler, Harold N. *A History of Roman Literature.* New York: D. Appleton and Company, 1909.

Gabba, Emilio. *Dionysius and the History of Archaic Rome.* Berkeley: University of California Press, 1991.

Galinsky, G. Karl, ed. *Perspectives of Roman Poetry: A Classics Symposium.* Austin, Tex.: University of Texas Press, 1974.

Grant, Sir Alexander. *Xenophon.* Edinburgh: William Blackwood and Sons, 1871.

Grant, Michael. *The Classical Greeks.* New York: Charles Scribner's Sons, 1989.

Grant, Michael. *Greek and Roman Historians: Information and Misinformation.* N.p.: Routledge, 1995. Brief articles on historians.

Hamilton, Mary Agnes, and A. W. F. Blunt. *An Outline of Ancient History to A.D. 180.* Oxford: Clarendon Press, 1927.

Hutchins, Robert M. "The Tradition of the West," published in *The Great Conversation, Volume 1, The Great Books of the Western World.* Chicago: Encyclopaedia Britannica, Inc., 1952.

Kelley, Michael W. *The Impulse for Power: Formative Ideals of Western Civilization.* Minneapolis, Minn.: Contra Mundum Books, 1998.

Le Glay, Marcel, et al. *A History of Rome.* Translated by Antonia Nevill. Malden, Mass.: Blackwell Publishers, 2001.

McFarlane, Patricia Anne. *Authors, Authors: A Chronological Annotated Bibliography of Authors and Literary Works of Western Literature from Ancient Times Through 1798.* Friendswood, Tex.: A Word in Season, 1996.

Mendell, Clarence W. *Latin Poetry: The New Poets and The Augustans.* London: Yale University Press, 1965.

Morgan, James. *The Importance of Tertullian in the Development of Christian Dogma.* London: Kegan Paul, Trench, Trubner and Co., 1928.

Murphy, Charles Theophilus, Kevin Guinagh, and Whitney Jennings Oates. *Greek and Roman Classics in Translation.* New York: Green and Company, 1947.

Nairn, John Arbuthnot. *Authors of Rome.* London: Jarrolds Publishers, 1924.

Osborn, Eric. *Tertullian, First Theologian of the West.* Cambridge: Cambridge University Press, 1997.

Payne, Elizabeth. *The Pharaohs of Ancient Egypt.* New York: Random House, 1992.

Putnam, Michael C.J. *Essays on Latin Lyric, Elegy, and Epic.* Princeton, N.J.: Princeton University Press, 1982.

Sandys, Sir John Edwin. *A Short History of Classical Scholarship.* Cambridge: University Press, 1915.

Showerman, Grant. *Rome and the Romans: A Survey and Interpretation.* New York: The Macmillan Company, 1932. Interesting old history which intersperses primary sources with the text.

Sider, Robert Dick. *Ancient Rhetoric and the Art of Tertullian.* London: Oxford University Press, 1971.

Thalheimer, M. E. *A Manual of Ancient History.* Cincinnati: Van Antwerp, Bragg and Company, 1872.

West, Willis Mason. *The Ancient World from the Earliest Times to 800 A.D.: Part II: Rome and the West.* Boston: Allyn and Bacon, 1913.

Wright, F. A. *Three Roman Poets: Plautus, Catullus, Ovid – Their Lives, Times, and Works.* New York: E. P. Dutton and Company, 1938.

CHRONOLOGY RESOURCES

Anstey, Martin. *Chronology of the Old Testament.* Grand Rapids, Mich.: Kregel Publications, originally published 1913, reprinted 1973. One of the standard Biblical chronologies. Anstey has a longer period for the Judges than Ussher. In his Introduction, Anstey reviews the many sources of data for constructing a chronology. Besides the Hebrew Masoretic Text of the Old Testament he lists: (1.) Other texts and versions such as the Septuagint and the Samaritan Pentateuch; (2.) Ancient literary remains such as Berosus, Manetho, the Old Testament Apocrypha, etc.; (3.) Ancient monumental inscriptions; (4.) Classic Greek and Roman literature; (5.) Astronomical observations and calculations; (6.) The works of ancient and modern chronologers.

Beechick, Ruth. *Adam and His Kin: The Lost History of Their Lives and Times.* Pollock Pines, Calif.: Arrow Press, 1990. This important book gives children a Biblically accurate overview of the book of Genesis, told in a narrative style.

Beechick, Ruth. *The Language Wars and Other Writings for Homeschoolers.* Pollock Pines, Calif.: Arrow Press, 1995. One chapter in this book addresses the chronology problem and describes several new developments in the study of chronology.

Clinton, Henry Fynes. *Fasti Hellenici* (1824-1834) and *Fasti Romani* (1845-1850). A Biblicist chronologer. His date for Creation is 4138 B.C.

Cooper, Bill. *After the Flood: The Early post-Flood History of Europe.* England: New Wine Press, 1995. This book shows how European history can be traced back to the Flood and the descendants of Japheth.

Courville, Donovan A. *The Exodus Problem and its Ramifications: Volumes I and II.* Loma Linda, Calif.: Challenge Books, 1971.

Curtis, E. L. "Chronology." In *A Dictionary of the Bible Dealing with its Language, Literature, and Contents Including the Biblical Theology,* edited by James Hastings. New York: Charles Scribner's Sons, 1908.

Down, David. "Searching for Moses." *Technical Journal* 15, no. 1 (2001): 53-57. Sets the Exodus at 1446 B.C.

Fairbairn, Patrick. "Chronology." In *The Imperial Bible-Dictionary: Historical, Biographical, Geographical, and Doctrinal.* London: Blackie and Son, 1889. Discusses the differences in the Hebrew text, the Samaritan Pentateuch, the Septuagint version and the writings of Josephus.

Grun, Bernard. *The Timetables of History: The world-famous reference that tells who did what when from 4500 B.C. to the present day – A Horizontal Linkage of People and Events.* 1946. Reprint, New York: Simon and Schuster, 1991. Based upon Werner Stein's Kulturfahrplan.

Horne, Thomas Hartwell. *An Introduction to the Critical Study and Knowledge of the Holy Scriptures: Volume 2, Parts 1 and 2.* 1839. Reprint, Grand Rapids, Mich.: Baker Book House, 1970.

Hull, Edward. *The Wall Chart of World History.* U.S.A.: Dorset Press, 1988. Large foldout timeline. Follows the chronology of Archbishop James Ussher.

James, Peter. *Centuries of Darkness: A Challenge to the Conventional Chronology of the Old World Archaeology.* New Brunswick, N.J.: Rutgers Univ. Press, 1991.

Jones, Floyd Nolen. *Chronology of the Old Testament: A Return to the Basics.* The Woodlands, Tex.: KingsWord Press, 1999. Book plus numerous charts. Follows Ussher. Refutes Thiele.

Jordon, James. *Biblical Chronology Newsletter.* www.biblicalhorizons.com Usually follows Anstey.

Klassen, Frank R. *The Chronology of the Bible.* Nashville, Tenn.: Regal Publishers, 1975. Colorful pictures included in this timeline. Puts creation at 3975 B.C.

M'Clintock, John, and James Strong. "Chronology." *Cyclopaedia of Biblical, Theological and Ecclesiastical Literature.* New York: Harper and Brothers, 1869.

Mauro, Philip. *The Wonders of Bible Chronology: From the Creation of Adam to the Resurrection of Jesus Christ.* Swengel, Penn.: Reiner Publications, 1970. Follows Anstey's chronology.

Orr, James, et al, eds. "Chronology." *The International Standard Bible Encyclopaedia.* Grand Rapids, Mich.: William B. Eerdmans Publishing Co., 1939.

Osgood, J. "Creation Education: The Date of Noah's Flood." *Creation, Ex Nihilo* 4, no. 1 (March, 1981): 10-13. Sets the date for the Exodus as 1447 B.C.

Pierce, Larry. "In the Days of Peleg." *Creation, Ex Nihilo* 22, no. 1 (1999-2000): 48-49. Discusses the consistency of ancient documents with the total accuracy of the Bible's chronology.

Pierce, Larry. "Evidentialism – the Bible and Assyrian Chronology." *Technical Journal* 15, no. 1 (2001): 62-68. Refutes Thiele. Follows Ussher.

Ptolemy. *The Canon or Table of Reigns.* A list of kings with the years of their reigns beginning 747 B.C. and ending at the reign of Antoninus Pius. Compiled A.D. second century.

Rice, David. *The Stream of Time: Bible Chronology and Time Prophecy.* San Diego, Calif.: n.p., 2002. Inquiries: 8060 Wing Span Drive, 92119. Generally follows Thiele. Sets the Exodus at 1445 B.C.

Rohl, David M. *Legend: The Genesis of Civilisation.* London: Random House, 1998. Concerns the Garden of Eden in northern Mesopotamia and various Biblical events.

Rohl, David M. *Pharaohs and Kings: A Biblical Quest.* New York: Crown Publishers, Inc., 1995. Rohl is an Egyptologist and ancient historian who, though not a Christian, believes that the Bible should be valued just like any other historical document – not rejected, as do most secular historians. His New Chronology, which is developed in this text, provides the archaeological evidence for the existence of many Old Testament characters, and redates Egyptian history. He places Dudimose as the pharaoh of the Exodus, and dates the Exodus at 1447 B.C. The e-mail list http://groups.yahoo.com/group/NewChronology is helpful in understanding the New Chronology.

Scroggie, W. Graham. *The Unfolding Drama of Redemption: The Bible as a Whole.* Grand Rapids, Mich.: Zondervan Publishing House, 1970.

Thiele, Edwin R. *A Chronology of the Hebrew Kings.* Grand Rapids, Mich.: Zondervan Publishing House, 1977. A Biblicist who synchronized the data of the kings of Israel and Judah.

Ussher, Archbishop James. *The Annals of the world deduced from the origin of time and continued to the beginning of the Emperor Vespasian's Reign and the total destruction and abolition of the temple and commonwealth of the Jews, containing the history of the Old and New Testament with that of the Maccabees, also all the most memorable affairs of Asia and Egypt, and the rise of the empire of the Roman Caesars, under Gaius Julius Caesar and Octavius Caesar collected from all history, as well as sacred, as profane and methodically organised.* First published in 1650-1654 in Latin, and in English in 1658. Recently revised and updated by Larry Pierce and to be republished by Master Books in July of 2003 with the title of *The Annals of the World* (ISBN # 0-89051-360-0). *The Annals* is a complete history of the world covering every major event from the time of creation to 70 A.D. In writing this history, Ussher read everything about ancient history that existed in the seventeenth century, and his work is extensively footnoted with thousands of references to ancient writers. Actually, this work is a summary of what the ancients wrote. Ussher constructed a system of chronology which is held to this day by many Biblicists. He dates the creation of the world in the year 4004 B.C. When this book is republished, it will prove to be the most valuable source of all time for the study of chronology.

Velikovsky, Immanuel. *Ages in Chaos.* Garden City, N.Y.: Doubleday and Company, Inc., 1952. This is a reconstruction of ancient history from the Exodus to King Akhenaten. Velikovsky reworked the traditional Egyptian chronology and placed the Exodus at the collapse of the Middle Kingdom of Egypt.

Velikovsky, Immanuel. *Peoples of the Sea: Sequel to Ages in Chaos.* Garden City, N.Y.: Doubleday and Company, Inc., 1977.

Velikovsky, Immanuel. *Ramses II and His Time.* N.p.: Doubleday, 1978.

Walton, John H. *Chronological and Background Charts of the Old Testament.* Grand Rapids, Mich.: Zondervan Publishing House, 1994. Dozens of charts which help us understand the history, literature, archaeology, theology, and chronology of the Old Testament.

CONSULTED FOR COVER PAINTING

Birt, Theodor. *Die Buchrolle In Der Kunst.* Leipzig: Druck Und Verlag Von B. G. Teubner, 1907.

Kenyon, Frederic G. *Books and Readers in Ancient Greece and Rome.* Oxford: Clarendon Press, 1932.

Schubart, Wilhelm. *Das Buch bei den Griechen und Romern.* Heidelberg: Lambert Schneider, 1960.

History Curricula
and Resources

Which Can Be Used with This Book

Please note: we do not necessarily agree with some of these curricula concerning choice of primary source literature to read.

Beechick, Ruth. *Adam and His Kin: The Lost History of Their Lives and Times.* Pollock Pines, Calif.: Arrow Press, 1990. This important book gives children a Biblically accurate overview of the book of Genesis, told in a narrative style. Read this book to your children before you begin your study of ancient history.

Bloom, Jan. *Who Should We Then Read: Authors of Good Books for Children and Young Adults.* Cokato, Minn.: BooksBloom, 1999. www.abebooks.com/home/booksbloom This 250-page reference guide contains information about 140 authors of great books for children and young adults, and it contains alphabetical lists of quality series such as Landmark, "We Were There," Vision Biographies, and Childhood of Famous Americans.

Dang, Katherine, ed. *Universal History: Volume 1: Ancient History, Law Without Liberty.* Oakland, Calif.: Katherine Dang, 2000. This large, beautiful volume, which matches the other "big, red books" published by the Principle Approach people, is a chronological compilation of excerpts from 18th, 19th, and early 20th century history textbooks. Included are numerous detailed timelines, maps, and genealogical charts. This text is the Principle Approach application to ancient history.

Grun, Bernard. *The Timetables of History: The world-famous reference that tells who did what when from 4500 B.C. to the present day – A Horizontal Linkage of People and Events.* 1946. Reprint, New York: Simon and Schuster, 1991. Based upon Werner Stein's Kulturfahrplan. This

book lists what happened in the world for every year since Creation. It covers politics, literature, theater, religion, philosophy, learning, visual arts, music, science, technology, growth, and daily life. You will find listed the titles of works by well known and lesser known scientists, historians, and fiction and nonfiction writers.

Guerber, H. A. *The Story of the Greeks.* 1896. Reprint, Ft. Collins, Colo.: Nothing New Press, 2001. www.nothingnewpress.com Here's another one of the great Guerber reprints. This one tells the history of the Greek culture in a way that everyone can understand. The black and white illustrations are lovely and can be used for copywork.

Guerber, H. A. *The Story of the Romans.* 1896. Reprint, Ft. Collins, Colo.: Nothing New Press, 2002. www.nothingnewpress.com If you could judge a book by its cover, then this reprint of Guerber's *Story of the Romans* would get an A+. But that's not the only great thing about this book – it's the literary quality which makes it valuable. Mrs. Guerber has turned dry history textbook facts into a fascinating yet accurate and literarily pleasing story that children and adults of all ages will enjoy. And there's no talking down to children – the vocabulary and sentence structure are complex enough to grab older kids and adults, yet younger children will be perfectly capable of understanding them.

Hobar, Linda Lacour. *The Mystery of History: Volume I – Creation to the Resurrection.* Dover, Del.: Bright Ideas Press, 2002. www.brightideaspress.com *The Mystery of History* combines a detailed historical narrative with lesson plans, tests, and projects. The Biblical emphasis, thoroughness, ease of use, and layout of this curriculum give it its value. The narrative is both historically accurate (she doesn't get into speculation or mythology) and entertaining. This curriculum is recommended for grades 4-8, but K-3 could also use it.

Hulcy, Jessica, Sarah Rose, and Carole Thaxton. *KONOS History of the World: Year One, The Ancient World.* Anna, Tex.: Konos, 1994. www.konos.com KONOS is the earliest model of the unit study curriculum from which all other unit study curricula have been patterned. *History of the World* consists of Bible study, timeline events, lists of noted people, map study, related vocabulary lists, and activities all taught chronologically beginning with Creation and ending with early Rome. Research, dialogue, reading classical literature, and writing are combined with creative and challenging activities to make the study of history light years away from the tedious way we studied history in our public school days. This curriculum says it is geared to students in grades 9-12, but some seventh and eighth graders could benefit from it also.

Hull, Edward. *The Wall Chart of World History.* U.S.A.: Dorset Press, 1988. Large foldout timeline. Follows the chronology of Archbishop James Ussher.

Miller, Christine. *All Through the Ages: A Guide to Experiencing History Through Literature.* Fort Collins, Colo.: Nothing New Press, 1997. www.nothingnewpress.com Extensive compilation of books arranged chronologically and geographically. For all ages.

Miller, Michelle. *TruthQuest History: Ancient Egypt and Ancient Greece* and *TruthQuest History: Ancient Rome.* Traverse City, Mich.: TruthQuest History, 1997-1999. These study guides, which can be used by students of all ages, contain short, concise historical commentary along with exhaustive book recommendations (both in-print and out-of-print) for every key person and event covered. Also included are writing exercises placed throughout the commentary. I love the cautions that Michelle gives us. At numerous points she suggests that we be careful in our study of ancient Egyptian, Greek, and Roman civilization, and she shows us which books would not be appropriate for young children or even some older students. There is just enough commentary throughout the books to guide us and keep us on the correct path so that we won't leave out any important historical events or people. A family is free to spend as long or as little time at each stop on the timeline as they wish.

Poland, A. B. and John H. Haaren. *Famous Men of Greece.* 1904. Revised by Rob and Cyndy Shearer. Lebanon, Tenn.: Greenleaf Press, 1989. www.greenleafpress.com

Poland, A. B. and John H. Haaren. *Famous Men of Rome.* 1904. Revised by Rob and Cyndy Shearer. Lebanon, Tenn.: Greenleaf Press, 1989. www.greenleafpress.com

Shukin, Barbara. *Ancient History Portfolio and Timeline.* N.p.: n.p. www.historyportfolio.com A sturdy spiral-bound book of blank maps and spaces for drawings, narrations or reports. Also contains a uniquely designed timeline for students to add dates and drawings. Can be used to supplement any history curriculum.

Somerville, Marcia. *Tapestry of Grace.* Derwood, Md.: Books'N Kids, Inc., 2001. www.tapestryofgrace.com This comprehensive unit-study curriculum combines the subjects of history (studied chronologically), literature, geography, writing, vocabulary, government, fine arts, and church history. Each week the student will read history and literature, discuss what he reads, and communicate what he has learned through writing projects, displays, activities, and oral presentations. This curriculum is thorough and detailed, and is an excellent application of the trivium approach, with the student activities divided into four levels: lower grammar, upper grammar, dialectic, and rhetoric.

Stanton, Mary, and Albert Hyma. *Streams of Civilization: Volume One.* Arlington Heights, Ill.: Christian Liberty Press, 1992. Good all-round history text from a Christian perspective.

Walton, John H. *Chronological and Background Charts of the Old Testament.* Grand Rapids, Mich.: Zondervan Publishing House, 1994. Dozens of charts which help us understand the history, literature, archaeology, theology, and chronology of the Old Testament.